Families and their Learning Environments

Kevin Marjoribanks

Department of Education
University of Adelaide

Families and their Learning Environments

An Empirical Analysis

Routledge & Kegan Paul

London, Boston and Henley

First published in 1979
by Routledge & Kegan Paul Ltd

39 Store Street,
London WC1E 7DD,

Broadway House,
Newtown Road,
Henley-on-Thames,
Oxon RG9 1EN and

9 Park Street,
Boston, Mass. 02108, USA

Set in Linocomp Plantin, 10/12
and printed in Great Britain by
Lowe & Brydone Printers Ltd,
Thetford, Norfolk

British Library Cataloguing in Publication Data

Marjoribanks, Kevin
    Families and their learning environments.
    1. Home and school   2. Academic achievement
    I. Title
    371.2'64   LC225   79-40051
ISBN 0 7100 0167 3

To Jan, Timothy, and Genevieve

you will remember that for you to
go to harvard has been your mothers
dream since you were born and no
compson has ever disappointed a
lady

WILLIAM FAULKNER

Contents

Figures

Tables

Acknowledgments

This book was written while I was a Visiting Professor in the Social Ecology Laboratory, Department of Psychiatry, Stanford University School of Medicine. I am indebted to Professor Rudolf Moos, the Director of the Laboratory, for his splendid hospitality, his generous provision of organizational support, and for the creation of a stimulating environment in which to write. Over the past few years I have enjoyed a fruitful research collaboration with Professor Herbert J. Walberg, of the University of Illinois at Chicago Circle. It is hoped that the benefits I have accrued from that partnership are reflected throughout the book. Also I am grateful to the University of Adelaide for supporting my work while I was at Stanford. I wish to acknowledge my debt to all the parents and children who have participated in the research projects that I have conducted, for it is hoped that their kind co-operation has enabled us to increase our understanding of the relations between family environments and children's school-related outcomes.

Stanford, 1978

1 Family environments: frameworks for analysis

Although most educators would agree with the proposition that families are one of the most pervasive influences on children's behaviours, only a relatively small number of educational researchers include detailed assessments of family environments in analyses of children's school outcomes. A number of studies that have attempted to increase our understanding of the relations between measures of family environments and children's academic performance are brought together in this book. The selection of studies, however, is quite idiosyncratic. I have presented much of my own research on data collected from families in Australia, Canada, and England. But in doing so I have endeavoured to integrate my findings with results from other family environment research. Also, I have attempted to explore social-psychological conceptual positions that might be relevant for further educational investigations. In this first chapter, general conceptual and statistical frameworks for examining family environments and their associations with children's behaviours are presented, followed by a review of some of the seminal family environment studies from education-related research.

Conceptual framework for analysis

In social-psychological and educational empirical research, children's behaviour has typically been examined in relation to one of the following three models: (a) the trait model, (b) the situationism position, and (c) the interactionism framework. In the trait model, factors determining behaviour are considered to be within the persons themselves. As Endler and Magnusson (1976, p. 6) suggest, in the 'classical' trait theory:

> It is sufficient to merely study the individual. Situations are taken into account, but the provoking and restricting effect of situational factors on behaviour is not supposed to change the rank orders of individuals for a given trait. This means that the rank order of individuals for any given trait is

supposed to be the same for different situations independent of the situational characteristics, except for errors of measurement.

Alternatively, the situationism position regards situational factors, or the stimuli in the situation, as the main determinants of individual behaviour. In some of the following chapters, a situationism position is adopted to investigate associations between children's academic achievement and different measures of family environments. It is the basic assumption of the book, however, that behaviour is the result of an indispensable, continuous interaction between persons and the situations they encounter. That is, children's school outcomes are explained most appropriately by examining an interactionism framework of behaviour. In this latter model it is assumed that not only do situations influence individuals but that individuals select and subsequently affect the situations with which they interact.

One of the earliest social-psychological forms of the interactionism framework was developed by Lewin in his field theory of personality. He proposes that '*the dynamics of environmental influences* can be investigated *only simultaneously with the determination of individual differences* and with *general psychological laws*.' Therefore, 'to understand or predict the psychological behavior (B) one has to determine for every kind of psychological environment . . . the momentary whole situation, that is, the momentary structure and the state of the person (P) and of the psychological environment (E). $B = f(PE)$' (Lewin, 1935, p. 79). As Moos (1976, p. 20) says, it 'made no sense to Lewin to analyze behavior without reference to the person and to his psychological environment'.

In a special adaptation of the interactionism framework, which is examined in Chapters 6 and 7, Thomas and Znaniecki (1958) propose that 'the social results of individual activity depend, not only on the action itself, but also on the social conditions in which it is performed; and therefore the cause of a social change must include both individual and social elements'. They declare that the fundamental methodological principle of both social psychology and sociology is: 'The cause of a social or individual phenomenon is never another social or individual phenomenon alone, but always a combination of a social and an individual phenomenon' (see Thomas, 1966, p. 277).

In Lewin's framework, the environment surrounding individuals is considered to be differentiated into regions. The regions may be defined along a continuum of 'nearness-remoteness' which is an indication of the extent of influence that one environmental region has on another. Also the boundaries of environment regions may be defined along the continua of 'firm-weak' and 'fluid-rigid'. If boundaries are firm then the environment regions have minimal interaction; but if the boundaries are weak, then the regions may exert considerable influence on each other. A fluid region is one that responds quickly to any influence brought to bear upon it, while a rigid medium resists change (see Lewin, 1935; Deutsch and Krauss, 1965; Hall and Lindzey, 1970). The environment constructs introduced by Lewin are adapted in the present book to suggest that the family environment surrounding an individual may be conceived of as a set of nested environments, ranging from: distal social environments and distal family structure variables to proximal social-psychological and socio-linguistic environments.

In the book the distal social environments of children are defined by social-status characteristics and ethnic group membership, while distal family structure is assessed by family size, birth order, and crowding within the home. Although these two sets of environment variables are defined as distal situations, it is shown in Chapters 3 and 4 that family environment research becomes more sensitive, enriched, and valid when children's school outcomes are examined not only in relation to proximal social-psychological measures but also in relation to global social environment characteristics.

Much of the impetus for educational research on family social-psychological environments was provided by Bloom (1964), who proposed that the environment may be regarded as providing a network of forces and factors which surround, engulf, and play on the individual. It is also suggested that the development of any particular human characteristic is related to a sub-set, or sub-environment, of the total set of environmental forces. In Figure 1.1, if A B C D represents, for example, the total set of family conditions surrounding an individual, then E F G H may represent a sub-environment of social-psychological process variables related to, say, the development of verbal ability. And J K L M may represent another sub-environment associated with, say, the development of achievement motivation. Then the task of researchers investigating relations between family environments and a particular human characteristic involves isolating, and then measuring, the pertinent sub-environment from the total set of environmental variables. It is shown later that families from different social-status and ethnic groups construct divergent sub-environments for children's academic achievement, and that between social groups the boundaries of environment regions may have quite variable qualities.

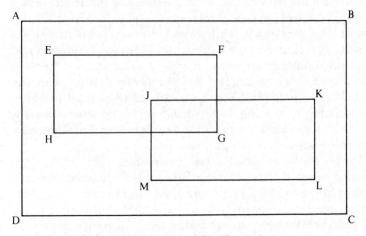

FIGURE I.I   *Sub-environments of family environments*

Within interactionism models of behaviour it is typically proposed that social conditions should be defined in relation to the meanings that the contexts have for individuals. It is suggested by Karabel and Halsey (1977, p. 58), however, that emphasis on the meanings that social conditions have for an individual 'often fails to take adequate account of the social constraints on human actors in everyday life'. They propose that in the examination of behaviour there is a need to integrate structural and interactional levels of analysis. The research presented in this book is within the framework of structural analyses of family environments. Detailed and sensitive studies, using an interpretative methodology, of the relations between academic performance and the meanings that family environments have for children from different social status and ethnic groups, have yet to be completed. Moos (1979) proposes, however, that person variables such as ability levels, cognitive and emotional development, ego strength, and self-esteem determine the meaning that an environment has for an individual. In subsequent chapters, studies are examined that investigate relations between academic achievement and measures of attitudes, personality, and intelligence at different levels of social-psychological family environment variables. These person variables may be considered to represent, in part, the results of interactions between children's perceptions of prior family environments and individual characteristics, and thus reflect, at least tentatively, the meanings that family environments have for children. But such measures are an initial approximation only of these meanings. Educational research is in need of investigations, using an interpretative framework, which examine relations between family learning environments and children's behaviour. Such research will provide data to embellish the findings from studies that observe the structural elements of families.

Ideally, research adopting an interactionism framework would incorporate a dynamic or organismic rather than a reactive or mechanistic model of the individual (see Harré and Secord, 1972). In mechanistic models, interactions are between causes rather than between chains of causes and effects. That is, the mechanistic framework is concerned with uni-directional causality and it assumes that independent variables influence dependent measures. Endler and Magnusson (1976, p. 13) indicate that the dynamic model 'is concerned with a reciprocal action (feedback) between environmental events and behavior. It is concerned with reciprocal causation so that not only do events affect the behavior of organisms, but the organism is also an active agent in influencing environmental events.' But they go on to suggest that in the social sciences we have not yet developed fully the methodology and technology to investigate the nature of dynamic interacton. While some of the reported research in later chapters examines longitudinal data and approximates a dynamic model of behaviour, most of the studies investigated reflect a mechanistic framework. Although it is assumed throughout the book that situations are as much a function of the person as the person's behaviour is a function of the situation, the research supports Endler's (1976, p. 66) contention that 'Concurrent with an investigation of dynamic interaction we must also examine how persons and situations interact (mechanistic interaction) in influencing behaviour'.

Statistical framework for analysis

Much of family environment research has relied on the use of restricted statistical techniques such as product-moment correlations which reveal only bivariate relations, and analysis of variance techniques that require the grouping of variables into levels. Regression models have been used, which concentrate on determining how much variance in children's behaviour is related to the addition of family measures to the equations. But the findings generated from these regression models depend on the order in which family environment is entered into the models (e.g., see Coleman *et al.*, 1966; Mosteller and Moynihan, 1972). Also, the regression models generally have not tested for the presence of interaction or curvilinear relations among the variables. In this book a variation of regression analysis is used in many of the studies that are examined. Regression surfaces are plotted using raw regression weights generated from equations of the form: $Z = a X + b Y + c X Y + d X^2 + e Y^2 + $ constant, where Z represents a measure of children's behaviour and X and Y are measures of family environments and person variables. Regression surface analysis allows a figural presentation of the relations between variables and is a useful methodology for testing an interactionism framework of analysis.

In the studies using regression surfaces simple random samples of families were not selected. Therefore in the analyses the design effect for each raw regression weight is generally estimated, using the Jack-knife technique (Mosteller and Tukey, 1968; Finifter, 1972). In the calculations the data on the families are divided randomly into sets of sub-samples, and then pseudo-values for the regression weights are computed by conducting the regression analyses on different combinations of sub-samples. Significance levels for the regression weights were recalculated using the formula: standard error of sample estimate = (design effect)½ × simple random standard error (Kish, 1965; Ross, 1976). Typically the application of the Jack-knife technique led to a reduction in the number of regression weights that were significant. Often the adjusted standard errors showed that the interaction and curvilinear terms were not significant. In such cases, a second stage of the regression analysis was conducted in which variables that no longer had significant associations with the measures of children's achievement were deleted from the regression models.

In the second analysis, the Jack-knife technique was used again to estimate design effects and adjust further the significance levels of the regression weights.

Seminal family environment studies

In the following section of the chapter a set of family environment studies is reviewed that have adopted various conceptual and methodological frameworks of analysis. The studies are considered to represent some of the most significant family environment research in educational literature. They have been categorized as either social-psychological or socio-linguistic family environment investigations. Within the former category, studies are divided further into those that have adopted variations of 'traditional' social science research methods (Burks, 1928; Rosen, 1956, 1959, 1961; Keeves, 1972, 1974), and those using intensive analyses of small samples of families (Kahl, 1961; Strodtbeck, 1958). The socio-linguistic studies include those labelled as: early-Bernstein, Hess and Shipman, Labov, and later-Bernstein.

Social-psychological family environments:
'traditional' research methodologies

1. In a Stanford doctoral dissertation presented in 1928, Burks completed a study of the relations between family environments and children's intelligence test scores, which for its sophistication of sampling design and measurement has rarely been replicated. Burks indicated that 'The investigation in hand approaches the aspect of the problem which concerns heredity and *home environment* through a comparison of mental test resemblances obtaining between parents and children on the one hand, with those obtaining between foster parents and their foster children on the other' (p. 221). The sample included 214 children who were placed with foster parents before the age of 12 months and a control group of 105 children and their natural parents. Ages of the children ranged from 5 to 14 years.

A comprehensive set of measures was adopted for the study, including intelligence tests, schedules to assess affective characteristics, and family environment questionnaires. Each family participated for a period of four to eight hours. Parents and children completed the Stanford Binet test. Also included were a home information blank, a personal information blank, the Woodworth-Cady questionnaire to test for emotional stability, and a statement by parents on their children's character. These scales are described below.

(a) The home-information blank was completed by the researchers; it consisted of the Whittier Scale for Home Grading and a culture scale constructed for the study. In the Whittier Scale five aspects of a home are evaluated, including: necessities, neatness, size, parental conditions, and parental supervision. Each of these aspects is scored on a five- or six-point scale. A score of six, for example, on parental supervision indicates that 'care given the children and provision made for their welfare very exceptional' while a two-point score suggests that there is a 'lack of discipline because parents away large proportion of time. No partiality (in dealing with children) as far as known. Parents good, hard-working people.' One further example is provided to indicate the nature of the Scale. A necessities score of one, assessed a family as having: 'Wages of driver of small express and transfer wagon. Old ragged dirty clothes. Little food, very plain. Three small rooms in basement of cheap tenement house. Hardly bare necessities. Old, cheap, broken, wooden chairs and tables. No pictures or decorations. Bare floors. No comforts or improvement,' while a home that obtained a five-point home necessities score was described as: 'Architect, well-to-do. Well-dressed. Table ware indicates abundant food. Large modern bungalow, frame construction, well finished. Furniture fine quality, plentiful. Fine carpets, rugs, and pictures. Modern conveniences, built-in cupboards, electric fixtures, plumbing' (p. 231).

The culture scale constructed for the investigation assessed the education of parents, outside activities and hobbies of parents, the speech of parents as measured by the vocabulary score on the Binet vocabulary test, the number of books in the parents' library, and a measure of parents' artistic taste.

(b) A personal information blank was filled out by each parent, and it attempted to gather data similar to that obtained in many subsequent investigations. The blank

    called for data on the following points: birthplace,
    occupation; highest school grade reached; special interests,

hobbies or accomplishments; positions of honor, trust or recognition which have been held; distribution of time during the day (at home or away from home); children's hobbies or interests; occupations which parents think may be suitable for child in future; where child spends his leisure time; discipline of child. In addition, the blank filled out by the mother asked for information upon the kind and amount of home reading done by the child at various ages; the home instruction or attention received by the child in such matters as reading or writing, story-telling to child, number work, or nature study; and the private tutoring received by the child (in music, dancing, or other subjects) (p. 229).

(c) Children 10 years old or over filled out the Woodworth-Cady questionnaire to test for emotional stability.

(d) Both parents gave independent ratings for their children on ten character and temperament traits.

Thus the study examined a wide range of environmental and individual characteristics. Results of the analysis for the intelligence test scores are summarized in Table 1.1, and they show that the parent intelligence and family environment scores have low concurrent validities in relation to the foster children's test scores but moderate to high associations for the control-group children's scores. For the vocabulary measure, the patterns of associations with environment scores show fewer significant differences between the two groups of children. When predictor variables were combined in regression models, Burks found that fathers' mental age, fathers' vocabulary, mothers' vocabulary, and family income had a multiple correlation of 0.42 with foster children's intelligence test scores, while fathers' mental age, fathers' vocabulary, mothers' mental age, and the Whittier index had a relation of 0.61 to the test scores of the control-group children.

Burks completed her analysis using path analysis, a technique that remained generally dormant in educational and sociological research for the following forty years. As she states, 'It is extremely interesting to apply the Wright path coefficient technique to the correlations for the Control Group, to find out how much of the children's I.Q. variance can be accounted for by the reference to parental intelligence alone' (p. 299). The results in the following figure show the strengths of relations between

TABLE 1.1 *Correlates of intelligence and vocabulary scores: from Burks (1928)*

Predictor variable	Foster children		Control children	
	Vocabulary	Intelligence	Vocabulary	Intelligence
Father's mental age		07 (09)		45 (55)
Mother's mental age		19 (23)		46 (57)
Father's vocabulary	28 (30)	13 (14)	51 (54)	47 (52)
Mother's vocabulary	34 (35)	23 (25)	12 (13)	43 (48)
Whittier index	25 (27)	21 (24)	26 (29)	42 (48)
Culture index	32 (34)	25 (29)	34 (36)	44 (49)
Father's education		01		27
Mother's education		17		27
Income		23 (26)		24 (26)
Number of books in home	22	16	17	34
Number of children's books	29	32	31	32

Note Decimal points of zero-order correlations have been omitted. Correlations in parentheses have been corrected for attenuation related to unreliability of measures.

the variables, with 'a' and 'b' representing path coefficients. Environment did not make a significant unique contribution to the differences in the test scores.

From her analyses of children of foster and natural parents, Burks concludes that 'close to 75 or 80 per cent of I.Q. variance is due to innate and heritable causes. This estimate makes allowance for the 17 per cent which the data of this study show is due to measurable home environment, plus an additional 5 or 10 per cent due to the possible "random somatic effects of environment"' (p. 304). Fifty years later, such findings continue to generate educational controversies.

Burks' study has been reviewed in some detail as variations in the measurement procedures and methodological and statistical techniques continue to form the basis of many family

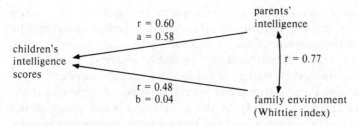

FIGURE I.2 *Children's intelligence, parents' intelligence and family environment*

investigations, often, it appears, without knowledge of Burks' pioneering efforts in relating family environments and children's outcomes.

2. In one of the few attempts that have been made to construct a social-psychological conceptual framework for the study of family environments, Rosen in a series of investigations developed the concept of the achievement syndrome. It is proposed that the learning environment of achievement-oriented families can be defined by three interrelated components: achievement motivation, achievement value orientations, and educational-vocational aspirations.

(a) Achievement motivation is considered to provide the internal psychological impetus to excel in situations involving standards of excellence. Rosen suggests that such motivation in children is generated by at least two kinds of family socialization practices that are labelled: achievement training and independence training. In the former socialization process 'parents, by imposing standards of excellence upon tasks, by setting high goals for their child, and by indicating their high evaluation of his competence to do a task well, communicate to him that they expect evidences of high achievement' (1959, p. 50). For independence training, parents indicate to children that they expect them to be self-reliant, and at the same time, the parents grant their children relative autonomy in decision-making situations. That is, while achievement training aims at getting children to do things well, independence training attempts to teach children to do things on their own.

(b) Achievement value orientations are defined as 'meaningful and affectively charged modes of organizing behavior – principles that guide human conduct. They establish criteria which influence the individual's preferences and goals' (p. 53). Rosen claims that the learning of achievement oriented values can be quite independent of the acquisition of the achievement motive. While value orientations are probably acquired when verbal communications within families are quite complex, it is considered that achievement motivation is generated from parent-child interactions early in the child's life when many of the interactions are emotional and non-verbal. Therefore within the achievement syndrome, achievement values focus 'the individual's attention on status improvement and help to shape his behavior so that achievement motivation can be translated into successful action'. Three sets of values are identified as components of the syndrome: activistic-passivistic orientations which encourage individuals to believe in their ability to manipulate the physical and social environment to their advantage; individualistic-collectivistic orientations that assess the extent to which individuals subordinate their needs to groups; and present-future orientations which stress either the merits of living in the present and emphasizing immediate gratifications or encourage the belief that planning and present sacrifices are worthwhile if future achievements are to be ensured.

(c) The third element of the achievement syndrome consists of educational-vocational aspirations. Rosen (1959, p. 57) states that 'Achievement motivation and values influence social mobility by affecting the individual's need to excel and his willingness to plan and work hard. But they do not determine the areas in which such excellence and effort take place.' It is considered that unless children have high educational and vocational goals, then positive value orientations and strong achievement motivation may not be related to successful achievement.

In studies of social mobility, Rosen has examined the achievement syndrome of families from French Canadian, Greek, Jewish, Negro, Southern Italian, and white Anglo-American Protestant ethnic groups. He found that the groups placed different emphases upon achievement and independence training within families; as a result, strong achievement motivation was more characteristic of Greek, Jewish, and Anglo-American children than of Italians, French Canadians, and Negroes. Generally, Jewish, Greek and Anglo-American parents were more likely to possess positive achievement-oriented values and higher aspirations than Southern Italian and French Canadian families.

The patterns for Negro families were not consistent for the three components of the syndrome.

As indicated earlier, the achievement syndrome provides a conceptual framework that includes some, but certainly not all, of the significant family environment process variables that are associated with children's academic achievement. In later studies, components of the syndrome are used in constructing schedules to assess the family environments of children from different social-status and ethnic groups.

3. In one of the most penetrating studies of family social psychological environments, Keeves (1972) combined stringent sampling procedures, refined measures of a set of learning environments, longitudinal data, and sophisticated statistical analysis. The path model shown in Figure 1.3 was used to examine the relations between the environment variables and measures of attitudes and achievement.

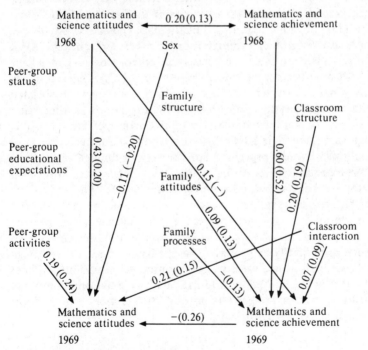

FIGURE 1.3 *Path model: Keeves analysis*

Note First coefficient relates to mathematics while coefficients in parentheses relate to science achievement and attitudes.

A simple random sample of 242 Australian children was included in the analysis. Data were collected when the children were in their final year of elementary school and again when they were in their first year of secondary school. Family structure was assessed using global social-status variables and sibsize; family attitudes by five variables that measured the parents' attitudes towards the child's present education and their ambitions for the child's future education and occupation. The process dimension of the family was defined by variables such as: the use of books and library facilities, arrangements made for doing homework assignments, and relations between teachers and parents. The peer-group and classroom variables are discussed in detail in Keeves (1972, 1974), and are not presented here.

In Figure 1.3 the results of the path analyses have been placed on the model. For mathematics achievement and attitudes, the 'major factor influencing final achievement was initial achievement, but both the attitudes of the home and the initial attitudes of the student to mathematics made a small but statistically significant contribution' (Keeves, 1974, p. 249). Also, the classroom structure and classroom interaction variables have significant direct relations to achievement. Attitudes towards mathematics measured during the second survey are associated with earlier attitudes, peer-group activities, classroom interaction and sex, but not related to earlier mathematics performance. The regression coefficients for science show a similar pattern of relations. Family processes are an extra influence on science achievement, while attitudes towards science have direct relations to the later science performance scores. The analysis is restricted to a consideration of direct effects and does not examine the possibility of the indirect effects of measures on the achievement and attitude variables. But the analysis goes beyond much prior family environment research as it specifies a model of analysis including a variety of environmental situations. In later chapters of this book longitudinal data from a national sample of English children are used to examine further models of the form presented in the Keeves' study.

Social-psychological family environments:
'intensive' research analyses

In the following two studies, Kahl (1961) and Strodtbeck (1958) use survey techniques followed by intensive investigations of small samples of families. The methodologies adopted provide possible guides for future researchers attempting to integrate structural and interactional analyses of the relations between children's behaviours and family environments.

1. The Kahl (1961) investigation gathered information from approximately 4,000 high school boys from the Boston metropolitan area. Assessments were made of the boys' current educational plans, intelligence, and family social status. Generally, boys who had high test scores or who came from high-status homes planned to go to college, while most boys with low intelligence scores or from low social-status families had no aspirations for higher education. But although the prediction of college plans was high at the extremes of intelligence and social-status scores, 'it was not good in the middle of the distribution. Of particular interest was the fact that if a boy had high intelligence and came from the most populous part of the status range – its lower middle section – one could not well predict his aspiration' (p. 350).

Kahl pursued his analysis of the relations between intelligence scores and the aspirations of boys from lower middle-status families, using intensive interviews of 24 boys and their parents. All 24 boys had test scores in the top three deciles of their school. Half the sample was enrolled in college preparatory courses, had grades in the top half of their respective classes and planned to go to college, while the remaining 12 boys were not in college preparatory classes and had no aspirations for college. Parents were interviewed from between one and two hours in their homes, while each boy had approximately five hours of interviews in school. As Kahl suggests, 'the interviews were designed to begin where the statistics left off' (p. 351).

The parental interviews did not follow a fixed schedule but were focused on attitudes towards work and school. In the interviews, parents identified a three-level social-status system based on the income and style of life of families. The parents perceived themselves as belonging to a middle group that Kahl labels as the 'common man' class. Above this group were the 'rich people', 'business class' or 'professionals', and there was a lower class beneath them which parents identified as including 'people who lived in slums, had rough manners and morals, and had tough kids who were a bad influence on their children' (p. 352). Within the 'common man' class two distinct groups of families were isolated. Fifteen families had a 'getting-by' core value reflecting a feeling that 'this way of life was not only to be accepted but to be preferred, that the competitive game to rise higher was not worth the candle', while the remaining nine families adopted a value of 'getting ahead', indicating a feeling of the parent that they 'had not risen quite as high as they should have' (p. 354).

The interviews revealed that the two groups of parents created different learning environments for their children. In the 'getting-by' families, boys were encouraged to enjoy themselves while they were young but to stay in high school 'because a diploma was pretty important in getting jobs nowadays, but they were allowed to pick their own curriculum according to taste' (p. 354). In these families, the possibility of pursuing a college education was rarely considered. By contrast, parents who believed in 'getting ahead' started to apply pressure to their sons from the beginning of the boys' school careers. 'They encouraged high marks, they paid attention to what was happening at school, they stressed that good performance was necessary for occupational success, they suggested various occupations that would be good for their sons' (p. 360). 'Getting ahead' fathers believed that their own lack of occupational success was related to their failure to receive sufficient education. 'Yet if they were blocked, their sons were not. Consequently, they encouraged their sons to take school seriously and to aim for college' (p. 355).

Interviews of the boys revealed two separate groups, which Kahl also labels as 'getting-by' and 'getting ahead'. Boys who believed in just 'getting-by' were bored with school, anticipated a 'common man' type of occupation, and found 'peer group activity to be the most important thing in life' (p. 359). Alternatively, the 'getting ahead' boys appeared to take schoolwork more seriously than recreational affairs, had more specific occupational goals, had educational aims to match their occupational aspirations, worked harder in school, thought more of the future, and 'believed they could somehow manage to pay their way through college and reach the middle class' (p. 363). That is, boys learned to an unusual degree to perceive the occupational and educational systems in relation to their parents' perspective.

By adopting an interview technique which was not overly structured, Kahl was able to generate an important explanatory variable for his analysis of the correlates of boys' college plans. As he states 'an intelligent common man boy was not college oriented in high school unless he had a very special reason for so being. Behind all the reasons stood one pre-eminent force: parental pressure' (p. 360). The investigation provides a sensitive example of educational research using an interpretative-type framework to enrich the findings from a large-scale statistical analysis.

2. Using a combination of questionnaires and family interviews, related to an experimental situation, Strodtbeck (1958) attempted to identify variables that might be associated with differential social mobility rates of American families. Italian and Jewish families were chosen for study, as 'In the United States as a whole, Jews consistently have higher occupational status than the population at large, while, in contrast, that of the Italians is lower' (p. 138). The stated aim of the research was 'to search their value systems and family life for clues as to why they differed in the population of achievement individuals in the United States' (p. 185).

From larger samples of students, 24 third-generation boys from both ethnic groups were selected for intensive analysis. The 48 boys were stratified according to social status and also were labelled as either under- or over-academic achievers in school. It was proposed that a family may be analysed in relation to a 'power system' and that a son's adjustment to the system should generalize to his extra-familial activities. An experimental situation was constructed to investigate the parents' and son's adjustment to the family 'power system'. In the 48 families, questionnaires were administered to the parents and the sons. The researchers included an experimenter and an assistant. As soon as the questionnaires were completed, the assistant compiled a set of answers for further discussion. The answers were placed into three coalition categories: mother and son agree on the answer, father disagrees; father and mother agree and son disagrees; father and son agree and mother disagrees. The parents and son were placed around recording equipment and asked to consider again some of the questions on which agreement was not complete. It was stated that 'We would like you to talk over the item until you understand clearly why each person marked the item as he did. We want you to try to agree on one choice which would best represent the opinion of the family, if this is possible' (p. 162).

Protocols were scored directly from the recordings of the family discussions to obtain power scores for mothers, fathers, and sons. Power scores were formed from the number of decisions won in the discussions. Scores were adjusted, 'so that winning, or holding one's position when in the minority, is weighed more heavily when one is an isolate than when one is a member of the larger coalition' (p. 166). As well as an assessment of family member's participation in the 'power system' of family decision making, Bales's interaction process categories were adopted to construct an index of supportiveness which indicated the amount of support one family member gave to the other two members in the discussion sessions.

Parents also completed a schedule which assessed achievement value orientations. Analysis of the responses generated two factors, labelled: mastery and independence of the family. The former factor loaded strongly on items such as: 'planning only makes a person unhappy since your plans hardly ever work out anyhow'; 'nowadays, with world conditions the way they are, the wise person lives for today and lets tomorrow take care of itself'; while the independence factor loads on items such as: 'even when teen-agers get married, their main loyalty still belongs to their fathers and mothers'; 'when the time comes for a boy to take a job, he should stay near his parents, even if it means giving up a good job opportunity'. The boys completed a thematic apperception-type test designed to assess achievement motivation.

The results showed that in relation to the Bales' interaction process categories, family patterns were not related to social status, ethnicity, value-orientation scores, achievement motivation, or over- and under-achievement. Strodtbeck states that 'The point to be emphasized is the very great similarity of Italian and Jewish interaction patterns. If there has been differential achievement – and according to our data this is indeed the case – then one must conclude that ethnic differences in family interaction are not of great relevance in explaining it' (p. 175). For the power scores, the findings revealed that the higher the social status of families the less was the power of sons and greater was the power of fathers. Mothers' power scores did not appear to be related to social status, but Jewish mothers had more power in the decision-making process than Italian mothers. No ethnic differences were found between fathers' and sons' scores and no differences in relations between sons' power scores and school achievement. After examining the associations between power and achievement value scores, Strodtbeck concludes that it is the relation between 'the son's power and the balance of power between father and mother which appears to affect the son's V-score' (p. 183). When the power and value scores of mothers were high, then the value scores of sons were also high. It is proposed that the less that mothers and sons are dominated by fathers within the family 'power system', the greater is the disposition of mothers and sons to believe that the world can be rationally mastered and that sons should risk separation from their families. Strodtbeck goes on to suggest that 'Knowing as we do that certain distributions of power in the family are conducive to achievement, we might even speak of certain families as being "talented" in developing their sons . . . in terms of the way they handle power' (p. 191).

Although both the Kahl and Strodtbeck investigations have limitations of measurement and design, which are expressed in the two studies, the research provides elegant methodologies for examining the potential influence of family social-psychological variables on children's behaviour. The variables of parental pressure and the family power system warrant continued analysis in educational research and the methodologies adopted are applicable for studying classroom and peer-group learning contexts as well as family environments.

Socio-linguistic family environments

During the second half of the 1960s, numerous educational programmes were developed for children who were labelled as disadvantaged or culturally deprived. The thrust of many of these ventures was to change children's language patterns. In the most extreme programmes it was assumed that children from certain social groups were bereft of a language that would allow them to learn in the classroom, and therefore it was decided to treat these children as if they had 'no language at all' (e.g., Bereiter *et al.*, 1966; Bereiter and Engelmann, 1966). Perhaps the most prominent socio-linguistic framework used by educators to support the construction of programmes was that formulated by Bernstein; and in this section of the chapter Bernstein's contribution is reviewed in two parts labelled as early- and later-Bernstein. In the introduction to a compilation of his work, Bernstein (1971, p. 1) indicates that the development of his theoretical position was in process for a period of at least twelve years. He says about one paper entitled 'Social class and linguistic development: a theory of social learning' (Bernstein, 1961): 'This paper I regard, despite the possible pretentiousness, as the end of the beginning stage.' The early-Bernstein review refers primarily to this 1961 publication.

During the early 1970s compensatory education programmes were criticized for directing the blame of children's failure at the family and the child rather than at the school curriculum and classroom environments. At the same time, Bernstein's socio-linguistic theory, and research generated from it, were attacked as it was claimed that they provided support for a theory of cultural deprivation within families (e.g., Baratz and Baratz, 1970; Labov, 1972; Rosen, 1974). In his later work, however, Bernstein (1971, p. 195) suggests that 'we should stop thinking in terms of "compensatory education" but consider instead most seriously and systematically the conditions and contents of the educational environment'. And he states that, 'If the culture of the teacher is to become part of the consciousness of the child, then the culture of the child must first be in the consciousness of the teacher' (p. 199).

Some of these developments in socio-linguistic theory are traced here briefly by reviewing the work of early-Bernstein, Hess and Shipman, who conducted an empirical analysis based on Bernstein's early formulations, Labov, and later-Bernstein. But readers are referred to three volumes of Bernstein's published work and related empirical studies for a more complete analysis of his contribution to educational research (Bernstein, 1971, 1973, 1975), and also to two very detailed volumes of Labov's research on youth from Central Harlem (Labov *et al.*, 1968a, 1968b).

1. Early-Bernstein: In the development of his socio-linguistic theory, Bernstein (1961, p. 288) was concerned with the questions: 'How does a given social structure become part of individual experience, what is the *main* process through which this is achieved, and what are the educational implications?' He proposes that within lower working-class and middle-class families different emphases are placed on language potential, resulting in two distinct forms of language being generated. And 'once the emphasis or stress is placed, then the resulting forms of speech progressively orient their speakers to distinct types of relationships of objects and persons' (p. 291). The typical mode of speech of the middle class was labelled formal language (elaborated code) and is considered to be a form of speech in which the structure and syntax are relatively difficult to predict for any one individual, and a speech where 'the formal possibilities of sentence organization are used to clarify meaning and make it explicit' (p. 291). In

contrast, the speech mode of the lower working class is considered to be characterized by a rigidity of syntax and as having a restricted use of structural possibilities for sentence organization. This latter mode of speech was called a public language (restricted code).

It was claimed by Bernstein that middle-class children learn both linguistic codes and are able to use them in appropriate contexts, while the working-class child is restricted to the public form of the language. In middle-class families, it is suggested that the early linguistic relations between mothers and children maximize 'cognitive and affective differentiation and discrimination, rather than affective inclusiveness and identity. The speech marks out a pattern of stimuli to which the child adapts . . . the child learns his social structure and introjects it from the very beginning of speech' (p. 294). For lower working-class families it is asserted that the linguistic relations between mothers and children are of a different order. 'It is essentially a verbal form, where, initially, personal qualifications are made through *expressive* symbolism; that is non-verbally, or through the possibilities of a limiting language structure. The child's relationship to the mother is of a direct, immediate nature' (p. 297).

Bernstein listed some of the implications for children possessing a public language, which aroused much of the criticism of the theoretical position. It is proposed that a public language is associated with:

> relatively low level of conceptualization, an orientation to a low order of causality, a disinterest in processes, a preference to be aroused by, and respond to, that which is immediately given, rather than to the implications of a matrix of relationships; and that this partly conditions the intensity and extent of curiosity as well as the mode of establishing relationships. A preference for a particular form of social relationship is engendered; a form where individual qualifications are non-verbally communicated, or mediated through the limited possibilities of a *public* language (p. 302).

It is stated, however, that the type of public language described and analysed is rarely found in the pure state. Instead, what is found empirically is an orientation to the described language form that is conditioned by socially induced preferences. But the following reaction by Labov (1972, p. 204) is typical of the criticisms made of the public and formal language descriptions: 'Bernstein's views are filtered through a strong bias against all forms of working-class behavior, so that middle-class language is seen as superior in every respect.'

Within school contexts, Bernstein proposes that the teaching of lower working-class children is often persecutory and exposes them to persistent attacks on their language and on their normal mode of orientation. And he warns that to develop educational programmes that simply attempt to substitute a formal for a public language 'is to cut off the individual from his traditional relationships and perhaps alienate him from them' (p. 308). Bernstein suggests the adoption of an educational strategy that preserves the public language but creates for children the possibility of using a formal language. But he states that such a change 'involves the whole personality of the individual, the very character of his social relationships, his points of emotional and logical reference, and his conception of himself' (p. 308). Although Labov is extremely critical of Bernstein's socio-linguistic framework, some of his own recommendations for educational practice are not too dissimilar from those just presented.

2. In a much cited study, Hess and Shipman (1965) used the Bernstein framework to examine relations between mothers' teaching styles and the learning styles and information-processing strategies of their children. Three propositions formed the structure for the analysis: (a) behaviour leading to social, economic, and educational poverty is learned in early childhood; (b) the lack of cognitive meaning in the mother-child communication system is the central quality involved in the effects of cultural deprivation; and (c) the growth of children's cognitive processes is facilitated in families that permit a wide range of alternatives of action and thought.

The sample for the study included 163 Negro mothers and their 4-year-old children, from four social-status groups. Mothers were interviewed in their homes and also taken to a university setting where they were taught three simple tasks and then asked to teach the tasks to their children. It is suggested that one of the greatest differences between mothers in the teaching-learning situations was related to patterns of language use. Middle social-status mothers gave protocols which were consistently longer in language productivity and of a greater quality, where quality was

assessed by the tendency to use abstract words and complex syn-
tactic structures such as co-ordinate and subordinate clauses,
unusual infinitive phrases, infinitive clauses, and participal
phrases. Hess and Shipman propose that the use of complex
grammatical forms and the elaboration of them into complex
sentences and clauses provides a highly elaborated (formal) code
with which to manipulate the family learning environment
symbolically. They suggest further that the elaborated code
encourages children to recognize the possibilities and subtleties
inherent in language both for communication and for carrying on
high-level cognitive procedures. In contrast, the effect of restricted (public) speech by the mothers was seen as foreclosing the
need by children for reflective weighing of alternatives and consequences, which resulted in children having relatively un-
developed verbal and conceptual abilities.

They conclude that:

> The meaning of deprivation is a deprivation of meaning – a
> cognitive environment in which behavior is controlled by
> status rules rather than by attention to the individual
> characteristics of a specific situation and one in which
> behavior is not mediated by verbal cues or by teaching that
> relates events to one another and the present to the future (p.
> 887).

Readers are referred to the volumes of Bernstein's work for
further empirical tests of the conceptual framework.

3. The Labov research is reviewed here as it opposes the Bern-
stein-type theoretical position, especially when applied to black
children. He claims that (1972, p. 201):

> The concept of verbal deprivation has no basis in social
> reality. In fact, black children in the urban ghettos receive a
> great deal of verbal stimulation, hear more well-formed
> sentences than middle-class children, and participate fully
> in a highly verbal culture. They have the same basic
> vocabulary, possess the same capacity for conceptual
> learning, and use the same logic as anyone else who learns to
> speak and understand English.

Labov's conclusions are generated from an intensive analysis of
the structural and functional differences between non-standard
Negro English (NNE) of northern American ghetto areas and the

standard English (SE) required in the classroom. The analyses
were conducted within peer-group settings rather than in families
as it is suggested that 'Many of the reports of "verbal deprivation"
of ghetto children are based on tests carried out under the most
unfavorable conditions' (Labov, 1968b, p. 340); that is, in adult-
oriented environments.

From an investigation of youth from Central Harlem, Labov
proposes that the major factor responsible for the reading failure
of ghetto children is a cultural conflict. 'The school environment
and school values are plainly not influencing the boys firmly
grounded in street culture' (1972, p. 252). He indicates that to view
the peer group as a mere substitute for school shows an unusual
lack of knowledge of adolescent culture. The findings indicated
that children who are rejected by peer groups are most likely to be
successful in school, while 'in ghetto areas it is the healthy,
vigorous, popular child with intelligence who cannot read and
fails all along the line' . . . 'somewhere between the time that
children first learn to talk and puberty, their language is restruc-
tured to fit the rules used by their peer group' (1972, p. 231). From
a linguistic viewpoint it is claimed that the peer group of ghetto
children is a more powerful influence than the family.

Labov *et al.* (1968b, p. 339) observe from structural linguistic
analyses of non-standard Negro English, that 'we do not find a
foreign language with syntax and semantics radically different
from SE: instead, we find a dialect of English with certain exten-
sions and modifications of rules to be found in other dialects'.
Indeed, it is claimed that the underlying differences between the
two forms of English are extremely subtle and that interference
between the two forms is more difficult to handle because of the
similarities in the two grammars. But, while they are closely
related, the two grammars form distinct sub-systems, which
means that the elements from one are not freely interchangeable
with the elements of the other grammar.

For school programmes, Labov *et al.* (1968b, p. 349) suggest
that teachers have to:

> show the NNE youngster that he can learn standard English
> for immediate advantage, as a means of getting other people
> to do what he wants them to do. Most importantly, there
> must be a strong program of breaking down the
> identification of standard English with white society. The

NNE youngster should be made to feel that he has as much claim to standard English as anyone else. If he is not being given the ability to read and write this language, then he is being cheated out of something that is rightfully his.

But Labov (1972, p. 213) cautions that, while there are undoubtedly many verbal skills that children from ghetto areas must learn in order to succeed in the school situation, before 'we impose middle-class verbal style upon children from other cultural groups, we should find out how much of this is useful for the main work of analyzing and generalizing, and how much is really stylistic – or even dysfunctional'.

4. Later-Bernstein: In a statement related to his own work, Bernstein (1971, p. 170) suggests that 'Looking back, I think I would have created less misunderstanding if I had written about socio-linguistic codes rather than linguistic codes'. He claims that 'using only the latter concept it gave the impression I was reifying syntax and suggesting that there was a one-to-one relationship between meaning and a given syntax. Also, by defining the codes in a context-free fashion, I robbed myself of properly understanding, at a theoretical level, their significance.'

Bernstein in his later analyses argues that, from a sociological position, the most formative influence upon socialization is social class, and that the class system has deeply delineated the distribution of knowledge within society. He claims that only a small proportion of people are socialized into knowledge which gives them access to the principles of intellectual change, while the mass of the population is denied such access and is socialized into knowledge at the level of context-tied operations. Two orders of meaning are distinguished and are defined as universalistic and particularistic. When 'meanings are universalistic, they are in principle available to all because the principles and operations have been made explicit and so public', but for particularistic meaning systems 'much of the meaning is embedded in the context and may be restricted to those who share a similar contextual history' (p. 176).

Bernstein then links socio-linguistic codes and meaning systems by proposing that elaborated linguistic codes 'orient their users towards universalistic meanings, whereas restricted codes orient, sensitize, their users to particularistic meanings (p. 176). Also linguistic codes are associated with family types, which are defined by the strength of the boundary maintaining procedures within families. If boundary procedures are strong, for example, it is proposed that the differentiation of family members and the authority structure are based upon unambiguous definitions of the status of the members. Such a family is labelled as positional. Alternatively, if boundary procedures are weak or flexible then the differentiation between members is based more upon differences between persons, and such families are defined as person-centred. In these latter families speech is considered to be a major form of control, while in positional families 'speech is relevant but it symbolizes the boundaries given by the formal structure of the relationships' (p. 185).

That is, a framework is constructed linking: (a) social structure, (b) socialization within family types that are defined by different social arrangements, (c) socio-linguistic codes which symbolize the form of the social relationships in families, and (d) access to particularistic and universalistic meanings. Bernstein cautions that one of the difficulties of socio-linguistic research is to avoid implicit value judgments about the relative worth of speech systems and the cultures which they symbolize:

> Let it be said immediately that a restricted code gives access to a vast potential of meanings, of delicacy, subtlety and diversity of cultural forms, to a unique aesthetic the basis of which in condensed symbols may influence the form of the imagining. Yet, in complex industrialized societies its differently-focused experience may be disvalued and humiliated in schools, or seen, at best, to be irrelevant to the educational endeavour. For the schools are predicated upon elaborated code and its system of social relationships (p. 186).

The analyses by Bernstein and Labov emphasize the importance for teachers to understand not only the linguistic patterns of children but also the social relationships from which the patterns are generated. Attempts to adjust language within schools means disrupting forms of social relations in families and peer groups. The failure of many educational programmes to achieve their goals may, in part, be related to a lack of appreciation and respect for the sub-stratum of a child's experiences.

The studies reviewed in this introductory chapter suggest that a model of the type shown in Figure 1.4 might be used to generate

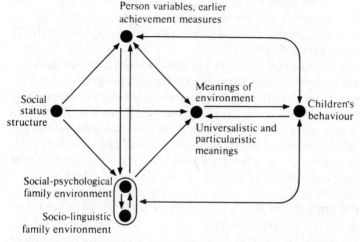

FIGURE I.4 *Model for family environment research*

research on the relations between family environments and children's behaviour. In the present book relationships are examined between social structure variables, social-psychological family environment measures, person variables, and children's achievement. Chapter 2 is a review of studies that have been labelled as belonging to either the 'Chicago' or 'British' schools of family environment research. A number of investigations that might have been included in the discussion of seminal studies (e.g., Fraser, 1959; Plowden, 1967), are examined in Chapter 2. In Chapters 3 and 4 relations between children's outcomes and distal social-status and sibling constellation variables are investigated. Although the book is concerned primarily with measures of family environments, relations between families and children's behaviours are explained more adequately when other environments also are considered. Thus, in Chapter 5 inter-relationships between families, school environments and children's outcomes are presented. The interactionism framework of analysis is specifically examined in Chapter 6, where associations are studied between person variables and children's achievement at different levels of family environments. In societies, ethnic group membership is one of the most significant sociological influences on children's school-related behaviour, and in Chapter 7 relations are examined between ethnicity, person variables, family environments, and academic performance. In the final chapter a path model is examined which attempts to bring together many of the variables that are discussed throughout the book. Some implications of the research for educational practice are considered also in the concluding chapter.

It is an assumption of the present book that, for the development of educational programmes that are meaningful for children, it is necessary to collect as much relevant information as possible relating to the environments in which children learn. Those who construct curricula need to understand how interactions between social structure and the social-psychological and socio-linguistic environments of families, peer groups and classrooms facilitate or constrain children's educational development. While this book is concerned primarily with relations between social-psychological family environments and the academic achievement of children from different social-status and ethnic groups, such an emphasis is not meant to infer any diminution of the influence of other environments. Instead, it is hoped that the present book might indicate the need to collect in other texts the findings from peer-group, classroom, and other family environment research, so that we may begin to develop sets of comparative data on the environmental correlates of children's behaviour.

2 The 'Chicago' and 'British' schools of family environment research

In the development of a theory of personality, Murray (1938, p. 16) suggests that if the behaviour of individuals is to be understood then it is necessary to devise a method of analysis that 'will lead to satisfactory dynamical formulations of external environments'. He proposes that an environment should be classified by the kinds of benefits or harms that it provides. If the environment has a potentially harmful effect Murray suggests that individuals attempt to prevent its occurrence by avoiding the environment or defending themselves against it, while if the environment has a potentially beneficial effect then individuals will typically approach the environment and attempt to interact with it. The directional tendency of the environment implied in Murray's framework is designated as the press of the environment. Each press is defined as having a qualitative aspect which is the kind of effect that the environment has or might have upon an individual. Also each press has a quantitative aspect, which is assessed by the variation in power that an environment has for either harming or benefiting different individuals, or the same individual at different times. In his framework, Murray (1938, p. 122) distinguishes between the alpha press of the environment 'which is the press that actually exists, as far as scientific discovery can determine it', and an environment's beta press, 'which is the subject's own interpretation of the phenomena that he perceives'. In the present chapter, research is examined that has investigated direct relationships between measures of the alpha press of family environments and children's cognitive performance and affective characteristics.

Family environment and the alpha press

In his own research, Murray concentrated on analysing the beta press of family environments. It was not until Bloom (1964), and a number of his doctoral students, examined the environmental correlates of children's cognitive and affective measures that a definite 'School' of research emerged to assess the alpha press of family environments. In what might be designated the 'Chicago' school of family environment research, Bloom defines the environment as the conditions, forces, and external stimuli that impinge upon the individual. It is proposed that these forces, which may be physical or social as well as intellectual, provide a network which surrounds, engulfs and plays on the individual. While it is acknowledged that some individuals may resist the network, it is considered likely that it will only be the extreme and rare individuals who can completely avoid or escape from the environmental forces. Thus the environment is conceived of as a shaping and a reinforcing force that acts upon individuals. As Bloom (1964, p. 187) suggests, 'such a view of the environment reduces it for analytical purposes to those aspects of the environment which are related to a particular characteristic or set of characteristics'. That is, the total environment surrounding an individual may be defined as being composed of a number of sub-environments. Then to understand the development of a particular characteristic it becomes necessary to identify that sub-environment of press variables which potentially is related to the characteristic. In later chapters of this book it is proposed that relations between family social-psychological sub-environments and children's school-related outcomes are explained more fully when social environment measures (such as social-status characteristics) and person

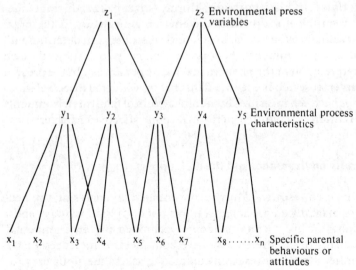

FIGURE 2.1 *Family environment model*

variables (such as children's attitudes and personality) are included in the analyses.

In the 'Chicago' studies, a family environment model of the form shown in Figure 2.1 has usually been adopted to guide the measurement of environments. That is, the press variables are defined by sets of social-psychological process variables, and then in interview schedules process characteristics are assessed by obtaining measures of specific behaviours or attitudes within the family.

As the research of the 'Chicago' school was undertaken, another set of studies, which may loosely be grouped together as the 'British' school, was being generated. Although these latter studies did not consciously adopt Murray's concept of the alpha press, nor generally use Bloom's model of sub-environments of press variables, they may be interpreted in relation to those constructs. The studies shown in Figure 2.2 are reviewed in the present chapter, as they are considered to reflect the development of the two schools of family environment research.

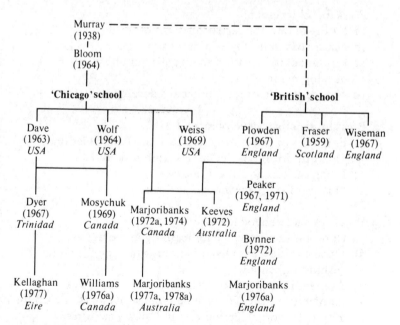

FIGURE 2.2 *The 'Chicago' and 'British' schools of family environment research*

The 'Chicago' school of family environment research

Family environment and cognitive performance

In the initial studies of the 'Chicago' school, Dave (1963) and Wolf (1964) examined relations between the family environment and measures of academic achievement and intelligence, respectively. Both investigations used the same 60 children, 32 girls and 28 boys. The children had an average age of 11 and were selected from 19 schools in an Illinois school system.

Wolf used the Henmon-Nelson Tests of Mental Ability to assess children's intelligence, and identified three press variables postulated to be related to the intelligence scores. The three press variables were labelled: press for achievement motivation, press for language development, and provisions for general learning, and were defined by the 13 process characteristics presented in the following list:

1 Press for achievement
  1a Nature of intellectual expectations of child
  1b Nature of intellectual aspirations for child
  1c Amount of information about child's intellectual development
  1d Nature of rewards for intellectual development

2 Press for language development
  2a Emphasis on use of language in a variety of situations
  2b Opportunities provided for enlarging vocabulary
  2c Emphasis on correctness of usage
  2d Quality of language models available

3 Provisions for general learning
  3a Opportunities provided for learning in the home
  3b Opportunities provided for learning outside the home (excluding school)
  3c Availability and encouragement of use of supplies
  3d Availability and encouragement of use of books (including reference works), periodicals and library facilities
  3e Nature and amount of assistance provided to facilitate learning in a variety of situations

A semi-structured home interview schedule was designed to measure the process characteristics and the press variables. Mothers were interviewed and their responses rated on 13 seven-point scales, one for each environmental process characteristic. Ratings for the three press variables were obtained by summing the ratings on the relevant process characteristics. When the relations between the three environment press variables were examined, using principal component analysis, the three measures loaded strongly on a general factor, which Wolf suggests supports the concept of a sub-environment for the development and maintenance of intelligence. The three press variables, when combined into a predictor set, accounted for 49 per cent of the variance in the intelligence test scores (see Table 2.3). In these discussions the phrase 'accounted for', which is typically used in regression analyses, may be substituted by 'associated with', to indicate that no causality is inferred by the findings that are presented.

In Dave's (1963) study the Metropolitan Achievement Tests were used to assess the academic achievement of the children. Out of the total set of conditions and processes that constitute the family environment, Dave identified a specific component which he labelled the educational environment of the family. Six press variables defined the family environment: achievement press, language models, academic guidance, activeness of the family, intellectuality in the home, and work habits in the family. These variables are defined by the 21 process characteristics shown in the following list, and a nine-point rating scale was devised for each characteristic.

1 Achievement press
   1a Parental aspirations for the education of the child
   1b Parents' own aspirations
   1c Parents' interest in academic achievement
   1d Social press for academic achievement
   1e Standards of reward for educational attainment
   1f Knowledge of the educational progress of the child
   1g Preparation and planning for the attainment of educational goals

2 Language models
   2a Quality of the language usage of the parents

2b Opportunities for the enlargement and use of vocabulary and sentence patterns

2c Keenness of the parents for correct and effective language usage

3 Academic guidance

3a Availability of guidance on matters relating to school work

3b Quality of guidance on matters relating to school work

3c Availability and use of materials and facilities related to school learning

4 Activeness of the family

4a The extent and content of the indoor activities of the family

4b The extent and content of the outdoor activities during weekends and vacations

4c Use of TV and such other media

4d Use of books, periodical literature, library and such other facilities

5 Intellectuality in the home

5a Nature and quality of toys, games, and hobbies made available to the child

5b Opportunities for thinking and imagination in daily activities

6 Work habits in the family

6a Degree of structure and routine in the home management

6b Preference for educational activities over other pleasurable things

Scores on the six press variables were obtained by averaging the ratings on the relevant process characteristics. The results in Table 2.3 show that the press variables have differential relations with performance in the academic subjects. For example, the environment accounts for over 50 per cent of the variance in arithmetic problem solving, reading, and word knowldge, but only 31 per cent of the variance in arithmetic computation scores. Also, the order of importance of the predictability of the six press variables was found to differ from subject to subject. In the case of word knowledge and reading, for example, achievement press was the most important variable in a step-wise regression analysis, while for arithmetic problem-solving the most important variable was intellectuality in the home. Thus as Dave (1963, p. 86) suggests, while factor analysis indicates that less than six press variables might be quite sufficient for the measurement of the educational environment of the family, the results show 'that if one is interested in the prediction of subject-wise achievement, one might even find more than six variables desirable on the environmental measure, so that different combinations of variables measured by the same instrument could be used for the optimal prediction of specific-subject achievement.'

The family environment measure devised by Dave has been used in other cultural settings. Dyer (1967), for example, examined the family environments of 60 11-year-old children from Port of Spain, Trinidad. The environment measure accounted for a large percentage of the variance in academic achievement scores, and generally had moderate relations to intelligence. In a study of 60 8-year-old Irish children, from a socially disadvantaged area of Dublin, Kellaghan (1977) accounted for moderate to large percentages of the variance in arithmetic, Irish reading, and English reading test scores, and found that the environment had moderate relations to 'crystallized' intelligence scores and smaller associations with 'fluid' ability measures.

The family environment and differential mental abilities

In studies of Canadian children, Mosychuk (1969) and Marjoribanks (1972a) moved beyond the examination of global intelligence scores and investigated relations between the family environment and sets of ability measures. Mosychuk examined the WISC scores of 100 10-year-old boys from Edmonton in Western Canada. A schedule assessing ten aspects of the family environment was used in interviews with mothers. The ten process characteristics were labelled: academic and vocational aspirations and expectations of parents; knowledge of, and interest in, child's academic and intellectual development; material and organizational opportunities for the use and development of language; quality of language in the home; female dominance in child rearing; planfulness, purposefulness, and harmony in the home; dependency fostering – overprotection; authoritarian home; interaction with physical environment; and opportunity for, and emphasis on, initiating and carrying through tasks. Factor analysis of the scores on the ten measures produced four factors which may be considered as press variables, and these were labelled: (a) aspirations-planfulness-harmony, (b) authoritarian-overprotective, (c) activity-environmental interaction, and (d) female-language. The first environment factor had moderate concurrent validities with the WISC verbal, performance, and full intelligence scores, while the other press variables had low to negligible associations with the WISC scores. When the ten WISC sub-test scores were factor-analysed, four factors emerged and these were defined as: reasoning, general memory, verbal-symbolic, and perceptual-motor-spatial. A significant canonical correlation of 0.57 was obtained between the four press variables and the four WISC factor scores.

Williams (1976a) extended the Mosychuk study by obtaining intelligence test scores from the children's parents, in order to investigate relations between parents' intellectual abilities, family environments, and children's abilities. A re-analysis of the family environment data generated factors which, Williams suggests, supports a social learning theory of environments. In such a theory (see Williams, 1976a, pp. 66–7) the postulated major dimensions of family environments are:

(a) the stimuli parents provide by specifically structuring opportunities for the child to interact with a wide variety of people and things in his environment;

(b) the reinforcement practices parents use to modify the child's performance on intellectually-relevant (i.e., school-related) behaviors; and

(c) the expectations they hold out for appropriate performance on these behaviors.

As well as these three dimensions, Williams obtained a further environment factor from the data which he labelled parental dominance, and which dealt with the relative dominance of one of the parents in child-rearing. Using path analytic techniques, Williams found that high-ability fathers, in relation to lower-ability fathers, provided more opportunities for their sons to interact with the environment, were more involved in child-rearing, tended to use more non-physical means of sanctioning, and had higher expectations for their son's performance. High-ability mothers provided more opportunities for environmental interaction, tended to have a more active role in child-rearing, but differed little from lower-ability mothers in the use of physical punishment as a sanction or in the expectations they had for their child's performance. Of the four dimensions of family environments, the stimulus and expectation measures exerted the strongest influence on the children's abilities. Williams found, however, that by far the greatest part of the parent-child ability correlation was explained by direct effects unmediated by family environments, and he suggests that 'the interpretation of these direct parent-child effects must remain equivocal as they represent the effects of biological inheritance and unmeasured environmental influences in some unknown mix' (Williams, 1976a, p. 91).

In a study of 11-year-old boys from Southern Ontario, Marjoribanks examined relations between the family environment and scores on tests of verbal, number, spatial, and reasoning ability. Approximately 500 boys were tested, using first the California Test of Mental Maturity and then the SRA Primary Mental Abilities Test (1962, revised edition). The first test-taking situation was used to establish examiner-examinee rapport, to ensure that all the boys were able to understand the test instructions, and to establish as far as possible uniform test-taking situations. The boys were assigned to two categories, one classified as middle social status and the other as lower social status. The social-status classification was based on an equally weighted combination of the head of the household's occupation and a rating of his (or her) education. As far as possible, two parallel pools of boys were formed. The purpose of the substitute pool was to provide a set of alternate families which could be included in the study if families from the first pool did not agree to participate. The final sample consisted of 90 boys and their parents classified as middle social status and 95 classified as lower social status. Both parents from each family participated in the interviewing sessions. The family environment schedule used in the interviews assessed eight press variables identified as press for: achievement, intellectuality, activeness, independence, English, a second language; father dominance, and mother dominance. The press variables were defined by the following process characteristics:

1 Press for achievement
   1a Parental expectations for the education of the child
   1b Social press
   1c Parents' aspirations for themselves
   1d Preparation and planning for child's education
   1e Knowledge of child's educational progress
   1f Valuing educational accomplishments
   1g Parental interest in school

2 Press for activeness
   2a Extent and content of indoor activities
   2b Extent and content of outdoor activities
   2c Extent and the purpose of the use of TV and other media

3 Press for intellectuality
   3a Number of thought-provoking activities engaged in by
      children
   3b Opportunities made available for thought-provoking
      discussions and thinking
   3c Use of books, periodicals, and other literature

4 Press for independence
   4a Freedom and encouragement to explore the environment
   4b Stress on early independence

5 Press for English
   5a Language (English) use and reinforcement in the home
   5b Opportunities available for language (English) use in
      the home

6 Press for second language
   6a Second language use and reinforcement in the home
   6b Opportunities available for second language use in the
      home

7 Father dominance
   7a Father's involvement in child's activities
   7b Father's role in family decision-making

8 Mother dominance
   8a Mother's involvement in child's activities
   8b Mother's role in family decision-making

TABLE 2.1 *Relations between family environment measures and mental abilities: Marjoribanks (1972a) study*

Environment measure	Ability Verbal	Number	Spatial	Reasoning
Press for achievement	0.66*	0.66*	0.28*	0.39*
Press for activeness	0.52*	0.41*	0.22*	0.26*
Press for intellectuality	0.61*	0.53*	0.26*	0.31*
Press for independence	0.42*	0.34*	0.10	0.23*
Press for English	0.50*	0.27*	0.18*	0.28*
Press for second language	0.35*	0.24*	0.09	0.19*
Father dominance	0.16†	0.10	0.09	0.11
Mother dominance	0.21*	0.16†	0.04	0.10
Multiple R	0.71*	0.71*	0.26	0.40*
100R²	50.4	50.4	6.7	16.0

Note $100R^2$ represents the percentage of total variance in the ability scores associated with the eight environment measures. The multiple correlations were corrected to allow for cumulative errors and for small sample size.

* $P < 0.001$
† $P < 0.01$

A six-point rating scale was developed to score each item in the interview schedule, and the score for each of the environmental characteristics was obtained by adding the scores on the relevant environmentl items. Each press variable score was the sum of the scores on the relevant environmental characteristics. (See Appendix for a revised form of the schedule.)

The findings in Table 2.1 show that, generally, the press variables have moderate to high concurrent validities for verbal and number scores, low to moderate concurrent validity for reasoning ability, and low to negligible relations to spatial ability. The lack of relations between spatial ability and the press for independence and father-dominance scores supports Vernon's (1969, p. 222) findings, from his analysis of different cultural groups, that 'there was only limited support for the hypothesis that masculine dominance in the home and encouragement of initiative are associated with perceptual-spatial abilities'. Also the results provide tentative support for Cattell's theory (Cattell, 1963; Cattell and Butcher, 1968), which proposes that crystallized abilities (verbal, number, and reasoning) are related more strongly to environmental factors than are fluid products (spatial ability).

But the analysis of zero-order and multiple correlations provides only a partial understanding of the covariate structure of the environment and ability measures. For a more enriched understanding of the relations between the two sets of measures, canonical correlations were computed (see Marjoribanks, 1974). Just as multiple correlation is a generalization of simple correlation in that it relates several predictors to a criterion, canonical correlation is a generalization of multiple correlation in that it relates several predictors to several criteria. Also, just as multiple correlation yields a set of weights for the predictors to form a linear composite that is correlated maximally with the criterion, one or more pairs of canonical variates for the predictors and criteria are calculated that maximize the simple correlation between the paired linear composite variables from each set. Well-worked-out inferential tests are available to test the significance of successive correlations, and the variates may be characterized by calculating the 'canonical loadings', that is, the correlations of each composite variate with its original set of variables (Bock and Haggard, 1968; Darlington et al., 1975).

When canonical correlations were computed between the four mental ability scores and measures of both global environment variables and the eight press variables, the first two canonical correlations 0.781 and 0.462 were significant (probabilities less than 0.001 and 0.005, respectively). The relations between the environment measures, mental abilities, and the two canonical variates are shown in Figure 2.3. With respect to the first canonical variate, verbal and number abilities and, to a lesser extent, reasoning ability, are associated more closely with the environment press variables than is spatial ability.

After removing the variance of the first canonical variate from predictors and criteria, the loadings on the second variate reveal that the social-status indicators and press variables are related significantly to differentially developed abilities. High ratings on press for English, father occupation, press for second language, and to a lesser extent, press for activeness and father dominance, are associated on the second variate with high scores on verbal, reasoning, and spatial abilities, but associated with lower number

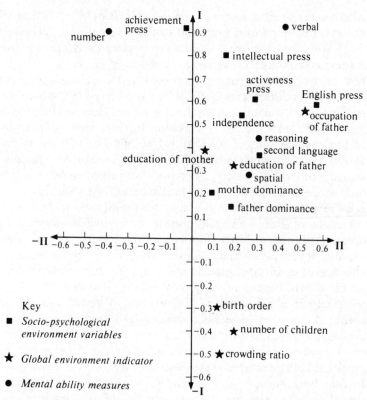

FIGURE 2.3 *Canonical loadings of environmental and mental ability measures*

ability scores. The two language press scales reflect, in particular, a measure of parent-son interaction in activities such as reading, conversations after school and at mealtime, purposeful teaching of vocabulary, and the correction of syntactical errors in language use. The press for activeness scale measures parent-son involvement in both academic and non-academic situations, while the father-dominance scale gauges the father's involvement in a son's activities.

Therefore, the second canonical variate suggests that the differential development of verbal, reasoning, and spatial abilities in relation to number ability might be facilitated in homes characterized by high parent-son interaction. The result is consistent with Bing's (1963) finding that mothers of high verbal boys (boys who had high verbal scores in relation to their number and spatial scores), in comparison to mothers of low verbal boys, provided more stimulation in early childhood, were more critical of poor academic achievement, provided more story books, and let the boys take a greater part in mealtime conversations. Bing suggested that for boys differential verbal ability is fostered by a close relation with a demanding, intrusive mother. Honzik (1967) also found that a close mother-son relationship is related significantly to the development of boys' verbal ability. For optimal verbal ability, Honzik proposes that a boy, at first, needs a close relation with a mother, followed by a relation with a male model who not only achieved himself but who is also concerned about his son's achievement. The canonical variate results suggest that an over-involvement with parents may impede the relative development of divergent number ability. Similarly, Bing found that divergent number ability is fostered in homes which allow boys a considerable degree of uninterrupted free time and freedom to experiment on their own. Ferguson and Maccoby (1966) also found that boys with higher number ability (in relation to verbal and spatial abilities) seem to have been discouraged from being overly dependent on their parents. Thus it is possible that environmental press variables may operate selectively to develop certain potential abilities and to leave others relatively underdeveloped. In fact, Ferguson (1954, 1956) and Lesser (1976) have proposed that if social groups are characterized by different learning environments then these environments may be related to differential patterns of cognitive performance among the groups. The proposition is examined in a later chapter.

The 'Chicago' school studies have measured family environments with greater precision than most prior investigations of the relations between family environments and children's cognitive performance. Generally the studies are limited, however, by using small samples, examining children from only one ethnic group, or by including children from only one sex group. In an attempt to overcome some of these methodological restrictions I collected data from over 900 Australian urban families during 1977. (Although the results, in Table 2.2, have not been published elsewhere, the study is designated as Marjoribanks (1977a) in Figure 2.2.) The sample included middle social-status Anglo-Australian families and lower social-status Anglo-Australian, English, Greek, Serbo-Croatian, and Southern Italian families (the sample and the measures are discussed in greater detail in Chapter 7). Each family had an 11-year-old child attending an urban elementary school. Among the variables used to define the family environment were: parents' educational and occupational aspirations for their children, the language environment of the family, press for independence, individual-collective value orientations of the parents (see Rosen, 1959), parents' satisfaction with the teaching in their child's school, and parents' general satisfaction with the school. The Raven's Progressive Matrices was used to measure the intellectual ability of the children, while tests devised by the Australian Council for Educational Research assessed achievement in mathematics, word knowledge, and word comprehension. These latter tests are labelled the Classroom Achievement Tests in Mathematics and the Primary Reading Survey Tests. The testing sessions were conducted by me to ensure, as far as possible, that the children were able to understand the test instructions, and to establish uniform test-taking conditions. Included in the sample were 447 girls and 471 boys. In Table 2.2, the findings show that the environment variables have

TABLE 2.2 *Relations between family environment measures and cognitive performance: Marjoribanks (1977a) study*

| Environment measure | Cognitive performance | | | |
	Intelligence	Mathematics	Word knowledge	Word comprehension
Parents' aspirations	*0.08* *(0.07)*[a]	0.12 (0.07)	0.10 (0.06)	0.10 *(0.03)*
Language in family	0.12 (0.13)	0.20 (0.20)	0.31 (0.36)	0.22 (0.34)
Value orientations	*0.08* *(0.06)*	0.14 (0.14)	0.26 (0.28)	0.26 (0.27)
Press for independence	−0.07 (−0.10)	−0.12 (−0.18)	−0.26 (−0.27)	−0.20 (−0.20)
Satisfaction with teaching	0.12 (0.14)	*0.06* *(0.09)*	0.20 (0.15)	0.16 (0.14)
Satisfaction with school	*0.06* *(0.08)*	0.10 (0.12)	0.18 (0.13)	0.21 (0.18)
Multiple R	*0.16* (0.19)	0.23 (0.22)	0.39 (0.39)	0.33 (0.38)
100R²	2.57 (3.50)	5.27 (4.83)	15.13 (15.13)	10.62 (14.26)

Note $100R^2$ represents the percentage of total variance in the performance measures associated with the six environment measures.
[a] Girls' scores are in parentheses.
Italicized coefficients are not significantly different from zero at the 0.05 level of confidence.

TABLE 2.3 *Relations between family environment and cognitive performance: 'Chicago' studies*

Study	Sample	Criterion measures	Multiple R^b	$100R^2$
Dave (1963)	Illinois N = 32 girls, 28 boys 11-yr-olds	Metropolitan Achievement Tests Word knowledge Reading Arithmetic problem solving Word discrimination Language Spelling Arithmetic computation	0.79 0.73 0.71 0.69 0.68 0.61 0.56	62.2 53.1 50.3 48.1 46.8 37.2 30.9
Wolf (1964)	Illinois N = 32 girls, 28 boys 11-yr-olds	Henmon-Nelson Test Intelligence	0.70	49.0
Dyer (1967)	Trinidad *Middle social status* N = 15 girls, 15 boys 11-yr-olds	Iowa Test of Basic Skills Total achievement Lorge-Thorndike Test Non-verbal ability Verbal ability	0.67 0.32 0.11	44.9 10.2 1.2
	Lower social status N = 15 girls, 15 boys 11-yr-olds	Total achievement Non-verbal ability Verbal ability	0.78 0.51 0.39	60.8 26.0 15.2
Kellaghan (1977)	Dublin N = 30 girls, 30 boys 8-yr-olds	Stanford-Binet Scale Intelligence Cattell Tests Culture fair ability Non-culture fair intelligence Marino Word Reading Irish Word Recognition Schonell Mechanical Arithmetic	0.51 0.35 0.50 0.63 0.60 0.55	26.0 12.3 25.0 39.7 36.0 30.3
Mosychuk (1969)	Edmonton N = 100 boys 11-yr-olds	WISC [a] Verbal Performance Total	0.39 0.32 0.42	15.2 10.2 17.6
Majoribanks (1972a)	Southern Ontario N = 185 boys 11-yr-olds	SRA Primary Mental Abilities Verbal Number Spatial Reasoning	0.71 0.71 0.26 0.40	50.4 50.4 6.7 16.0

TABLE 2.3 *cont.*

Study	Sample	Criterion measures	Multiple R[b]	100R²
Majoribanks (1977a)	Australia N = 447 girls, 471 boys 11-yr-olds	Intelligence	*0.16* (0.19)	2.6 (3.5)
		Word knowledge	0.39 (0.39)	15.1 (15.1)
		Word comprehension	0.33 (0.38)	10.6 (14.3)
		Mathematics	0.23 (0.22)	5.3 (4.8)

[a] Only the relations between one environmental press variable and the WISC scores are shown.
[b] Italicized coefficients are not significantly different from zero at the 0.05 level of confidence.

low to moderate relations to the academic achievement scores and negligible to low associations with intelligence. When the measures are combined they account for moderate percentages of the variance in the word achievement scores and low percentages of the variation in the mathematics and intelligence scores. Relations between the family environment, person variables, and cognitive performance within the different ethnic groups, are presented in Chapter 7.

The results of the 'Chicago' school studies are summarized in Table 2.3. In general, the findings show that the environment measures have moderate to high relations to verbal performance scores, moderate associations with mathematics achievement, and lower relations to non-verbal intelligence scores. The more modest findings with the larger sample of Australian children suggest, however, that the correlations in many of the 'Chicago' studies may be biased upwards because of the effects of cumulative errors associated with the nature and sizes of the samples that were selected.

All of the studies reported in Table 2.3 are restricted to an investigation of the correlates of cognitive measures. In the following set of studies from the 'Chicago' school the environmental correlates of affective characteristics were examined also.

Family environment, affective characteristics and cognitive performance

Weiss (1969) investigated relations between the family environment and measures of achievement motivation and self-esteem for 27 boys and 29 girls, from a community in Illinois. The average

age of the children was approximately 11. Three press variables were used to define the sub-environment for achievement motivation: generation of standards of excellence and expectations, independence training, and parental approval; and the sub-environment for self-esteem was defined by: parental acceptance, evaluation of child, and opportunities for self-enhancement. Three measures assessed each of the affective characteristics: a self report, a rating by the child's current teacher, and a projective technique. The sub-environment for achievement motivation included:

1 Generation of standards of excellence and expectations
    1a Level of parental aspirations for themselves
    1b Level of parental aspirations for the child
    1c Emphasis on parents doing things well
    1d Risk-taking behaviour of parents
    1e Parents' level of competitiveness
    1f Expectations of competitiveness held for child
    1g Work habits of parents
    1h Expectations of work habits for child

2 Independence training
    2a Freedom given to child for exploring environment
    2b Amount of aid given to child
    2c Extent of dominance of parent of same or opposite sex

3 Parent approval
    3a Awareness of child's activities and behaviours
    3b Involvement in child's activities
    3c Extent of child's participation in decision-making
    3d Quality and quantity of rewards and punishments

The sub-environment for self-esteem included:

1 Parental acceptance
    1a Awareness of child's activities
    1b Involvement in child's activities
    1c Quality and quantity of rewards and punishments
    1d Extent of parental self-acceptance

2 Evaluation of child
  2a Evaluation of child's physical characteristics
  2b Evaluation of child's intellectual qualities
  2c Evaluation of child's personality
  2d Evaluation of child's psychomotor competencies
  2e Evaluation of child's social skills

3 Opportunities for self-enhancement
  3a Extent of privacy for each person in family
  3b Encouragement given to child to explore new places
      and interests
  3c Child's participation in decision-making

In the family interviews questions were arranged in three categories: those asked of the mother alone, those asked of father alone, and those directed at the mother and father together. Rating scales were constructed for each question in the schedule, with many of the questions being pre-coded to facilitate the rating of responses. A score for an environment process characteristic was composed of the sum of scores on the rating scales for each question that was part of the characteristic. Scores on the environmental press variables were principal component scores calculated from each cluster of characteristics that comprised each press variable. The results in Table 2.4 show that after correcting multiple correlations for unreliability of predictor and criterion measures there are a set of moderate relations between family environment and the measures of achievement motivation and self-esteem. As Weiss (1974, p. 147) suggests, generally,

> these results support the thesis that a sub-set of the total
> environment can be identified and measured for individual
> personality characteristics. However, the results were
> dependent upon the criterion utilized. Unlike studies of
> cognitive characteristics, it is more difficult to establish
> validity of criterion instruments for personality charac-
> teristics.

Two studies of Australian children, by Keeves (1972) and Marjoribanks (1978a) have examined relations between family environments and measures of both cognitive and affective characteristics. Using a simple random sample of 242 children who were in their final year of elementary school, Keeves

TABLE 2.4 *Relations between family environment and measures of cognitive performance and affective characteristics*

Study	Sample	Criterion measures	Multiple R^a	$100R^2$
Weiss (1969)[b]	Illinois	Achievement motivation		
	N = 29 girls,	Self report	0.57 (0.27)	32.5 (7.3)
	27 boys	Teacher rating	0.66 (0.54)	43.6 (29.2)
	11-yr-olds	Projective technique	0.81 (0.70)	65.6 (49.0)
		Self-esteem		
		Self report	0.47 (0.72)	22.1 (51.8)
		Teacher rating	0.80 (0.79)	64.0 (62.4)
		Projective technique	0.65 (0.43)	42.3 (18.5)
Keeves (1972)	Australia	Mathematics achievement	0.58	33.6
	N = 215	Science achievement	0.59	34.8
	11-12-yr-olds	Attitudes to mathematics	0.29	8.4
		Attitudes to science	0.14	2.0
Marjoribanks (1978a)	Australia	Otis Intermediate Test		
	N = 120 girls,	Intelligence	0.43 (0.33)	18.5 (10.9)
	130 boys			
	12-yr-olds	Enthusiasm for school	0.33 (0.19)	10.9 (3.8)
		Academic self concept	0.24 (0.36)	5.9 (13.2)
		Friendliness of school	0.31 (0.25)	9.4 (6.3)
		Dislike for disruptive behaviour	0.33 (0.23)	11.1 (5.4)
		Educational and occupational aspirations	0.44 (0.36)	19.4 (13.3)
		Commitment to school	0.28 (0.36)	7.7 (12.7)
		Academic orientation	0.25 (0.16)	7.3 (2.7)

[a] Italicized coefficients are not significantly different from zero at the 0.05 level of confidence.

[b] Correlations in the Weiss study have been corrected for unreliability of measures.
  Coefficients for girls are in parentheses.

examined the environmental correlates of children's science and mathematics achievement and their attitudes towards science and mathematics. The family environment was assessed when the children were in their final year of elementary school and in their first year of secondary school. The achievement and attitude measures were administered at the end of the first year of secondary school. Five attitudinal and four process variables were gauged by the family environment schedule. The attitudinal variables were: father's and mother's attitudes towards child's present education; father's and mother's ambitions for the child's future education and occupation; and parents' hopes and aspirations for themselves. The process variables were identified as: relations between home and school, use of books and library facilities, provision to help with formal schoolwork, and arrangements made for tackling home assignments. Principal component analysis was used to construct an environment press score for each of the two general family dimensions. The results (see Table 2.4) indicate that when the attitudinal and process variables are combined into a predictor set they have moderate relations to science and mathematics achievement and lower concurrent validities in relation to the attitude scores.

In a study of 550 12-year-old children, from towns in rural parts of Australia, Marjoribanks (1978a, 1979a) examined the environmental correlates of intelligence scores, measures of personality, and school-related affective characteristics. Family environment data were collected from interviews with the parents of 250 children, 130 boys and 120 girls. Where possible two parallel pools of families, based on social-status background, were formed. The substitute pool provided a set of alternate families which could be used in the study if families from the first pool did not agree to participate. Family environment was assessed in terms of six press variables which were labelled: parents' expectations for the child, expectations for themselves, concern for the use of language within the family, reinforcement of educational expectations, knowledge of child's educational progress, and the family involvement in educational activities. The interview schedule which is an adaptation of a previous instrument (see Marjoribanks, 1972a) is presented in the Appendix for the use of other researchers who may be interested in adapting it for further investigations. Factor scaling techniques (Armor, 1974) were used to examine the structure of the six press variables. Scores on the items that made up each of the variables were analysed using principal component analysis. After eliminating items with small factor loadings (< 0.40), the remaining items were refactored, producing six factor scales that all had theta reliability estimates greater than 0.75. Form A of the CPQ devised by Cattell (see Cattell *et al.*, 1970) used to assess children's personality. Data on 14 personality constructs are provided by the schedule. When the scores on the variables were factor-analysed and the factors rotated, four second-stratum personality factors were identified. There is a modest correspondence between these four factors and second-stratum factors isolated in previous studies (e.g., see

Gorsuch and Cattell, 1967; Warburton, 1972; Nesselroade and Baltes, 1975; Howarth, 1976). The factors were labelled: contemplative-impatience (loaded strongly on conscientious (G^+), dependent (I^+), apprehensive (O^+), controlled (Q_3^+)); self-reliant-subduedness (excitability (D^+), assertive (E^+), circumspect-individualism (J^+), shrewdness (N^+), high ergic tension (Q_4^+), enthusiastic (F^+)); adjustment-anxiety (participating (A^+), emotionally stable (C^+), self-assured (O^-), adventurous (H^+)); and extraversion-introversion (aggressive (E^+), enthusiastic (F^+), worldly (N^+)). Factor scores were obtained on the four second-stratum personality factors for each child. Measures constructed by Barker Lunn (1969, 1970) and Sumner (1972), and modified for the study, were used to assess children's school-related affective characteristics. Both scales are of a Likert-type format and each of 50 items. Factor-scaling techniques were adopted to examine the responses to the schedules. From the first schedule five factor scales were isolated and identified as: enthusiasm for school, academic self-concept, loneliness at school, enthusiasm for disruptive behaviour, and children's educational and occupational expectations. From the second schedule two factors were identified and labelled: alienation from school, and child's academic orientation. The general intellectual ability of the children was assessed using the Otis Intermediate Test-Form AB.

When the environment variables were combined they accounted for a low to moderate percentage of the variance in the intelligence test scores and had small but differential sex associations with the affective measures. The relations between environment and the personality variables were not significant. Thus, in Table 2.4 only the relations between the environment and the measures of intelligence and affective characteristics are shown. Relations between the personality factors and children's academic and affective outcomes, at different family environment levels, are discussed in detail in Chapter 6.

The findings from the 'Chicago' school studies, presented in Tables 2.3 and 2.4, show that generally the environment measures have moderate concurrent validities in relation to academic achievement, low to moderate concurrent validities for intelligence test scores, and negligible to moderate associations with measures of affective characteristics. As Bloom (1974, p. 10) suggests, there have been some major exceptions in the predictive power of some measures, 'especially with personality and attitudinal measures. We still have much to learn about how to measure some environments and some characteristics.'

The 'British' school of family environment research

The results of studies in British settings by Fraser (1959), Wiseman (1967), Plowden (1967), and Marjoribanks (1976a) are presented in Table 2.5, and they show that the family environment measures have moderate associations with cognitive performance. The academic achievement measure used in the Fraser study was a combined assessment of children's performance during secondary school, while the intelligence test score was obtained during the children's last year of elementary school. The family environment schedule assessed the cultural, material, motivational and emotional aspects of the children's homes, but the environment schedule was not as refined and detailed as those developed in the 'Chicago' studies. In the Wiseman investigation the children were selected from 22 elementary schools in Manchester, England. In Table 2.5 the relations represent averages of correlations between the family environments of children, assessed when they were 10, and measures of cognitive performance obtained when the children were 7, 8, 9, and 10. Only the behaviour or attitude items, from the family environment schedule, that had the strongest relations to the cognitive scores are presented. As Wiseman (1967, p. 373) indicates, 'what is very significant is the presence in the "top seven" of the four variables dealing with reading, with average correlations with all tests ranging from 0.272 to 0.341, and an overall average of 0.312.'

In the Plowden (1967) survey, the environmental correlates of cognitive performance were examined for three age cohorts of a national sample of English children. The sampling procedure in the survey had two stages. First, a stratified random sample was taken from all types of government-supported elementary schools in England, which resulted in the selection of 173 schools. Second, a systematic sample of children was chosen from the schools producing three age cohorts each of approximately 1,000 children. The average age of the children in the senior cohort was approximately 11, of the middle cohort 8, and of the junior group 7 years. From an analysis of 80 attitude and behaviour items, 14

TABLE 2.5 *Relations between family environment and children's characteristics: the 'British' school*

Study	Sample	Environment variables	Criterion measures	Multiple R		$100R^2$	
Fraser (1959)	Aberdeen, Scotland N = 427 12-15-yr-olds	Reading habits of family	Intelligence Achievement	0.28 0.33		7.8 10.9	
		Parents' attitudes to education and future occupation of child	Intelligence Achievement	0.30 0.39		9.0 15.2	
		Impression of home environment	Intelligence Achievement	0.39 0.46		15.2 21.2	
Wiseman (1967) [a]	Manchester, England N = 186 11-yr-olds	Preferred age of leaving school	Total achievement	0.41		16.8	
		Child's reading		0.34		11.6	
		Parents members of library		0.34		11.6	
		Prefer grammar school		0.31		9.6	
		Whether parents read		0.29		8.4	
		Number of books in home		0.27		7.3	
		Complaints against teacher		−0.24		5.8	
Plowden (1967) Peaker (1967)	England Junior cohort N = 1,053	Total family environment	Reading girls boys	0.46 0.51		22.0 26.0	
	Middle cohort N = 1,016	Total family environment	Reading girls boys	0.44 0.45		19.0 20.0	
	Senior cohort N = 1,023	Total family environment	Reading girls boys	0.57 0.67		32.0 45.0	
Marjoribanks (1976a) [b]	England Plowden senior cohort N = 396 girls 383 boys 11-15-yr-olds	Family environment, measured during first survey	Intelligence English Mathematics Aspirations	0.34 0.45 0.45 0.45	(0.30) (0.49) (0.50) (0.48)	11.6 20.3 20.3 20.3	(9.0) (24.0) (25.0) (23.0)
			Self-expectations	0.21	(0.23)	4.4	(5.3)
		Family environment, measured during second survey	Intelligence	0.29	(0.27)	8.4	(7.3)
			English	0.45	(0.48)	20.3	(23.0)
			Mathematics	0.45	(0.46)	20.3	(21.2)
			Aspirations	0.46	(0.45)	21.2	(20.3)
			Self-expectations	0.26	(0.25)	6.8	(6.3)

[a] Total achievement represents a combination of intelligence, arithmetic, and English scores.
[b] Coefficients for girls are in parentheses.

press variables were identified by factor analysis. For the results in Table 2.5 the press variables were combined into a predictor set in a multiple regression model (Peaker, 1967).

Four years after the original Plowden study, the children and their families were surveyed again (see Bynner, 1972; Peaker, 1971). In an analysis of the data from the senior cohort, which included 396 girls and 383 boys with an average age of 15, Marjoribanks (1976a) examined the relations between the family environment, measured during both surveys, and assessments of the cognitive and affective characteristics of the children which were assessed during the second survey. In the latter survey, cognitive performance was measured using the Alice Heim general intelligence test (AH4), the Watts-Vernon English comprehension test, and the Vernon graded mathematics test. Two scales constructed by the National Foundation for Educational Research measured the children's educational and occupational aspirations and their self-expectations.

In both the Plowden survey and in the follow-up study a structured interview schedule was used to gather information about the family environments of the children. In the Marjoribanks study, factor scaling was used to construct environment press variables. From the first survey eight variables were identified, and nine from the second survey. The variables were labelled: parental aspirations for child, literacy of home, parental interest and support in child's education, responsibility and initiative taken by parents in relation to child's schooling, relations between parents and teachers, parents' time to do things with child, interest in helping with schoolwork, parents' belief in value of school, satisfaction with present school, child's viewing of TV, and parents' knowledge of child's schoolwork.

The two sets of press variables were refactored, and in each case the variables loaded strongly on general factors which had theta reliabilities of approximately 0.85. Two family environment scores for each child were obtained by summing the scores on the press variables that made up the two general factors. The correlations in Table 2.5 show that the family environment measures account for more of the variance in the achievement scores than in the intelligence test scores, which supports the findings from the 'Chicago' studies. Also, the environment accounts for only a low to moderate percentage of the variance in the self-expectation scores but a moderate to large percentage of the variance in aspiration scores. In the study of Australian rural children, Marjoribanks (1978a) also found that, from a set of affective characteristics, children's aspirations had the strongest associations with family environment (see Table 2.4). Only a small number of relations from the Plowden and follow-up studies are presented in Table 2.5. But in later chapters the Plowden material is investigated in much greater detail.

This review of the 'Chicago' and 'British' studies indicates that the environment measures constructed for the research generally have been successful in accounting for variation in academic achievement scores, but less successful in 'explaining' variance in non-verbal, personality, and school-related affective measures. In many of the studies the construct validities of the family environment measures have been examined by testing the proposition that 'the measure of the family environment accounts for more of the variance in children's cognitive and affective scores than other environment measures such as social-status characteristics and family structure variables'. Typically, it has been found that the global measures are relatively poorer predictors of children's outcomes when compared with the more sensitive parent interview measures. It will be argued in the following two chapters, however, that family environment research becomes more sensitive, enriched and valid when children's outcomes are examined in relation to both global social environment variables and refined social-psychological family measures. In Chapter 3 the relations between social status, refined measures of the family environment and children's outcomes are examined.

3 Social status and children's outcomes: analytic models for research

Many family environment studies have concluded that: (a) social-status measures are relatively poor predictors of children's outcomes when compared with more sensitive parent interview measures of the family environment; and (b) the family environment affects children's outcomes to an important extent independently of social status. The findings in a recent investigation by Bradley, Caldwell, and Elardo (1977, p. 699) are typical of the research. They suggest that their 'results provide further evidence that measures of specific environment processes are more strongly associated with cognitive measures than measures of social status'. Such interpretations of the relations between social status, family environments, and children's school-related outcomes have been subject to trenchant criticism (e.g., see Bernstein and Davies, 1969; Connell, 1972, 1974; Halsey, 1975). The criticism proposes that in much of the environment research the concept of social status has been trivialized to such an extent that differences in parents' attitudes and behaviours are conceived of as separate factors rather than as an integral part of the social background of children's families. It is suggested by Halsey (1975, p. 17), for example, that 'it is essential to insist that the effect of class on educational experience is not to be thought of as one factor from which parental attitudes and motivations to succeed in education are independent'.

TABLE 3.1 *Some models for research on children's social status and school-related outcomes*

1 Social status $\longrightarrow$ cognitive and affective characteristics

2 f (Social status, sibsize) $\longrightarrow$ intellectual abilities

3 f (Social status, social-psychological family environment) $\longrightarrow$ cognitive and affective outcomes

4 f (Social status, intelligence) $\longrightarrow$ academic achievement

5 f (Status, sibling variables, family environment, early achievement) $\longrightarrow$ later academic achievement

6 f (Social status, teacher attitudes) $\longrightarrow$ academic achievement

In the present chapter research is reviewed, and new analyses presented, in an examination of relations between social status and children's outcomes at different family environment levels. Associations between social status and children's outcomes are investigated further by including in analyses measures of intellectual ability and teachers' attitudes towards children. The six research models shown in Table 3.1 are used as a framework for the presentation of the studies.

Model 1: Social status ⟶ children's cognitive and affective characteristics

One of the few consistent findings in educational research is that social-status measures have moderate concurrent validities with

TABLE 3.2 *Relations between social-status characteristics and children's outcomes*

		Outcomes			
	Social status	English	Mathematics	Intelligence	Self-expectations
Senior cohort	Father occupation	26 (30)	23 (37)	21 (23)	13 (20)
	Father education	25 (23)	28 (31)	19 (17)	13 (17)
	Family income	16 (26)	17 (29)	10 (22)	06 (19)
	Housing index [a]	26 (29)	25 (28)	21 (18)	11 (10)
Middle cohort	Father occupation	36 (30)	33 (27)	27 (22)	14 (16)
	Father education	33 (20)	32 (20)	26 (16)	21 (09)
	Family income	33 (34)	28 (27)	24 (27)	13 (17)
	Housing index [a]	28 (25)	20 (28)	20 (22)	18 (08)
Junior cohort	Father occupation	31 (26)	26 (21)	20 (20)	21 (17)
	Father education	19 (17)	22 (19)	14 (09)	14 (17)
	Family income	27 (15)	24 (12)	16 (05)	19 (06)
	Housing index [a]	29 (22)	24 (17)	22 (25)	24 (09)

Note Coefficients for girls are in parentheses. Italicized coefficients are not significantly different from zero at the 0.05 level of confidence.

[a] The housing index assesses whether the family owns its own dwelling, the amenities in the home, and the crowding within the home.

school-related outcomes. Generally the associations with academic achievement scores are strongest, while the relations to intelligence and affective characteristics are of a lower order. The zero-order correlations shown in Table 3.2 have been computed from the Plowden data, and they are representative of the relations which typically are found between social status and children's outcomes. Social-status data were collected when the ages of the children in the three age-cohorts were approximately 11, 8, and 7 years. The outcomes were measured four years later (see Chapter 2 for a more complete account of the Plowden data). In Table 3.2, the findings show that, generally, the amount of variance associated with the social-status indicators is about 4 to 9 per cent (the square of the correlations) for the achievement scores, 4 to 6 per cent for intelligence, and 2 to 4 per cent for the self-expectation measure. When the status characteristics are combined in regression models they are associated with approximately 16, 8, and 5 per cent of the variance in the achievement, intelligence, and self-expectation scores, respectively, which replicates much previous research.

Model 2: f(social status, sibsize) ——→children's intellectual abilities

Sibling constellation variables such as sibsize and birth order have been used in numerous studies as an indicator of children's family environments (see Forer, 1977, for a bibliography of approximately 400 birth order and sibsize studies completed since 1970). Although investigations of relations between sibling variables and children's behaviours have produced inconsistent and often ambiguous results, it generally has been found that higher achievement scores, especially verbal performance, of school-age students occur more often in families with fewer children (e.g., Nisbet, 1953; Fraser, 1959; Dandes and Dow, 1969; Eysenck and Cookson, 1969; Waller, 1971; Belmont and Marolla, 1973; Nuttall *et al.*, 1976; Breland, 1977). Some investigators have attempted to account for the relations between sibsize and cognitive performance by controlling for the effects of factors such as maternal age and social status (e.g., Record *et al.*, 1969; Lichtenwalner and Maxwell, 1969; Murray, 1971). But even when such influences have been controlled the overall findings remain equivocal. The inconsistencies in the studies may be related partly to the restricted statistical techniques that have been used. Typically the research has relied on the use of product-moment correlations which reveal only bivariate relations, or on analysis of variance techniques which require the grouping of variables into levels. As a result the full range of possible relations between social status, sibling variables, and children's cognitive performance has not been revealed by the research. The study reported below was an attempt to overcome some of the statistical restrictions of prior research and it is presented as an illustration of how social status and sibling variables may interact to affect children's performances.

Using data collected from 185 11-year-old Canadian boys (see Marjoribanks (1972a) in Chapter 2 for a discussion of the nature of the study), Marjoribanks, Walberg, and Bargen (1975) examined relations between sibsize and measures of verbal, number, spatial, and reasoning ability at different levels of father occupation. In the analysis a new sibling variable was introduced: the inverse of sibsize. It was reasoned that since children share adult resources of intellectual stimulation in the home, the mathematical relationship between sibsize and parents' stimulation is not linear but is of a hyperbolic form involving the term: one divided by the number of children in the family. That is, the amount of parental attention which each child receives decreases as the number of children in the family increases in such a way that with each additional child the successive decrements in shared attention become smaller. Therefore the 'expected' percentages of parental attention given children in, say, one-, two-, three-, four-, and five-child families would approximate 100, 50, 33, 25, and 20, respectively. Thus, single children in families may score higher on cognitive tests because they receive all available parental stimulation, whereas children with four siblings may have lower performance scores because they receive more like one-fifth of the available stimulation. A significant relation between cognitive performance and the inverse of sibsize would suggest a possible explanation for the correlations that are found between cognitive scores and birth-order position. Such an explanation does not take into account important variables such as sex-related differences in parental attention, age-spacing between siblings, ages of parents, and the presence of other adults in the home. Zajonc and Markus

(1975), however, have proposed a confluence theory of sibling effects on intellectual ability. The theory, which relates sibling variables, age-spacing between siblings, environment variables, and the intellectual performance of children, is examined in the following chapter.

In regression models, the inverse of sibsize was not related to the reasoning and spatial ability scores of the Canadian children, at different levels of father occupation. Verbal and number scores had significant associations with father occupation, inverse of sibsize, and the interaction of the two variables. Squared-terms, to test for non-linearity, were not significant in any of the regression models. The findings from the analysis are summarized in Figure 3.1, which shows the regression-fitted relations between the inverse of sibsize and the verbal and reasoning scores at different levels of father occupation. The shape of the surface for the verbal scores (the relations are similar for number ability) shows that at low levels of father occupation, increases in sibsize are associated

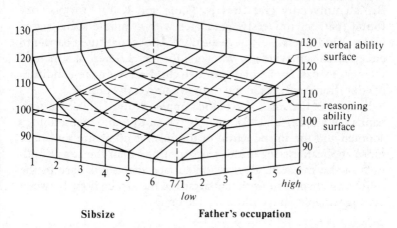

Sibsize   Father's occupation

FIGURE 3.1 *Fitted-ability scores in relation to sibsize and father's occupation*

with decrements in the verbal scores. At a low father occupation level of one, for example, the regression-fitted verbal scores for boys in one-child families and in seven-child families are 120 and 89, respectively. There is apparently little sibsize effect, however, on the fitted-verbal values at the highest levels of father occupation. The attenuation of sibsize influences on verbal scores at high social-status levels supports both the findings of Record *et al.*

(1969) and the conclusion which Anastasi (1956) reached after her extensive review of studies relating sibsize and intelligence.

The surface for reasoning ability (and similarly for spatial scores) indicates that at each sibsize level increases in social status are associated with increments in reasoning scores; but at each social-status level, changes in sibsize are not related to changes in reasoning ability. Both surfaces are drawn from regression models in which the sibsize data were converted into the inverse of sibsize scores.

The above analysis suggests the interesting possibility that the relations between social status and children's outcomes may be relatively modest because of the attenuating effect that lower social-status children, with few siblings, may have on outcome measures. In Figure 3.1, the surfaces show that lower social-status children from one-child families perform as well as children from higher social-status families. Such a finding may provide the beginnings of an explanation for the results of an investigation of British university graduates by Poole and Kuhn (1973). They found that, for university graduates with a middle social-status background, a relatively large family did not constitute a barrier to educational achievement, whereas, for the children of a manual worker, a small family of one or two children was a pre-condition of educational success in the form of a university degree.

Because of the small size of the sample involved in the Marjoribanks, Walberg, and Bargen (1975) study, the methodology adopted and the introduction of the inverse of sibsize may have more applications for future investigations than the actual findings of the research. Regression surface analysis is used in the following chapter in further analyses of the associations between sibling variables and children's outcomes.

Model 3: f(social status, social-psychological family environment) ⟶ children's cognitive and affective outcomes

In Chapter 2 it was suggested that the construct validities of family environment measures have often been examined by testing the proposition that refined family environment measures account for more of the variance in children's outcomes than other environment measures such as social status. It was proposed, however, that family environment research would be more sensitive and enriched if children's outcomes were considered in relation to both social environment characteristics and social-psychological family environment measures.

In the present model, the Plowden data are used to examine the proposition that 'family social status is related to children's school-related outcomes at different levels of refined family environment measures'. Social status is defined by an equally weighted composite of father occupation, father education, and family income. Parents were interviewed in their homes by government social survey interviewers in both the original Plowden and the follow-up studies. The same five parent socialization variables were assessed within each cohort during both surveys. Each socialization scale consists of six to eight items. The following list includes the labels used for the scales with some sample items provided, to indicate the nature of the measures: (a) responsibility and initiative taken by parents over child's education (whether parents had talked to teachers about teaching methods used, asked for work for child to do or how to help the child at home, discussed educational matters with principal); (b) parents' interest and support (whether husband helps with the control of the child, whether parents do things with the child at weekends, whether husband takes an interest in how child is progressing at school); (c) literacy of the home (number of books in the home, whether parents read, whether child has library books at home); (d) relations between parents and teachers (whether parents are happy with the arrangements for seeing teachers, feel teachers are interested in what they think about their child's education, feel teachers would prefer to keep parents out of the school); and (e) educational and occupational aspirations (parents want child to stay on at school, to have a professional occupation, to take university entrance examinations). For the present analysis the family socialization measures from each time period are combined to provide a modest approximation of the cumulative nature of the family environment between the two time periods. English, mathematics, and intelligence test scores which were assessed in the follow-up survey, as well as the educational and occupational aspirations of the senior children, are used as assessments of outcomes. The measure of aspirations is of a Likert-type format, consisting of 10 items of the form: what academic level the student wanted to attain in English and mathematics, what school examinations the student wanted to take, the type of occupation desired, age at which the student wanted to leave school, and whether the student wanted to undertake tertiary education. Aspirations were not assessed for the junior and middle-age group children.

Regression surfaces are plotted using the raw regression weights generated from models of the form: $Z = aX + bY +$ constant, where Z, X, and Y represent measures of children's outcomes, social status, and the social-psychological family environment, respectively. In more complex regression models, product terms (to test for interactions) and quadratic terms (to test for non-linearity) were not related to the outcomes. Results of the regression analysis are presented in Table 3.3. They show that for

TABLE 3.3 *Raw regression weights for multiple regression of children's outcomes on social status and family environment*

	Senior girls				Middle girls			Junior girls		
Predictor variable	Intel.	Eng.	Math.	Asp.	Intel.	Eng.	Math.	Intel.	Eng.	Math.
Social status	0.50*	0.41*	0.81*	0.49*	0.68*	0.68*	0.77*	0.03†	0.28†	0.33†
Family environment	0.41*	0.48*	0.70*	0.29*	0.43*	0.27*	0.32*	0.01†	0.16*	0.27*
Multiple R [a]	0.42	0.59	0.65	0.56	0.39	0.45	0.40	0.23	0.36	0.36

	Senior boys				Middle boys			Junior boys		
Predictor variable	Intel.	Eng.	Math.	Asp.	Intel.	Eng.	Math.	Intel.	Eng.	Math.
Social status	0.09	0.03	0.11	0.20	0.75*	0.65*	0.72*	0.04†	0.38*	0.51†
Family environment	0.37*	0.44*	0.67*	0.36*	0.39*	0.44*	0.60*	0.01†	0.20*	0.33*
Multiple R [a]	0.40	0.59	0.57	0.53	0.38	0.53	0.51	0.26	0.43	0.41

Abbreviations Intel.=Intelligence; Eng.=English; Math.=Mathematics; Asp.=Aspirations
* Value of raw regression weight exceeds three times its standard error.
† Value of raw regression weight exceeds twice its standard error.
[a] All multiple correlations significant beyond 0.05 level of confidence.

both sexes and within the three cohorts there are strong relations between the socialization influences and the outcome scores at each social-status level. Also, except in the senior boys' cohort, social status is related significantly to the outcomes at each family environment level. The latter finding provides substantial support for the proposition of the present analysis. The most significant differences occur between senior girls and senior boys. At different family environment levels, social status of senior boys' families is not related directly to the outcome scores, while for the senior girls (and for girls and boys in the other cohorts), social status continues to have direct effects on the outcomes. The findings in the senior cohort provide some support for Alexander and Eckland (1974, p. 668), who in a longitudinal study of the educational attainment of American students found that 'status background influences were a double liability for women in that such influences were found to be considerably more determinant of high school process and outcome variables for females'.

As it is not possible in the space available to present all the regression surfaces generated from the data, only four planes have been plotted in two figures. The surfaces show the differential social-status relations to the outcome scores, at different levels of family environment. In Figure 3.2, the surfaces reflect the regression-fitted relations between social status and the intelligence scores of senior girls and boys at different family environment levels. At each social-status level, increases in family

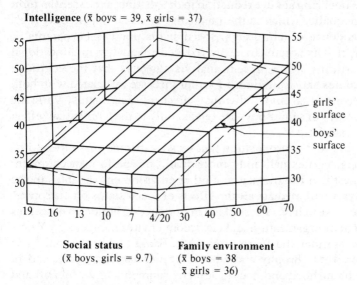

FIGURE 3.2 *Fitted-intelligence scores in relation to social status and family environment: senior group girls and boys*

environment are associated with sizeable increments in intelligence scores. In the boys' sample, for example, as the family environment scores increase from 30 to 60, the regression-estimated intelligence scores change by approximately 10 points at each status level. At each environment score the shapes of the surfaces show that for girls increases in status are related to increments in intelligence, while for boys changes in status are not associated with variation in the intelligence test scores.

The relations in the senior cohort suggest that social status may have two separate influences on achievement and affective scores. First, a 'contextual effect' which is the indirect influence that social status has on children's outcomes. The 'contextual effect' is mediated through the social-psychological family environment. Second, an 'individual effect' which is assessed by the direct effects of social status on outcomes, after accounting for the mediated influence of status. It is possible that the 'individual effects' represent an interpretation by children of the social-status position of their family which results in children adapting their behaviours and performances. Such a proposition is related, in part, to Boudon's (1977, p. 196) conclusion that '. . . under extremely general conditions, expansion of educational opportunity does not bring about a reduction in that distinct and essential form of inequality which is the inequality of social opportunity (i.e., dependence of (children's) social status upon (their parents')), even if it is accompanied by reduced inequality in educational opportunity'. The present analysis suggests that the cognitive outcomes and aspirations of senior girls are associated with both the 'contextual' and 'individual' effects of social status, while the outcomes of senior boys are related only to the 'contextual' effect of social status.

Critics of the proposition that social status may have these dual effects, 'contextual' and 'individual', on performances might suggest that the inclusion of other environment variables in the analysis will mediate all the effects of social status on outcomes. Other research has stressed the importance on childen's outcomes of school organization and classroom environments (e.g., Yates, 1966; Sumner and Warburton, 1972; Banks and Finlayson, 1973; Nash, 1973; Brophy and Good, 1974; Delamont, 1976), and of neighbourhood and peer group environments (e.g., McDill and Coleman, 1965; Kandel and Lesser, 1969; Haller and Portes, 1973; Lambert *et al.*, 1973; Bain and Anderson, 1974; Picou and Carter,

1976; Alwin and Otto, 1977). In Chapter 8, a longitudinal model is examined which includes some of these other potentially mediating mechanisms.

In Figure 3.3, the surfaces show the regression-fitted relations between social status and the English achievement of junior children. The Figures reflect the shapes of most of the regression surfaces in which there are significant relations between the outcome scores and measures of social status and family socialization variables. At each social-status level, increases in family environment scores are related to increments in English achievement; and at each level of family environment, changes in social status are associated with changes in English performance.

The results of the analysis indicate the importance of considering both social status and social-psychological family environment measures if a more complete understanding of the variation in children's school-related outcomes is to be obtained (also see Marjoribanks, 1977b, 1977c). Later, in Model 5, the relations between social status, social-psychological family measures, and children's cognitive outcomes are examined in further detail, using a path analytic model.

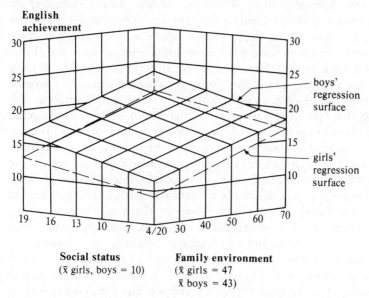

FIGURE 3.3 *Fitted-English scores in relation to social status and family environment: junior group girls and boys*

Model 4: f(social status, intelligence) ⟶ academic achievement

It was suggested in Model I that one of the most consistent findings in educational research is that social status has moderate associations with children's school-related outcomes. An even more consistent, and not surprising finding, is that intelligence test scores have high concurrent validities in relation to children's school achievement. When social status, intelligence, and children's outcomes have been included in the same analyses, however, the findings from the research have been inconsistent. There is no clear understanding of how measures of social status are related to school performance scores at different levels of intellectual ability. For example, a set of path analytic studies using the 'Wisconsin' sociological model of educational and occupational attainment (a model which shall be investigated in detail in Chapter 5) has shown that social-status measures have little or no influence on the academic performance of students of equal intellectual ability (e.g., see Alexander *et al.*, 1975; Sewell and Hauser, 1975; Wilson and Portes, 1975; Sewell and Hauser, 1976; Spencer, 1976; Williams, 1976b). The conclusion by Alexander, Eckland and Griffin (1975, p. 334) indicates the nature of the findings of these studies when they suggest that their results 'indicate the considerable importance of measured ability and the essential irrelevance of social origins (net of ability) for class standing. Thus, status origins do not influence the academic performance of boys of equal ability.' Similarly Alexander and McDill (1976, p. 974) propose that 'the pattern of background influences upon academic performance actually obtained is quite consistent with previous research on these issues. Academic aptitude is, by a considerable margin, the major direct determinant of both rank and achievement . . . we obtain little evidence of appreciable direct SES bias in the allocation of grades.' Featherman and Carter (1976, p. 141) found, however, that while 'mental ability emerges as the most dominant causal antecedent of grade point averages, both mother's education and paternal occupation affect grade point averages directly'. Also, from an analysis of the educational attainment of black and white American students, Kerckhoff and Campbell (1977, p. 23) suggest that the effect of intelligence on grade-nine achievement scores was 'about the same for both races, but the SES measures have a clear effect on grades for whites'. In an investigation of fifth- and sixth-grade Chicago children, Gordon (1976a, p. 10) proposes 'that among children of similar IQs, there is under- and over-achievement associated with their race and social class'. From a review of studies, Banks (1976, p. 69) concludes that 'there is a great deal of evidence that socio-economic status has a considerable effect on academic achievement even when measured ability is controlled'. The intricacies in the relations involving social status, intelligence, and school-related outcomes are highlighted by Bowles and Gintis (1977, p. 221) in their analysis of 'IQ in the U.S. Class Structure'. They propose that 'although IQs and economic success tend to go together, higher IQs are not an important cause of economic success'. It is suggested that 'the statistical association between adult IQ and economic success, while substantial, derives largely from the common association of both of these variables with social class background and level of schooling'.

The equivocal nature of the findings relating social status, intelligence, and achievement may be associated, in part, with the failure of many of the studies to include samples of both females and males. In many of the 'Wisconsin'-type analyses, for example, only samples of males have been investigated; this possibly is a major restriction in socialization research as it is often proposed that family background experiences may be related to differential school performances of girls and boys (e.g., see Moore, 1967, 1968; Hoffman, 1972; Hutt, 1972; Lee and Gropper, 1974; Hout and Morgan, 1975; Epstein and McPartland, 1977). Also, the studies typically examine only one age-cohort of children, which prevents the detection of age-differential relations between family background characteristics and children's performances. A further restriction of much of the research has been the analysis of linear relationships without testing for possible interaction and curvilinear relations between the variables.

In an attempt to overcome some of these limitations of prior research, the present analysis examines relations between social status, intelligence, and the academic achievement of children from the three age-cohorts of the Plowden data. Social status is defined by an equally weighted composite of father occupation, father education, and family income, all assessed during the initial survey. Academic achievement was measured in the follow-up study using the Vernon English comprehension test and the Vernon graded mathematics test while the Alice-Heim general intelligence test (AH4) was used to measure intellectual ability (see Marjoribanks, 1979b).

Regression surfaces are constructed using raw regression weights generated from models of the form:

$$Z = aX + bY + cXY + dX^2 + eY^2 + \text{constant, where}$$

Z, X, and Y represent measures of academic achievement, intelligence, and social status, respectively. As indicated in Chapter 1, the Design Effects for regression weights are calculated for most of the regression surfaces constructed in the book. For the present investigation, within each age-cohort and sex group, Jack-knife estimates were based on four sub-samples which were formed by randomly allocating children to the four groups. Pseudo-values for the regression weights were obtained from four sets of computations. In successive analyses different combinations of subsamples, taken three at a time, were used. The significance levels for the regression weights were recalculated using the formula: standard error for sample estimate = (design effect)^{½} x simple random sample standard error. The Jack-knife estimates led to a substantial reduction in the number of regression weights that were significant. Therefore a second stage of the regression analysis was conducted in which variables that no longer had significant associations with the English and mathematics measures were deleted from the regression models. In the second analysis the Jack-knife technique was used again to estimate Design Effects and thus to adjust further the significance levels of the regression weights.

Regression surfaces were generated from equations including the raw regression weights shown in Table 3.4. As well as significant linear associations the findings show that intelligence has significant curvilinear relations to some of the achievement scores at different social-status levels. The surfaces portrayed in Figure 3.4 have been presented as they are representative of the shapes of the other regression surfaces in the analysis. For the construction of the planes the data were converted to standard scores with a mean of 50 and a standard deviation of 10. In Figure 3.4, the regression-fitted relations between intelligence and mathematics are shown at different social-status levels, for the senior children. The shape of the girls' surface reflects those equations in which social status is not related to the achievement

TABLE 3.4 *Raw regression weights for multiple regression of academic achievement on intelligence and social status*

Predictor variables	Senior Cohort		Middle Cohort		Junior Cohort	
	Mathematics	English	Mathematics	English	Mathematics	English
Intelligence	0.69* (1.36†)	0.76† (1.04†)	0.54† (0.49†)	0.40† (0.36†)	1.05† (1.09†)	0.63† (0.29†)
Social status	0.73* (0.10)	−0.38 (0.66)	0.63† (0.40†)	0.61† (0.48†)	−0.21 (−0.66)	0.33 (0.31†)
Intelligence × status	a (0.01)	0.01 (0.02)	a(a)	a(a)	0.01 (−0.01)	0.01(a)
(Intelligence)²	a (−0.01†)	−0.006* (−0.01†)	a(a)	a(a)	−0.008* (−0.009†)	−0.005†(a)
(Social status)²	a (0.03)	0.01 (−0.04)	a(a)	a(a)	0.02 (0.05)	0.01(a)
Multiple R	0.60 (0.67)	0.59 (0.60)	0.67 (0.62)	0.68 (0.63)	0.73 (0.63)	0.63 (0.51)

Note Coefficients for girls are in parentheses.
* Value of raw regression weight exceeds twice its standard error.
† Value of raw regression weight exceeds three times its standard error.
a Indicates that the variables were not entered into analysis after calculating design effects and adjusting significance levels.

scores at different ability levels. At an ability level of 40, for example, the regression-fitted mathematics scores for senior girls

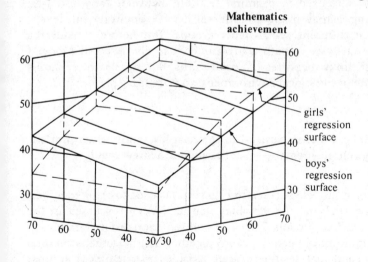

FIGURE 3.4 *Fitted-mathematics scores in relation to intelligence and social status: senior cohort girls and boys*

is approximately 42 at each social-status level. In the senior boys' sample, however, increments in the social-status levels of families are associated with increases in mathematics scores at each level of intelligence. As the social-status level changes from a low of 30 to a high of 70, the regression-estimated mathematics scores increase by approximately nine points at each level of ability. The shapes of the planes also indicate that at each level of social status, increments in ability scores are associated with sizeable increases in the achievement scores. In the girls' surface there is a slightly negative curvilinear relation between social status and achievement at each social-status level.

The findings indicate that at each social-status level, intelligence has strong direct linear relations, and sometimes slightly curvilinear associations, with academic performance. In half the regression models, social status continues to affect the achievement scores at each ability level. The relations between family environment measures and outcomes at different levels of cognitive scores are examined further in later chapters. For example, in Chapter 6 the associations between intelligence and achievement are investigated at different levels of refined family environment measures. Also, in Chapter 6 regression surface analysis is used to examine relations between early and later reading achievement at different family environment levels, within different social-status groups. But before considering those analyses, a path analytic model is discussed in Model 5 which links measures of social status, sibling variables, family social-psychological environment, and cognitive performance.

Model 5: f(social status, sibling variables, family environment, early achievement) ——→later academic achievement

The path model specified in Figure 3.5 is used to bring together, in one analysis, the variables that have been discussed in the previous four models. For ease of presentation certain variables in the figure have been 'blocked' together. In the actual structural model and analyses the separate variables operate on one another as diagrammed. The data used to test the model were selected from the senior-age cohort children in the Plowden studies. As the model shows, during the first Plowden survey, data were

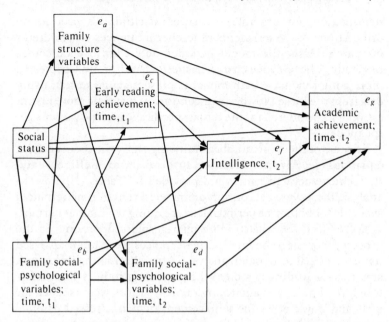

FIGURE 3.5 *Schematic path model for relations between social status, family environment and cognitive performance*

collected on: social-status characteristics of the family, sibsize, crowding ratio in the home (which is a ratio of the number of people inhabiting the household to the number of rooms), family environment variables, and reading achievement (the Watts-Vernon reading test). In the second survey the family environment was remeasured, as well as children's intelligence, mathematics, and English achievement. The model proposes that the famly structure variables were affected by the social-status measures and that the early social-psychological family environment is influenced by the two sets of social background measures. It is assumed that the early reading scores are influenced by all the prior environment measures. The family environment, measured in the second survey, is considered to be affected by all the variables assessed during the initial Plowden study. Intelligence has been placed as a mediating variable between the achievement outcomes and all the preceding variables in the model (Marjoribanks, 1977c).

The path model suffers from an under-identification as it does not include, for example, measures of children's peer group orientations nor assessments of teacher influences on children's outcomes. Also, the model includes only cognitive outcomes neglecting the affective characteristics of children. In Chapter 8 a more comprehensive path model is presented and tested, using data from the three Plowden age-cohorts. At that time more justification will be offered for the actual specification of the variables in the model.

Because of the large number of findings only the reduced-form equations (see Alwin and Hauser, 1975) related to intelligence and the achievement measures are provided in Table 3.5. For the analysis there were data on approximately 20 environment indices available for both time periods. Factor-scaling techniques (Armor, 1974) reduced the data to more manageable proportions. In the process, scores on the environment indices were factor analysed using principal component analysis. After eliminating items with small factor loadings (<0.40) the remaining indices were refactored. At time 2, two environment press factors were isolated for girls and boys: press for achievement (which assessed parents' aspirations for their children and the literacy of the home) and parent-teacher interaction. Two environment variables were identified for boys at time 1: parents' aspirations for children and press for intellectuality (a measure of parent-child activeness within a family and parents' knowledge of the child's school environment). For girls at time 1 three factors emerged, and these were labelled: parents' aspirations for children, parent-child activeness, and knowledge of child's school environment.

(a) Associations with intelligence: In Table 3.5 the regression coefficients show that the influence of father occupation on boys' intelligence scores is mediated via the early parent socialization factors (line 3). Similarly, for girls, the effects of father occupation and family income on intelligence are transmitted through the early socialization measures (line 20). Early reading achievement and later family environment factors are the only variables that have significant direct effects on boys' intelligence. For girls, reading achievement (t_1) and educational aspirations (t_1) have direct effects on intelligence, but the later environment variables do not add significantly to an explanation of the differences in intelligence scores. That is, in relation to family environment influences, intelligence may become more stable at an earlier age for girls than for boys.

TABLE 3.5 *Regression coefficients in standard form for analysis of path model: reduced form equations*

Predetermined variables: senior boys

Dependent variables	A	B	C	D	E	F	G	J	K	L	M	R²
Intelligence (M)	153	007	112									0.053
Intelligence	137	017	108	-149	007							0.076
Intelligence	080	-034	064	-085	003	136	188					0.130
Intelligence	086	-030	058	-082	-005	106	164	145				0.149
Intelligence	042	-030	035	-082	-003	041	072	106	228	112		0.189
English	174	045	154									0.091
English	155	060	153	-226	-026							0.136
English	067	-023	-083	-124	-024	296	230					0.282
English	082	-014	070	-116	-045	228	174	330				0.380
English	013	-019	032	-114	-041	111	024	266	396	119		0.472
English	001	-009	020	-086	-040	098	001	231	321	082	329	0.560
Mathematics	123	057	197									0.093
Mathematics	109	068	195	-167	-016							0.118
Mathematics	024	-013	128	-067	-011	319	197					0.263
Mathematics	037	-006	117	-061	-027	264	153	262				0.324
Mathematics	-025	-005	087	-064	-023	180	029	209	300	181		0.403
Mathematics	-041	007	073	-032	-022	165	001	168	211	138	387	0.525

Predetermined variables: senior girls

Dependent variables	A	B	C	D	E	F	H	I	J	K	L	M	R²
Intelligence (M)	133	145	063										0.073
Intelligence	128	153	069	-070	-037								0.077
Intelligence	070	095	008	-019	018	313	135	-030					0.184
Intelligence	062	081	-003	029	022	218	105	-030	242				0.225
Intelligence	043	083	-007	027	017	192	071	-044	216	079	087		0.235
English	194	140	102										0.118
English	170	153	111	-248	-062								0.168
English	096	077	032	-174	002	364	176	022					0.327
English	079	046	009	-074	010	164	113	021	507				0.509
English	058	025	-041	-052	001	063	075	-016	435	324	025		0.567
English	049	006	-040	-048	-003	019	059	-006	386	306	005	230	0.607
Mathematics	248	120	170										0.179
Mathematics	231	143	190	-234	-123								0.220
Mathematics	149	057	106	-153	-048	394	241	011					0.430
Mathematics	136	035	089	-080	-041	250	196	010	365				0.525
Mathematics	111	033	075	-077	-049	200	150	-012	321	156	103		0.548
Mathematics	097	005	077	-086	-054	137	126	002	249	130	074	333	0.633

Italicized coefficients are not significant at the 0.05 level of confidence. Decimal points for the coefficients have been omitted. Variable labels are: A, father occupation; B, family income; C, father education; D, sibsize; E, crowding ratio; F, educational aspirations t_1; G, press for intellectuality t_1; H, knowledge of child's school environment t_1; I, parent-child activeness t_1; J, early reading achievement t_1; K, press for achievement t_2; L, parent-teacher interaction t_2; M, intelligence t_2.

(b) Associations with English: For both girls and boys, reading (t_1), press for achievement (t_2), and intelligence (t_2) have the strongest direct effects on English performance. The direct effects of father occupation and father education on boys' English scores are absorbed by the addition of the early socialization measures to the path model (line 8). While much of the effect of sibsize is mediated by the early family measures, it continues to have a small but significant direct effect on boys' scores. In the girls' sample, the social status and sibsize effects on English achievement are transmitted via the early family and reading scores.

(c) Associations with mathematics: The pattern of associations with mathematics performance, for girls and boys, is quite different. Father occupation, father education, and sibsize continue to have direct effects on girls' mathematics scores after the addition of the intervening measures (last line in Table 3.5). For boys, the effects of sibsize are absorbed by the early environment measures, while the influence of father education on mathematics performance is mediated by the famly socialization variables.

The results of the path model show the presence of a network of strong inter-relationships between social status, parent socialization influences, and children's achievement, thus providing support for Halsey's (1975, p. 17) contention that 'a theory which explains educational achievement as the outcome of a set of individual attributes has lost the meaning of those structural forces which we know as class'.

Model 6: f(social status, teacher attitudes) ⟶ academic achievement

The studies examined in this chapter have been restricted to analyses of the inter-relationships among social status, family socialization variables, and children's school-related outcomes. Although the purpose of the present book is not to examine in detail the influence of school environments on children, an attempt is made to show how school measures are related to children's outcomes at different levels of family environment measures. There is a burgeoning interest in investigations linking children's background characteristics, teacher attitudes, and children's performances (e.g. Elashoff and Snow, 1971; Finn,

1972; Rubovits and Maehr, 1973; Kehle, 1974; Cooper *et al.*, 1975; Dusek, 1975; Hargreaves, *et al.* 1975; Wilkins, 1976; Williams 1976b; Rist, 1977). From a review of related research Braun (1976, p. 194) concludes that 'an apparently potent source of input (to teachers' attitudes) is that of race and socio-economic status'. He goes on to suggest that 'the degree to which social class and race signal differential expectancy cues either in isolation or in inter-action with each other is an area of much needed research'. In Chapter 8 the relations between background characteristics, teacher attitudes, and children's outcomes are analysed in a path model. The following investigation is an initial analysis of the extent that teacher attitudes are related to children's achievement at different social-status levels.

Again, data from the three Plowden cohorts are used. Teacher attitude is the only variable which has not previously been described. In the follow-up Plowden survey, teachers were asked to rate their students on a questionnaire designed by the National Foundation for Educational Research in England. It consisted of 10 items of the form: whether the teacher thought the student was a hard worker, obedient in class, participation in class and school activities, concentrated on schoolwork, was restless in class and aggressive in school. A teacher attitude score was obtained by a simple summation of the item-scores.

The regression surfaces constructed in Figure 3.6 relate only to the senior group English scores, but they reflect the findings of the analyses within each cohort, and they are similar to the surfaces for mathematics. At each social-status level increases in the favourableness of teacher attitudes are associated with incre-ments in performance on the tests. Also, at each level of teacher attitude, changes in social status are related to changes in achieve-ment. Thus if children come from low social-status families and they are perceived by teachers as exhibiting unfavourable school-related behaviour then, within the school context, the children appear to suffer a compounded liability in relation to academic achievement. If children who come from lower social-status families are not perceived by teachers as having unfavourable attitudes then the children perform at a relatively higher level. Unfortunately, the correlational nature of the analysis does not permit any inferences regarding how teacher attitudes, at different social-status levels, are translated into academic performance. In an attempt to apply labelling theory to an understanding of the

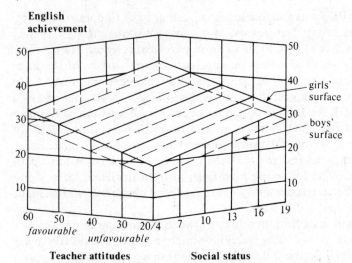

FIGURE 3.6 *Fitted-English scores in relation to social status and teacher attitudes: senior group girls and boys*

process of schooling, Rist (1977, p. 302) suggests that 'to extend the research on the educational experience of those students who are differentially labeled by teachers, what is needed is a theoretical framework which can clearly isolate the influences and effects of certain kinds of teacher reactions on certain types of students, producing certain typical outcomes'. He proposes that 'the labeling perspective appears particularly well-suited for this expansion of both research and theoretical development on teacher expectations'. In later chapters the discussion of the relations between teachers' attitudes and children's outcomes will be pursued further. The present analysis offers a caveat, that any such research needs to be undertaken in the context of the social environment of the children.

The studies in this chapter indicate the necessity of integrating measures of global social-status characteristics, refined social-psychological measures, and person variables for a more complete understanding of children's school-related outcomes.

4 Sibling variables: insignificant or meaningful family environment measures

Social scientists have had a long, if somewhat unproductive, fascination with exploring the relations between sibling constellation variables and measures of children's behaviour. Adler (1959), Toman (1969), and Zajonc (1976), for example, have used sibling variables as central elements in constructing theories to explain variation in individuals' personalities and social behaviour. But, typically, studies have included sibling measures as peripheral rather than as major explanatory variables. In a discussion of the complexities surrounding the inclusion of birth order in research, Schooler (1972, p. 174) provides a clear statement of the status of sibling variables in much recent research. He suggests that 'I suspect that future investigators, including myself, will not be able to resist the temptation of taking a cheap bet on a long shot by collecting birth order data on their subjects as they pursue studies more central to their interests'.

The present chapter argues that research on sibling variables can lead to a more meaningful understanding of the variation in children's characteristics. Research is reviewed that has included sibling measures as primary variables in examinations of a social-psychological theory of sibling effects on children's cognitive and affective outcomes. It is postulated in the theory: (a) that parents provide differential environmental experiences for children of different birth-order positions and for children within families of different sizes, and (b) that these family-related environment treatments are associated with sibling differences in children's school-related outcomes. The following five sets of relations are analysed in the chapter, using data from various national settings:

(a) Sibsize, social status, and changing national ability

(b) Social-psychological theory: birth order effects (Canadian 11-year-old children)

(c) Social-psychological theory: sibsize effects (Canadian and English data)

(d) Sibsize, birth order, social status and intelligence (Dutch sample of 19-year-old males)

(e) The confluence model of sibling constellation effects on children's cognitive performance (Australian 11-year-old children)

Sibsize, social status, and changing national ability

About 1925, three statistical findings confronted psychologists in Western Europe and North America (see Walberg and Marjoribanks, 1976).

1. Sibsize had been found to correlate about −0.3 with the mean ability scores of children in the family: the larger the sibsize, the lower the children's abilities (see Model 2 in Chapter 3). That is, sibsize was associated with approximately 9 per cent of the variance in ability scores, even though the relations were subject to exceptions.

2. Children's abilities had been shown to correlate about 0.3 to 0.4 with parents' social status (see Model 1 in Chapter 3). That is, social status was associated with about 9 to 16 per cent of the variance in ability scores.

3. On the average, parents in lower social-status groups were found to marry earlier than parents from other social-status groups, bear children more quickly, and continue to conceive children to a later age. On hereditarian grounds, some psychologists inferred that because of such differential reproductive rates, national intelligence levels might be declining by as much as 2 or 3 points per generation.

Several large-scale studies were undertaken to investigate the possibility of declining national ability. Samples of children in relatively stable population districts in England and Scotland were obtained at two time periods more than ten years apart (Scottish Council, 1949; Emmett, 1950). To the surprise of the original investigators, ability levels had risen slightly. An environmental explanation was advanced to defend the validity of the hereditarian influence, namely, that while the national gene pool of ability was deteriorating, education was improving and the sum of the two opposing effects maintained the level of measured ability or raised it slightly.

It was shown later, however, that such longitudinal studies can be highly misleading when changes in national gene pools of ability are investigated. Spurious results are obtained because correlations between the mean ability of siblings in the family and the number of siblings fail to take into account the non-contribution of barren adults to gene pools (Cole, 1954). Anastasi (1956) also observed that spurious findings would result if the research failed to start with a sample of adults with and without children, if it did not obtain a record of parents' abilities, and did not ascertain fertility rates at various ability levels. Two research groups recognized and attempted to avoid these errors. Higgens, Reed and Reed (1962) sampled children and grandchildren of non-epileptic patients in a Minnesota psychiatric hospital, and Bajema (1963) studied the offsprings of former public schoolchildren in Kalamazoo, Michigan. Both studies agree that adults at the highest levels of intelligence (scores above 130) have the highest average fertility rates and about three offspring, and that feeble-minded adults (intelligence test scores of 55 and below) have very low fertility. These studies suggest that, for the populations surveyed, average intelligence, in so far as it is genetically determined, had been at least stable and possibly rising.

Another interesting though unanticipated finding in both the Minnesota and the Michigan studies was bimodal (double peaked) fertility rates across the range of intelligence levels. In the larger sample of 1,966 individuals (Higgens *et al.*, 1962), for example, the groups with intelligence test scores from 56 to 85 had reproductive rates of 2.42; the group from 86 to 115, 2.21; and the group above 116, 2.60. Bajema (1963) found bimodal fertility with respect to the number of years of school completed by the parents. Although bimodality of these fertility rates is not sufficient to produce bimodal intelligence test score distributions in the offspring generation, it is likely to increase the standard deviation of the scores. That is, bimodal fertility rates are likely to spread the offspring intelligence test scores farther from the mean, and to make the distribution platykurtic, or flatter than the normal curve. These tendencies may also be increased by assortative mating. Warren (1966), for example, found the correlation of spouses' years of education to be about 0.60, and the correlation of their social statuses (as indexed by father's occupation) to be about 0.30. Since both years of education and father occupation are correlated with intelligence test scores, assortative mating could be increasing intelligence test score variation from parent to offspring generations.

An analysis by Walberg (1974) of the Higgens *et al.* (1962) data revealed a significant increase in the standard deviations of intelligence scores from parents to offsprings. Unfortunately, the initial study was based on a special population, children and grandchildren of psychiatric patients. In longitudinal research in Britain, the Scottish Council for Research in Education and Population Investigaton Committee (1949) found a significant increase, from 15.48 to 16.10, in the standard deviations of intelligence test scores from 1932 to 1947 in a nearly complete sample of population cohorts in Scotland; and Emmett (1950) found a slightly higher increase, from 14.21 to 15.00, in a large-scale sample of English districts during the same period.

It is well established in genetic theory and research that assortative mating and bimodal fertility produce greater variation in characteristics in offsprings. Since these mechanisms operate with respect to intelligence test scores, years of education, and social status, and since studies of changes in verbal intelligence scores reveal increasing standard deviations, it appears that in so far as it is genetically determined, variation in intelligence may be increasing.

It was noted earlier that the longitudinal surveys carried out in England and Scotland, on very large numbers of children, had shown slight increases in intelligence scores over time. Two somewhat comparable sets of data on young men have been reported in the United States. Tuddenham (1948) found that the mean intelligence test scores of draftees for military service rose by about one standard deviation between World War I and World War II, while Tupes and Shaycoft (1964) reported a half-standard deviation increase between World War II and 1963. That is, on the average, intelligence scores appear to have risen by about a half point a year. By the standards of a hypothetical intelligence test normed early in the twentieth century, the typical young adult in the United States would now rank high in measured verbal intelligence. Better nutrition, more verbal stimulation inside and outside the home, and additional years of schooling are all factors that probably have contributed to such a rise. In addition the general reduction of family size that has accompanied urbanization may have enabled parents to concentrate their intellectual energies on fewer children.

The early doubts regarding inter-relationships between social status, sibsize, and a possible decline in national ability levels have generated much interesting sibling research. From the research a social-psychological theory of sibling influences on children's outcomes has been formulated which, as indicated at the beginning of the chapter, proposes that family configurations are related to differential family learning environments for children and that the learning environments are related to differences in children's cognitive and affective outcomes. Aspects of the theory are examined in the following sections of the chapter.

Social-psychological theory: birth-order effects

Investigations of the relations between the birth order of children and measures of cognitive performance have usually shown that firstborns tend to have slightly higher scores, especially on verbal tests, than laterborn children (e.g. Clausen, 1966; Warren, 1966; Kellaghan and Macnamarra, 1972; Belmont and Marolla, 1973; Skovholt *et al.*, 1973; Zajonc and Markus, 1975; Nuttall *et al.*, 1976; Breland, 1977). Attempts to support a social-psychological explanation of the birth-order differences, in relation to social-status characteristics and other family structure variables, have not been particularly successful in generating consistent findings. Record, McKeown and Edwards (1969) reported, for example, that birth-order differences in the verbal reasoning scores of approximately 37,000 11-year-old English children were related primarily to between-family differences in father's occupation and maternal age at child's birth. Similarly, from an analysis of data on over 40,000 American children who were tested in the Project Talent study, Burton (1968) concluded that among social-status categories and among family size groups there were no consistent relations between birth order and intelligence test scores. And Murray (1971), who examined high school students in England, found that for each level of family size, with some control exercised over social status, there was no significant difference between first- and laterborn children on verbal and non-verbal intelligence test scores.

Kellaghan and Macnamarra (1972) in a study of the family correlates of the verbal reasoning scores of 11-year-old Irish children concluded, however, that after accounting for the influence of family size and social status, birth order still made a significant contribution to the variation in the reasoning scores. Also,

Eysenck and Cookson (1969), who studied 4,000 11-year-old English children, showed that on mathematics and English achievement tests there was a significant trend for early-born children to do better than laterborn children when family size was held constant; whereas, after accounting for the influence of family size, there was no relation between birth-order position and measures of intelligence or reading achievement. In an investigation of approximately 500 families from four suburban Boston communities, Nuttall and his associates (1976) investigated relations between a 'firstborn index' and grade-point averages. After accounting for the effects of family size and intelligence test scores, the firstborn index continued to be associated with the academic achievement of girls but not of boys. Using data on 400,000 19-year-old Dutch males (data which will be examined in more detail later in the chapter), Belmont and Marolla (1973) revealed that, at each family-size level, scores on the Raven's Progressive Matrices Test declined with birth order.

Because of the equivocal findings from investigations of the relations between birth order, other family configuration variables, social status, and children's cognitive abilities, researchers have proposed that studies should investigate associations between birth order and children's outcomes at different levels of social-psychological family environment measures (e.g., see Altus, 1966; Clausen, 1966; Bayer and Folger, 1967; Burton, 1968; Jensen, 1969; Poole and Kuhn, 1973; Cicirelli, 1977a). In an attempt to overcome some of the environmental restrictions of prior investigations, Marjoribanks and Walberg (1975a) and Marjoribanks (1976b) examined the birth order and environmental correlates of the mental ability scores of a sample of Canadian 11-year-old boys. The family environment measure in the Marjoribanks and Walberg (1975a) study was defined by the parent-sibling interaction variables of press for: achievement, activeness, intellectuality, English, independence; and mother dominance and father dominance. The parents of the 185 boys in the sample were interviewed in their homes, and the final sample consisted of 95 families classified as lower social status and 90 classified as middle social status (see Marjoribanks (1972a) in Chapter 2 for a more complete description of the sample and the environment measure). Mental ability performance was assessed using the SRA Primary Mental Abilities Test, which provides verbal, number, spatial, and reasoning scores.

In the first analysis of the social-psychological theoretical position, Marjoribanks and Walberg (1975a) investigated relations between: (a) birth order and mental abilities, (b) birth order and the family environment measures, (c) the family environment and mental abilities, and (d) birth order, family environment, and mental abilities. Only the results for the total sample are considered as there were no significant differences in the relations between the two social-status groups. The findings indicated that birth order was related only to the verbal and number scores. That is, earlier-born children tended to have higher scores on those two ability measures. Press for independence and mother dominance were the only parent-sibling interaction variables not to be related to birth order. Thus, in relation to laterborn boys, earlier-borns had a family environment that: (a) exerted a stronger press for: achievement, activeness, intellectuality, and English; and in which, (b) relative to mothers, fathers were more dominant in family decision-making and more involved in their sons' activities. The correlations that were reported in Table 2.1 showed that the parent-sibling variables that are being examined here were associated with about 50 per cent of the variance in the boys' verbal and number scores. Therefore, in relation to verbal and number abilities these findings provide initial support for the theoretical position which states that parents create differential learning environments for children of different birth-order positions, and that the environments are related to variations in cognitive performance.

The theoretical position was tested further using multiple regression models to examine the unique contribution of birth order to variation in the ability scores after 'accounting for' the unique contribution of the environment measures and also the joint contribution of birth order and family environment. In the regression analysis, the environment was defined by two sets of measures. First, a combination of the social-status measures: father occupation, father education, and mother education. Second, a combination of the family-sibling interaction variables. Initially, birth order was associated with approximately 7 per cent of the variance in the verbal and number ability scores. After the addition of the social-status measures, birth order continued to make a significant contribution of approximately 3 per cent to the differences in the cognitive measures. When the parent-sibling interaction variables were added, birth order no longer had a unique association with the variation in the test scores. That is, by using more refined family environment measures the study provides support for the acceptance of the social-psychological theoretical position.

The study just examined is limited, as are many other birth-order investigations, by the use of restricted statistical techniques. In a more detailed examination of the Canadian data, Marjoribanks (1976b) used regression surface analysis to investigate relations between birth order and ability scores at different family environment levels. A principal component analysis of the family environment scales revealed that press for achievement, activeness, English, intellectuality, and independence loaded strongly on a general factor that had a theta reliability estimate of approximately 0.85. A family environment score for each boy was calculated from an equally weighted composite of the five parent-sibling interaction variables. Regression models included linear, product (to test for interactions), and squared terms (to test for curvilinearity). Except for spatial ability, family environment had significant linear and curvilinear relations to the ability scores. Birth order was not related to the abilities at any level of the family environment measure.

The findings of the surface analysis are summarized in Figure 4.1, which shows the relations between birth order and the fitted-

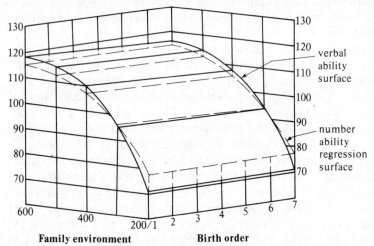

FIGURE 4.1 *Fitted-verbal and number ability scores in relation to birth order and family environment*

verbal and number scores at different family environment levels. The curvature of the surfaces indicates that, at each environment level, increases in birth order are not associated with significant changes in the ability scores. At a low environment level of 300, for example, the regression-estimated values of verbal ability are 95 for boys who are firstborn and 93 for boys who are seventh-born, while the comparable estimated verbal values are 118 and 116 at an enriched environment level of 600.

If the between-family data are considered to reflect within-family mechanisms, the surfaces indicate that if parents create differential learning environments for successive children then the regression-estimated ability values vary. At a family environment score of 400, say, the estimated verbal and number scores of a firstborn are 110 and 107, respectively. If a second-born son grows up in a more enriched family environment, perhaps as the result of a change in parents' economic conditions or because the parents have learned from their experiences with the firstborn how to create more stimulating learning environments for successive children, then the estimated verbal and number scores are higher than those of firstborn sons. The regression-estimated verbal and number ability values for a second-born boy at an environment level of 600, for example, are 117 and 114, respectively; that is, seven points higher in both ability measures than firstborn boys with an environment level of 400. In the development of a confluence model of birth-order effects on intelligence, which will be examined later in the chapter, Zajonc and Markus (1975) and Zajonc (1976), propose that unless there is sufficient age-spacing between successive children in a family, the intellectual environment for children will tend to become more diluted rather than enriched. In relation to Figure 4.1, if after the birth of the second child parents are unable to provide as stimulating a learning environment as they did for the firstborn, then the estimated ability scores of the second-born are lower than those of the firstborn. At an environment level of 300, for example, the regression-fitted verbal and number scores for second-borns are 95, while they were 110 and 107, respectively, for firstborn boys at an environment level of 400.

Studies which concentrate on examining the amount of variance in ability scores associated with birth order typically conclude that, after environment measures are included in the analysis, birth order is no longer a significant variable in family environment research. The regression surface analysis suggests, however, that our understanding of the relations between refined family measures and children's outcomes may be enhanced if these relations are examined in the context of family configurations. As Adler (1959) and much of Adlerian psychology suggests, individuals' positions in the family structure may greatly affect the kinds of definition they develop and upon which they operate. And, indeed, in a number of interesting experimental situations, Cicirelli (1975, 1977a, 1977b) has shown that the effectiveness of a mother in helping a child to develop problem-solving techniques depends on the sibling structure of the family. He suggests that 'interactions within the family can be viewed as constituting an interactional system consisting of three sub-systems: parent-parent interactions, parent-child interactions, and sibling-sibling interactions' (Cicirelli, 1977b, p. 310). In any such system it is proposed that 'the interaction between any two members of the family is qualified by the interactions involving other members of the family'. In an investigation of problem solving tasks, for example, Cicirelli found that when a child was being helped by an older sibling, older sisters provided much more assistance than did older brothers. When the child was being helped by the mother, it was revealed that mothers provided much greater information to children who had older brothers and not older sisters. Cicirelli suggests that mothers relinquish part of their helping role towards a given child when the child has an older sister. From his investigations, Cicirelli (1977b, p. 316) concludes that 'sibling effects should be studied within the context of the entire interactional system of the family'.

Therefore, perhaps birth order should not be included in family research as a peripheral variable, as Schooler (1972) predicts will be the fate of the variable. Instead, studies should examine in greater detail the complexities surrounding the relations between birth order and children's personality and social behaviour.

Social-psychological theory: sibsize effects

In the analysis of Model 2 in Chapter 3, it was shown that sibsize and the inverse of sibsize had significant (linear and interaction) relations with cognitive performance. Social-psychological explanations of the relations propose that large sibships are associated with poorer family learning environments (see Hunt, 1961; Rosen, 1961; Sampson, 1965; Oldman *et al.*, 1971; Adams and Phillips, 1972); and that sibsize is merely an unreliable indicator of more specific processes that operate within families. Again, using the data from the Canadian sample that was discussed in the previous section of the chapter, Marjoribanks and Walberg (1975b) provided the first real test of the above explanation by analysing relations between sibsize and parent-sibling interaction variables, at different social-status levels. Both sibsize and the inverse of sibsize were included in the investigation. In regression models, product and quadratic terms among the variables were not significant. At each level of the two sibsize measures, social status was related to the parent-sibling variables. Also, at each social-status level, sibsize had significant linear associations with press for achievement, activeness, intellectuality, and father dominance, while the inverse of sibsize had significant associations with press for achievement, activeness, intellectuality, and English. Press for independence and mother dominance were not related to either of the sibsize variables at different status levels. In Figures 4.2 and 4.3, the surfaces reflect the associations with the two sibsize variables. At each social-status level, parents' press for

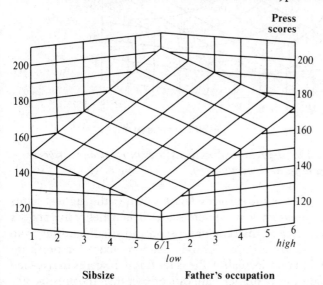

FIGURE 4.2 *Fitted-press for achievement scores in relation to sibsize and father's occupation*

achievement decreases with increments in sibsize (see Figure 4.2). At a low social-status level of one, for example, the regression-estimated press for achievement scores for boys in one- and six- child families are 150 and 124 respectively, while the corresponding press values at a high social-status level of six are 202 and 174. The hyperbolic form of the relation between press for English and the inverse of sibsize is shown in Figure 4.3, indicating that at each social-status level the decrements in press for English, which are associated with increases in sibsize, are greatest at low sibsize levels. As sibsize increases from one to two, for example, there is a decrease in press for English of approximately 18 points, at each level of social status. When sibsize increases from four to five, however, the decrease in the press for English scores at each status level is only about two points.

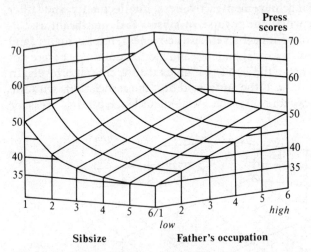

FIGURE 4.3 *Fitted-press for English scores in relation to inverse of sibsize and father's occupation*

The curvature of the surfaces denotes that, in the highest status groups, the press for achievement scores in families of five and six children are greater than the press scores in small families from the lowest status groups. Similar relations exist for press for activeness and intellectuality. Press for English scores in five- and six-child families of higher status are greater than the press scores in lower social-status families with two or more children. If the environment acts as a threshold variable in relation to cognitive performance (see Jensen, 1969) such that after a certain environmental level is reached additional environment increments have increasingly less influence on performance, then the associations in Figures 4.2 and 4.3 may provide a possible explanation of the finding mentioned in Chapter 3 (also see Anastasi, 1956; Douglas, 1964; Cicirelli, 1967; Kennett and Cropley, 1970) that the influence of sibsize on ability diminishes as social status increases. Also, by showing that the amount of parental attention that second- and laterborn children receive in families of lower social status is less than that for first-born children in such families, and also much lower than the attention that fifth- and sixth-born children receive in families of higher social status, the results of the analysis provide a further explanation for Poole and Kuhn's (1973) results (see Chapter 3). That is, for British university graduates with a middle social-status background a relatively large family does not constitute a barrier to obtaining a degree, whereas for children of manual workers a small family of one or two children is virtually a precondition of educational success. The findings also provide partial support for Rosen's (1961) contention that the small family of one or two children, the 'planned unit driven by ambition', may be necessary if children from lower social-status families are to be academically mobile.

The above tentative explanations do not take into account, of course, many of the other possible interpretations of the relations between social status and the educational and occupational attainment of children. While differences in family environments may account for much of the variation in children's attainments it is assumed throughout the present book that families are only one, albeit extremely important, influence on a child's school-related outcomes. As Halsey (1975, p. 21) contends, 'the association of social class with educational achievement will not be explained by a theory or eliminated by a policy which falls short of including changes in public support for learning in the family and neighbourhood, the training of teachers, the production of relevant curriculum, the fostering of parental participation, the raising of standards of housing and employment prospects, and, above all, the allocation of educational resources'.

For a more complete test of the social-psychological theory of sibsize relations with children's characteristics it is necessary to examine the association between sibsize and children's outcomes at different levels of refined environment measures. Using the children from the Plowden senior cohort Marjoribanks examined to what extent relationships between sibsize and children's cognitive and affective characteristics are mediated by family environment measures. From 383 boys and 396 girls, who were approximately 15 years old, measures were obtained on intelligence, mathematics, English, educational and occupational aspirations, and self-expectations (see Marjoribanks, 1976a). The family environment measures included both distal indicators and more proximal social-psychological variables. Factor scaling techniques were adopted to combine the indices that had been assessed in the initial Plowden and follow-up surveys. Included in the final environment measure were (a) the distal variables: father's occupation, father's education, family income, crowding in the home, and home amenities (all measured during the initial survey), and (b) the proximal measures: parents' aspirations for children, literacy of the home, parents' interest and support of schooling, initiative and responsibilities taken by parents towards education, and interest in helping with schoolwork (measured during both surveys).

In the boys' sample, sibsize had low to moderate zero-order correlations of -0.16, -0.20, -0.15, -0.15, and -0.13 with intelligence, English, mathematics, aspirations, and self-expectations. The corresponding correlations between these five outcome variables and the rather inclusive family environment measure were: 0.37, 0.51, 0.49, 0.49, and 0.24. For girls, the relations between the outcomes and sibsize (in the same order) are: -0.08 (not significant), -0.24, -0.23, -0.27, and -0.13, while the associations with family environment are: 0.32, 0.53, 0.53, 0.54, and 0.28. Thus the performance measures generally have low to moderate concurrent validities with sibsize and moderate to high relations to family environment.

Regression models disclosed that after adjusting raw regression weights for design effects, only linear relations between the variables were significant. For both sex groups, family environment is related strongly to the outcome measures at each sibsize level. Sibsize is related, however, only to boys' English achievement and girls' English and aspiration scores, at different family environment levels.

Results of the regression analysis are summarized in Figures 4.4 and 4.5. In Figure 4.4, the surfaces show the regression-fitted sibsize association with mathematics achievement. The shapes

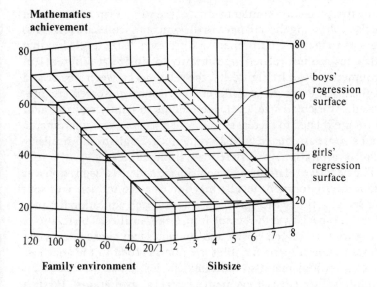

FIGURE 4.4 *Fitted-mathematics scores in relation to sibsize and family environment: girls and boys*

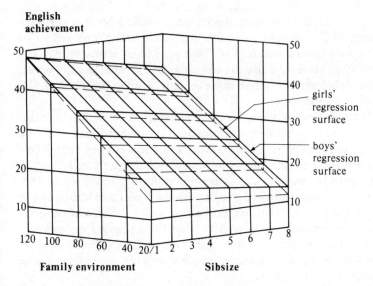

FIGURE 4.5 *Fitted-English scores in relation to sibsize and family environment: girls and boys*

of the two planes are similar to most of the surfaces generated from the data, showing that changes in the outcome scores are related to changes in family environment at different sibsize levels but that outcomes are not related significantly to sibsize at different environment levels. In Figure 4.5, the relations between sibsize and English achievement at different environment scores are presented. At each sibsize level, increments in family environment scores are related to increases in English scores. Also, increments in sibsize are associated with decrements in English (and similarly for girls' aspirations) at different environment levels.

The negative relations between sibsize and girls' aspirations, at different environment levels, may indicate the influence of sex-role socialization which prescribes a restricted educational career for girls, especially if they come from large families. The relations in Figure 4.5 between sibsize and outcomes may signify that some relevant environment variables are not included in the analysis. But the findings may also indicate that sibsize has two effects on children's English achievement and girls' aspirations. First, a 'contextual effect' in which sibsize influences are mediated by other environment measures. Second, an 'individual effect' which is the remaining unmediated influence of sibsize on the outcome variables. A similar argument was proposed in Chapter 3 regarding the relations between social status and children's performances. In the present study the 'individual effect' may reflect an interpretation by children of their positional status within the family which results in girls adapting their aspirations and which affects children's English achievement, even at enriched family environment levels.

If the between-family data are considered to capture within-family relationships, as was proposed in the examination of the birth-order findings, then the sibsize surfaces suggest that differential family environments for successive children are related to variations in outcomes. At a family environment score of, say, 100, the regression-estimated mathematics score of a firstborn boy is 60. If the second-born son grows up in a less enriched environment, for example, at a level of 80, then the estimated mathematics score is 50, which is lower than that of the firstborn. The regression-estimated mathematics score for a second-born son at an enriched level of 120 is 70.

As for the birth-order studies, the present findings emphasize the need for more refined analyses to examine the socialization of children of different birth-order positions within families of different sizes. Bernstein (1973, 1977) suggests a theoretical framework which might be useful in guiding such future research. In the development of a theory relating social class, language, and socialization, he examines relations between family types and their communication structures (see also Chapter 1). Families are distinguished according to the strength of their boundary-maintaining structures and they are classified as either positional or personal. In positional families, boundary procedures are strong and as a result the differentiation of family members and the authority structures within the family are based upon unambiguous definitions of the status of family members. Boundary procedures are much weaker in person-centred families and 'the differentiation between members is based more upon differences between persons' (Bernstein, 1977, p. 483). It is proposed by Bernstein (1977, p. 484) that the social identities of members in positional-type families are a function of their age, sex, and age-related status, while members of person-oriented families make their roles rather than step into them. For a child, 'in positional families he attains a strong sense of social identity at the cost of autonomy; in person-centred families, the child attains a strong sense of autonomy but his social identity may be weak'.

From the conceptual framework and the studies reviewed in this chapter, hypotheses may be generated such as: at different levels of family environment, laterborn children in large families attain a stronger sense of social identity but have lower autonomy when compared with children in smaller families, but the differences are attenuated at high family environment levels. That is, as already stated, sibling variables need not be peripheral in family environment research.

Sibsize, birth order, social status and intelligence

Although the studies that have been presented in this chapter have attempted to overcome some of the measurement and statistical limitations of much previous sibling research, the studies are themselves restricted by small sample sizes. Also, as in many prior sibling investigations, the studies do not examine inter-relationships between different sibling variables and outcome measures. Schooler (1972, p. 172) submits, for example, that 'it is also possible that a more consistent pattern of birth order effects would be discovered if other sibling structure variables were taken into account'. In the following study (see Marjoribanks and Walberg, 1975c), relations are examined between intelligence and measures of sibsize, birth order, and the interaction of these two variables within different social-status groups, for a large sample of males. Included in the sample were approximately 400,000 19-year-old males representing nearly all male survivors of the children born in the Netherlands from 1944 to 1947, and who were still living in the Netherlands at the time they reached 19 years of age. (Also see Belmont and Marolla (1973) for a different analysis of the same data.) It is reasonable to assume that virtually all of their respective families were complete at that time. When the males reached the age of 19 they were required to complete a battery of tests as part of an examination to assess fitness for military training. In the present investigation, scores from the

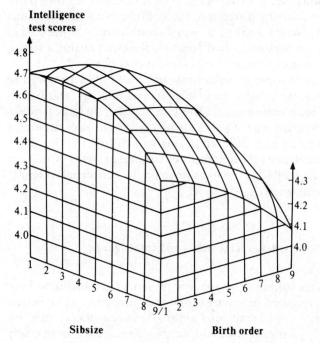

FIGURE 4.6 *Fitted-intelligence test scores in relation to sibsize and birth order in non-manual social-status group: Dutch sample*

Raven's Progressive Matrices Test (Dutch modification with 40 items) were used to assess intelligence. Raw scores from the test were grouped by the Dutch military into six classifications with the scores ranging from a low of one to a high six. Three broad social-status categories are used and labelled: non-manual, manual, and farm group. The three regression surfaces generated for the social-status groups have all been presented, as they are based on such a large and rare sample and because they stress the possible complexity of relations between family configuration indicators and performance measures. The regression models contained linear, product, and squared birth order and sibsize predictor variables.

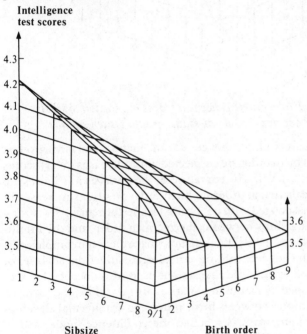

FIGURE 4.7 *Fitted-intelligence test scores in relation to sibsize and birth order in manual social-status group: Dutch sample*

In the non-manual social-status group birth order is not related to the intelligence scores at low sibsize levels. At a sibsize level of four, for example, the regression-fitted intelligence values are approximiately 4.7 for each of the birth-order positions. At high sibsize levels, increases in birth order are associated with increas-

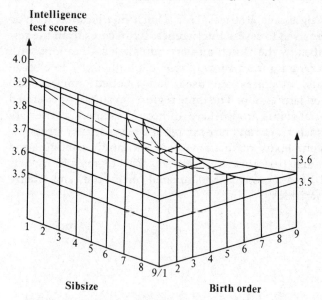

FIGURE 4.8 *Fitted-intelligence test scores in relation to sibsize and birth order in farm social-status group: Dutch sample*

ing decrements in intelligence. For the manual and farm groups, increases in birth order are connected with decreases in test scores at each sibsize level. The curvature of the surfaces in Figures 4.6 and 4.7 reveals that at different birth-order positions increases in sibsize are associated with declining test performance.

The relationships between sibsize, birth order, and the intelligence test scores in the Dutch sample make clear the complexities that may exist between sibling variables. Results from analyses of the Dutch males provided, in part, the basis of a conceptual framework developed by Zajonc and Markus (1975) and Zajonc (1976) to explain relations between birth order and intellectual development. The framework is labelled the confluence model and is examined in the following section of the chapter.

The confluence model of sibling constellation effects on children's cognitive performance

In the development of the confluence model, Zajonc and Markus (1975) and Zajonc (1976) submit that the relations between birth order and intelligence can be accounted for by the age spacing

between siblings. According to the model, 'intellectual performance decreases with birth order but only when there is a close
spacing between successive children. Under these conditions
each successive child has access to a less favorable intellectual
environment. With larger gaps between children this pattern can
be arrested and even reversed' (Zajonc and Markus, 1975, p. 85). As
Zajonc (1976, p. 230) says, 'Long birth intervals give older
children the benefits of being in a small family for a longer period
of time and during an early phase of growth, which is sensitive to
environmental effects.' For younger children it is claimed that it is
to their intellectual advantage to have their births postponed, as
the later they arrive the more mature will be the family environment into which they enter and in which they will develop.

The confluence model introduces the concept of a 'non-teacher
deficit' to explain some of the unpredicted associations that are
revealed between birth order and intelligence test scores. Sometimes it is found, for example, that only-children and lastborn
children have depressed achievement scores relative to other
children. The confluence model contends that only-children do
not usually have opportunities to serve as intellectual resources
for other children within the family and, similarly, lastborns are
not likely to be teachers to older siblings. For lastborn children it
is proposed that the 'non-teacher deficit' may be compensated for,
if lastborns enter families many years after the birth of the next-to-
last siblings. In such situations, lastborns enter environments of
intellectually more mature children which may atone for the 'non-
teacher deficit'.

In the following study (Marjoribanks, 1978b), regression
surface analysis is used to consider the confluence model by
investigating relations between birth order, age spacing between
adjacent siblings, and children's cognitive performance. Also,
relationships between birth order, age spacing, and family environment are studied to test the proposition that the learning
environments which parents fashion for children of different
birth-order positions are related to the age spacing between
adjacent siblings.

The sample for the study included 500 (240 girls and 260 boys)
11-year-old Anglo-Australian children from both lower and
middle social-status families. There were 12 children from one-
child families, 140 families with two children, 153 with three
children, 103 four-child families, 54 families with five children, 22

with six children, and 16 seven-child families. Intellectual ability was assessed using the Raven's Progressive Matrices, while standardized tests measured performance in word knowledge, word comprehension, and mathematics.

A semi-structured interview schedule was used to elicit responses from both parents of the 11-year-olds (see Chapter 6 for a more detailed discussion of the schedule). Two measures from the schedule are used in the present study: parents' expectations for their child and the language environment of the family. Both environment variables have been shown (see Chapter 2) to have moderate to strong relations to cognitive performance. Six questions were combined into a parents' expectations factor scale; they assessed the educational and occupational expectations parents had for their 11-year-old child and how long the expectations had been held. Ten questions assessed: how much reading the parents did, how often they read to the child before she/he started school, how often they read to the child now, how often they assist the child with English grammar, how particular parents are about the way the child speaks English, and how often parents check to see what the child is reading. The questions were incorporated into a language environment factor scale with a theta reliability estimate of approximately 0.85.

Also, parents were asked: 'if the child has older brothers or sisters how often does the child get together with them to help with homework or reading?' and 'if the child has younger brothers or sisters how often does the child get together with them in a teaching situation?' These two questions are used as an initial, if somewhat tentative, analysis of the relations between birth order and the concept of the 'non-teacher deficit' of children. In the interviews with the parents, data were collected on the birth-order positions of the 11-year-old children and on the birth dates of siblings. From the birth dates, the age spacing between the 11-year-old children and any adjacent siblings was calculated.

Birth order has low but significant zero-order correlations with mathematics and word knowledge scores, but is not related to intelligence and word comprehension. Increases in birth order are associated with slightly lower parental expectations and a less favourable language environment. Parents' expectations have significant relations to each of the cognitive measures, while the language environment scores have moderate concurrent validities with the two reading scores. Increases in age spacing between the 11-year-olds and older adjacent siblings are associated with small increments in the children's cognitive performance and in parents' expectations. Also, the wider the space between the 11-year-olds and older adjacent siblings the less often do the children receive assistance from older siblings, but the more often do they interact in a teaching situation with their younger brothers and sisters.

Decreases in age spacing between the 11-year-old children and younger adjacent siblings are associated with decrements in the children's mathematics and word knowledge scores. The correlations show that the smaller the spacing to the younger siblings, the more often the child interacts with the younger children in a teaching situation. But the amount of teaching by the child to younger siblings is related only to intelligence scores and to the language environment of the family. Also, the amount of assistance children receive from older siblings is inversely related to their performance on the achievement measures and parents' expectations. This latter result may indicate that those children who are in the greatest need of help, because of poor performances at school, and have parents with low expectations, seek more assistance from older siblings. Although the zero-order correlations are of a low order the results do provide some initial and tentative support for the acceptance of the confluence model.

Relations between the measures were examined further by plotting regression surfaces. Sex was not a significant variable in accounting for differences in relationships, so the surfaces were constructed only for the total sample. The nature of the relationships are summarized in Figures 4.9 and 4.10, in which the cognitive and environment scores have been converted to standard scores with a mean of 50 and a standard deviation of 10. In Figure 4.9, the surfaces show the regression-fitted birth-order relationships with word comprehension and mathematics at different levels of age spacing to the older adjacent sibling. The curvature of the surface for the comprehension scores is similar to that for the word knowledge scores. At each age-spacing level, increases in birth order are associated initially with decrements in word scores, but eventually they are related to slight increments in performance. For each birth-order position, however, increases in age spacing between the 11-years-olds and adjacent older siblings are not related to changes in word scores. That is, the results for the word measures do not provide support for the proposition that

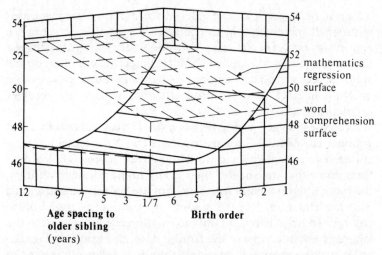

FIGURE 4.9 *Fitted-word comprehension and mathematics scores in relation to birth order and age spacing to older adjacent sibling*

birth-order relations to cognitive performance are mediated by the age spacing between adjacent siblings. Partial support for the confluence model is provided by the regression plane for mathematics in Figure 4.9. At birth-order positions, increases in age spacing to adjacent siblings are associated with increments to

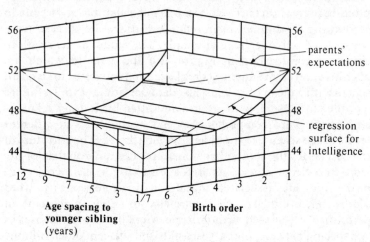

FIGURE 4.10 *Fitted-intelligence and expectation scores in relation to birth order and age spacing to younger adjacent sibling*

mathematics scores, while there is no relationship between birth order and mathematics at each age-spacing level.

In Figure 4.10 the surfaces show the regression-birth order associations with intelligence and parents' expectations at different age-spacing levels to the younger adjacent siblings. Highest fitted-intelligence scores are achieved by firstborn children who are separated by only a year from their younger sibling, and by seventh-borns who are the lastborn in the family. For earlier-born children, increments in age-spacing intervals are associated with decrements in intelligence scores, with the only-child having depressed regression-fitted scores. Birth order has negative relations to intelligence when age-spacing intervals are less than approximately seven years. After that age-spacing level has been reached the relationship between birth order and intelligence is reversed. These results support the confluence model. In the surface for parents' expectations, age spacing is not associated with expectations at different birth-order positions; but at each age-spacing level birth order has a curvilinear relation to expectations.

The original construction of the confluence model was concerned with relations between family configurations and intelligence. Results of the present analysis support the model when relations between birth order, age spacing to younger adjacent siblings, and intelligence are examined. But generally the propositions of the model are not upheld when birth order and measures of academic achievement and family environment are analysed. The present study is restricted, however, as it examines only the age spacing to nearest siblings and does not investigate spacings to more distant siblings. What are required now are more comprehensive analyses of the confluence model which examine in greater detail: the 'non-teacher deficit' of children, the birth-order positions of children from different age groups and different sibsize levels, and age spacing among all siblings in families. Also the 'sibling density' of a child which is some yet-to-be-worked-out function of a child's birth-order position and age spacing with all other siblings may be a useful sibling variable for future research. Only when more refined studies are completed will there be a clearer understanding of the confluence model.

In Chapter 3 it was concluded that an enriched understanding of the variation in children's school-related outcomes would eventuate if research integrated measures of social-status indicators, more refined social psychological family environment measures, and person-characteristics. The findings of the present chapter suggest that if the complexities of sibling variables are recognised, then they can be meaningful indicators of children's family environments and should also be integrated into family environment research that is seeking to understand variation in children's cognitive and affective characteristics.

5 Families, schools and children's outcomes

One of the most influential and controversial investigations in recent educational research has been the study of *Equality of Educational Opportunity* by Coleman *et al.* (1966). As Spady (1976, p. 188) indicates 'No other study of its kind, including the equally formidable Project Talent survey . . . has generated so much discussion, controversy, and re-examination of methodologies and data'. (See Harvard Educational Review, 1968, Winter issue for criticisms of the study; Mosteller and Moynihan, 1972; and Jencks, 1972 for re-analyses of the data.) From their study of some 570,000 children and 60,000 teachers from 4,000 American schools, Coleman and his associates (1966, p. 316) concluded that: 'Differences in school facilities and curriculum, which are the major variables by which attempts are made to improve schools, are so little related to differences in achievement levels of students that, with few exceptions, their effects fail to appear in a survey of this magnitude.' Instead it was revealed that family background was much more important than school characteristics in explaining differences in achievement among children. But as Karabel and Halsey (1977, p. 21) indicate:

> The conclusion that families rather than schools are responsible for relative failure does not necessarily follow from the data. For there may be something characteristic of *all* the schools that tends to inhibit the academic achievement of poor and black children; the fact that differences between schools fail to account for such variation would be decisive only if the schools did in fact differ significantly among themselves.

Since the Coleman study, many investigators have attempted to identify characteristics that differentiate between schools and which are related to variation in children's cognitive and affective behaviours. In the present chapter five sets of studies are reviewed that have adopted divergent methodological, measurement, and statistical approaches to the examination of relations between children's outcomes and measures of classroom and school environments. Not all of the studies, however, have included family environment measures. The research is grouped under the following five headings:

(a) Path analytic models of children's attainments
(b) Refined social-psychological measures of school and classroom environments
(c) Teachers' attitudes and children's outcomes
(d) Ethnographic studies of schools
(e) Regression surface analysis of family and school relations with children's performances

Path analytic models of children's attainments

There now exists a large set of studies that have adopted path analytic techniques to examine relations between children's social-status background and measures of their educational and occupational attainment. Many of these studies use adaptations of what has become known as the 'Wisconsin' model of educational attainment. The specification of variables in the basic model is shown in Figure 5.1. In attempting to explain how social-status origins affect educational and social-status attainments the model focuses on socialization mechanisms and on their importance in shaping children's aspirations and academic achievement.

Using the model in a longitudinal study of male Wisconsin high school students, Sewell and Hauser (1976, p. 21) found, for example, that parents' encouragement and friends' plans for college depended heavily on the son's social-status origin, while teachers' encouragement was more strongly dependent on the student's academic ability and school achievement. They propose that: 'Indeed, teachers apparently do not engage in direct socio-economic discrimination, as parents and peers seem to do, but rather depend mainly on judgments of the student's academic ability in school performance'. Furthermore, Sewell and Hauser (1976, p. 22) show, as do many of the Wisconsin-model studies, that the influence on student outcomes of parents and peers is greater than that of teachers. In their analysis they conclude that:

> Holding constant all other factors included in the model up to this point (the four socio-economic origin variables: academic ability, school performance, parental encouragement, and friends' plans), we find that strong

Earnings

Occupational attainment

Educational attainment

Father's education

Parental encouragement

Mother's education

Teachers' encouragement

College plans

Occupational aspiration

High school grades

Friends' plans

Father's occupation

Mental ability

Parental income

Students' expectations

Social-status attainments

Social background measures

Early cognitive measures

Significant others' influence

FIGURE 5.1 *Specification of variables in the general Wisconsin path model*

teachers' encouragement is worth an additional quarter of a year of higher education, whereas the net value of strong parental encouragement and of having friends who plan to go to college are six-tenths and three-quarters of a year, respectively.'

The Wisconsin model has had a strong influence on educational research, particularly American sociological research relating to education (e.g., see Sewell and Hauser, 1972; Haller and Portes, 1973; Alexander *et al.*, 1975; Wilson and Portes, 1975; Hauser *et al.*, 1976; Picou and Carter, 1976; Portes and Wilson, 1976; Alwin and Otto, 1977; De Bord *et al.*, 1977). Implications that are generated from the research must be considered as extremely tentative, however, as the studies have relied on inadequate measures of the socialization processes. Typically the parent, teacher, and peer indices are assessed only by single items which require students to respond to questions such as: 'how much encouragement have you received from your parents (or teachers) to attend college?' and 'are your best friends planning to go to college?' Also it has been claimed that the basic Wisconsin model is inadequately specified as it omits a consideration of organizational and structural arrangements of schools that may constrain educational opportunities and outcomes. Alexander and his associates (1978, p. 47) recommend, for example, that there is a need for a research model which complements the social-psychological perspective of the Wisconsin framework and examines 'structural constraints in the social organization of schooling which may condition educational outcomes entirely independent of the kinds of interpersonal and subjective processes so important to the Wisconsin model'. These concerns have led sociologists to: (a) introduce curriculum differentiation, school selection, and allocation mechanisms into their analyses, and (b) examine how teaching in high schools provides access to various educational resources and thus promotes or retards achievement (e.g., Heyns, 1974; Alexander and Eckland, 1975; Rosenbaum, 1975; Alexander and McDill, 1976; Alexander *et al.*, 1978; Marjoribanks, 1978c). Alexander and Eckland (1975, p. 414) concluded, for example, that:

> With individual ability and status characteristics constant, a 'benefit' accrues to students in educational institutions characterized by a high status-low ability student body in terms of

increased likelihood of enrollment in a college preparatory curriculum, of involvement with college-oriented peers, and of enhanced academic self concept, college plans and actual attainment. Competing with relatively low status-high ability peers, on the other hand, has the opposite effects.

In a further analysis of curriculum differentiation, Alexander and McDill (1976, p. 977) found evidence of considerable status ascription in curriculum placement in schools which was net of status differences in measured ability. They observe 'that curriculum membership has considerable consequence for a broad range of schooling outcomes and, by implication, for school retention as well'. Such studies suggest that there are important organizational constraints in schools affecting children's academic and affective outcomes. The interpretations from the research, however, are not unequivocal. In a large scale longitudinal study, Hauser, Sewell and Alwin (1976, p. 334) found that the type of curriculum completed in school is 'absolutely and relatively more dependent on socio-economic background and less dependent on mental ability than are grades in school'. But they state that 'the importance of curriculum choice as a factor in the organization of school . . . is mitigated by the fact that its effects on aspirations and on later schooling are less than those of high school grades'. And they proffer that the influence of the curriculum variable has 'been largely played out by the time a student leaves school'.

In perhaps the most comprehensive path analytic study of the effects of tracking, or curriculum membership, on children's outcomes Alexander, Cook and McDill (1978, p. 48) constructed the path model specified in Figure 5.2. The model was used to elaborate on previous analyses that had shown curriculum placement to be associated with student outcomes. Also, the study investigated whether the advantages which accrue to students in college-oriented tracks 'may well have existed prior to their curriculum placement, and hence did not derive from such placement and attendant educational experiences'. They observed that even with pre-enrolment controls 'the importance of curriculum placement for junior-year and senior-year outcomes is marked' (p. 62). Fathers' and mothers' encouragement generally were not related to the final outcome measures. But the path models that have focused on curriculum placement are circumscribed by inade-

Social background measures	Early ability measures	Intervening mechanisms, time 1	Curriculum placement, time 2	Socialization and achievement measures, time 2	Outcome measures, senior year
Father's education		Achievement		Achievement	Verbal achievement
Mother's education		Curriculum plans			Mathematics achievement
Father's occupation	Ability, time 1	Educational expectations	Curriculum enrolment		Educational expectations
Family acquisition index		Father's encouragement		Father's encouragement	Application to college
Sex		Mother's encouragement		Mother's encouragement	Acceptance by college
Race		Friends' plans		Friends' plans	Senior class rank

FIGURE 5.2 *Specification of structural model of curriculum placement influences in the adolescent educational attainment process*

quate measures of family and peer influences. Typically, the variable of primary concern, curriculum placement, is restricted also by dichotomized measures indicating either 'academic/other' or 'college oriented/other' placement. Because of these measurement limitations it is not unexpected that the parent variables have restrained associations with the outcome measures. And it is not surprising that the general conclusions from the various studies suggest that: (a) there is a tendency for higher-social status students to be streamed disproportionately into college preparatory curricula, and (b) placement in a college track accrues educational benefits which increase the probability of successful academic achievement, application to and acceptance in college.

Until path analytic studies include more refined measures of parent, teacher, and peer socialization influences and more elegant and comprehensive school-structure variables, the 'Wisconsin-Alexander' type models may not lead to any further enrichment in our understanding of the variation in children's educational attainments.

An alternative methodology to the large-scale path analytic approach is to examine relations between children's outcomes and organizational constraints within individual schools. In a study of an American high school, for example, Rosenbaum (1975) investigated the effects of the school's tracking system on intelligence test scores, between the eighth and tenth grades. From the investigation a theoretical perspective was generated, suggesting that stratification by intellectual ability has two very different socialization influences on children. First, tracks for higher-ability children represent differentiating settings in which the children are allowed to be self-directed and are encouraged to give expression to the different backgrounds and interests they bring to the school. Second, streams for lower-ability students encourage conformity rather than self-direction which leads to an homogenizing effect of stratification on the children. The propositions were developed, however, from an examination of the changes in only the verbal intelligence test scores of students who were in a stratified socialization setting. In a replication and extension of the study, Marjoribanks (1978c) compared the homogenizing and differentiating effects of school structures on higher-ability and lower-ability group children in both stratified and mixed-ability group settings. For the analysis, the sample included children from the only secondary school in an English provincial town.

The school has a federal concept of organization, consisting of four administratively independent junior secondary schools which are all linked to the same senior secondary school. Children in the town are allocated to the four junior schools on a random basis, with each school having an annual entry of approximately IIO children. Two of the schools are organized into mixed-ability teaching groups. Within these two schools children are assigned randomly to four classes on the basis of a general ability score. The other two schools are stratified into three ability streams with an upper-ability class, two parallel middle-ability tracks, and a lower-ability class. For each teaching subject a common curriculum is adopted for the four schools. In the analysis, data on the children in the mixed-ability schools were grouped into three ability levels. Student scores were assigned to those ability groups into which the children would have been placed if the schools had been stratified originally into streams.

A battery of cognitive and affective measures was administered to 440 12-year-old children during their first year of junior high school and again to the same children at the end of their second year in the schools. At the beginning of the first year and at the end of the second year, assessments were made of intelligence (a verbal reasoning and a non-verbal reasoning test) and creativity (measures of originality, fluency, and flexibility). During the first year and at the end of the second year, school-related affective characteristics were measured. From responses to attitude questionnaires, two factor scales were identified and labelled: (a) children's school-related attitudes (loaded on the sub-scales: attitude to class, attitude to school, interest in schoolwork, importance of doing well, and conforming versus non-conforming school attitudes), and (b) social adjustment to school (loading on sub-scales: children's relationships with teacher, anxiety in the classroom situation, getting on well with classmates, and academic self-image). At the end of both the first and second years of secondary school, English comprehension and mathematics understanding were assessed using standardized tests. Teacher-constructed tests, which were related to the content of the common curricula being taught in the four schools, were adopted to assess performance in French, and physical and biological sciences. Thus the study investigated changes in performances on ten cognitive and two affective measures for English children, from both stratified and mixed-ability socialization structures.

At the end of the second year there were no differences in mean scores on seven of the measures for the two higher-ability groups, but the higher-ability children in the stratified system had higher mean scores on non-verbal ability, fluency, French, and biological science. In both physical and biological sciences the higher-ability children from the mixed-ability structure had signicantly higher mean scores than the children from the stratified structures at the end of the first year but by the end of the second year the streamed children had made up the differences and, as already indicated, in biological science they were scoring significantly higher than the mixed-ability children. For the middle-ability groups there were no significant differences in mean scores on ten of the tests, at the end of the second year. Only in French and biological science were there significant mean differences and these were in favour of the streamed children. On the three creativity measures, the stratified middle-ability children had higher mean scores at the beginning of the first year of the study but there were no significant differences between the two groups by the end of the second year. For the lower-ability groups, there were no significant mean differences at the end of the second year, on nine of the measures. There were mean differences, in favour of the mixed-ability groups, for scores in French, and biological and physical sciences. In the physical and biological sciences, a significant difference in favour of the stratified group at the end of the first year was reversed in favour of the mixed-ability group by the end of the second year. Within each of the six ability groups there were significant decreases in children's school-related attitudes, during the period of the study.

The initial results suggest that, in relation to cognitive performance, there appear to be some advantages for higher-ability children to be taught in an homogeneous-ability setting while for lower-ability group children there may be advantages in being taught in an heterogeneous-ability environment. But, as Rosenbaum (1975) suggests, the examination of changes in mean scores provides only a limited analysis of the effects of ability stratification on the performance of children. Therefore the propositions that the stratification of children into ability groups provides a differentiating socialization process for higher-ability students and has an homogenizing effect on lower-ability students, were examined further by investigating changes in the variances in the cognitive and affective scores. The results of the analysis provided no consistent support for Rosenbaum's framework. Within the two stratification structures, there was a differentiation, for example, in English performance in each ability group between the two time periods, while for middle- and lower-ability children the biological science scores, for example, become increasingly homogeneous. That is, the same patterns of variation within certain subjects occur whether the children are taught in a stratified or mixed-ability structure. Also, within ability groups some teaching subjects exhibited increasing differentiation while others showed greater homogenization. Thus, instead of replicating the findings of the Rosenbaum investigation, the study suggests that school environments may have differential homogenizing and differentiating socialization influences on student outcomes that are independent of the stratification structures of the schools. Where there were significant differences, for example, in the variance for English, mathematics, French, and physical science the changes all reflected increased differentiation, while for fluency, biological science, and attitudes to school the significant changes indicated increased homogeneity. In analyses of English schoolchildren, Hudson (1966, 1968) distinguishes two types of student, the converger and the diverger. The converger excels in conventional intelligence tests and performs well in subjects such as mathematics, physical sciences, and French, while the divergers excel in open-ended creativity-type tests and perform well in arts subjects and also biological science. The findings of the present investigation suggest, somewhat provisionally, that where there are significant changes in the variation of children's school outcomes there is a tendency for a differentiation in those school subjects that distinguish the converger and an homogenization of scores in tests which characterize the diverger.

The rather extended analysis of the relations between school organizational and structural arrangements and children's outcomes has been presented to show the limitations and the equivocal nature of the findings that have been generated from much of the research. It is likely that such research will be embellished substantially when investigations of school curriculum structures are associated with analyses of the content of the curriculum. A number of sociologists (e.g., Davies, 1971; Young, 1971; Bernstein, 1971; Eggleston, 1973; Cicourel *et al.*, 1974) have urged that research in education should de-emphasize analyses of the structural characteristics of schools and concentrate on investigations of the content of what is taught. As Banks (1976, p. 174) indicates, the new research directions wish to explore 'the implications of treating knowledge as socially constructed, and the curriculum as socially organized knowledge . . . schools are seen as knowledge-processing as well as people-processing organizations'. She indicates further that 'stratification is still a major theme but it is now the stratification of *knowledge* which is of central concern. At the same time, culture, rather than structure becomes the chief organizing principle.'

A useful summary of school-effects research has been provided by Sørenson and Hallinan (1977). They indicate that:

> A considerable body of research accumulated over the last decade has failed to establish strong school effects.
> Schools seem to make little difference in educational outcomes, when a child's ability and family background are adequately controlled. Particularly research on the effect of schools' instructional resources (facilities, curriculum and staff characteristics) has produced results of this nature, while research on school environmental variables – measured by student body characteristics – has been only slightly more successful (pp. 273–4).

In the development of a differential equation model for the analysis of school effects on learning, Sørenson and Hallinan (1977, p. 282; also see Sørenson, 1977; Hauser, 1978) propose that in future school-effects research 'only those school characteristics that directly affect ability and effort should be used as independent variables'. They cite a study by McDill and associates (1969) as providing an example of research that has generated refined school environment variables which continue to be related to children's outcomes, after other characteristics have been controlled. In the following section of the chapter, the McDill *et al.* (1969) study is examined, along with other research that has adopted refined school environment measures.

Refined social-psychological measures of school and classroom environments

A number of researchers have developed schedules to assess the social-psychological environments of classrooms and schools.

Three of these measures are discussed here, namely those constructed by McDill and Rigsby (1973), Anderson and Walberg (1974), and Moos (1975).

1. In an investigation involving 20 American high schools and approximately 20,000 students from diverse communities, McDill and Rigsby (1973, p. 2) examined whether the quantity and quality of school and community resources have an influence on the academic behaviour of the students. The research was guided by three questions:

(a) To what extent do the educational and social environments or 'climates' (as perceived by students and staffs) of high schools vary?
(b) What are the consequences of such variations for the academic achievement and college plans for students?
(c) What are some of the sources of these variations in educational climates?

The school climate measure included attributes of the school environment which earlier research and theory suggested had direct effects on the development of children's academic achievement and aspirations. From analyses of responses to questionnaire items, six school environment factors were isolated and identified as:

(a) Academic emulation (indicated a concern for general academic and intellectual tone of the school environment).

(b) Student perception of intellectualism-estheticism (a high score suggests the school has a climate which places an intrinsic value on the acquisition of knowledge).

(c) Cohesive and egalitarian estheticism (the extent to which the student social system emphasizes intellectual criteria for status as opposed to the ascribed criteria of students' social background).

(d) Scientism (a high score indicates that the school has a scientific emphasis).

(e) Humanistic excellence (deals with staff and student pressures towards creating and maintaining student interest in art, humanities, social studies, and current social issues).

(f) Academically-oriented student status system (schools with high positive scores have student bodies which socially reward intellectualism and academic performance more than low-scoring schools).

McDill and Rigsby (1973, p. 87) found the school climate

measures had significant associations with a set of achievement and affective characteristics. When measures of ability, social status, and children's academic values were controlled, academic evaluation continued to be associated with students' college plans and mathematics achievement. The authors suggest, however, that:

> One could argue that this measure of family background is inadequate and that therefore the climate effects are spurious, for two reasons. The first is that the single indicator of family SES employed, father's education, is not a valid measure of family socio-economic status and that if a more comprehensive measure were used, the effects of school climate might either disappear or be drastically reduced. . . . The second argument one could make is that family SES, regardless of how adequately it is measured, is not a valid indicator of the quality of the intellectual environment of the home.

In response to these criticisms, McDill and Rigsby added two additional measures of family social status (mother's education and father's occupation) and measures of: the structural integrity of the home (that is, which parents live in the child's household), sibsize, whether or not the child's mother is employed, and the number of books in the home. When the six extra family environment measures were added to regression equations, academic emulation was still associated with mathematics performance and college plans. Although the study uses a refined social-psychological school environment measure, it is constrained by restricted family environment indicators. Even with their refined school measure, McDill and Rigsby (1973, p. 128) conclude that 'school quality (regardless of how it is measured) can have only modest effects on the achievement of students', and that within-school factors, such as ability, child-rearing practices and peer-group membership, act as the major influences in accounting for variation in achievement. Similarly from their own research, and in support of other studies, Alwin and Otto (1977, p. 269) conclude that 'differences among schools are generally less important than factors which vary within schools. . . . For most dependent variables considered here, we can account for from 70 to 95 per cent of the between-school variance using the within-school structural equation model'. And, as Mosteller and Moynihan (1972, p. 19) observe, 'the idea that school-to-school variation might be well under 50 per cent, even as small as 5 to 10 per cent, is not outrageous'.

The conclusion, that most of the variation in children's school outcomes is related to variables that vary within schools and that between-school measures are associated with only modest proportions of the variance in outcomes, should not impede the search for those variables that do differentiate between schools. Indeed, future research should include more comprehensive coverages of student outcomes and also incorporate traditional independent schools, 'alternative' schools, atypical school settings such as correspondence schools and radio-contact contexts, as well as general government-supported schools. Only when such research is completed can upper limits begin to be placed on the influence of between-school factors on children's outcomes.

2.   One of the most widely used measures of classroom environments is the Learning Environment Inventory (LEI), devised by Anderson and Walberg (1974). The initial version of the schedule was patterned by Walberg on Hemphill's (1956) Group Dimensions Description Questionnaire. Although the measure was shown to have satisfactory concurrent and construct validities (Anderson and Walberg, 1968; Walberg and Anderson, 1968), content, item, and factor analyses suggested a number of improvements, and a new schedule was designed and validated (Anderson, 1970; Walberg, 1971; Anderson, 1971). The questionnaire is administered to children and consists of 15 sub-scales, each of seven items scored on four-point Likert scales. The sub-scales are labelled: cohesiveness, diversity, formality, speed, environment, friction, goal direction, favouritism, difficulty, apathy, democratic, cliqueness, satisfaction, disorganization, and competitiveness.

The LEI scales are 'high-inference' measures as they require subjective ratings of perceived behaviour in the classroom, unlike 'low-inference' instruments which are objective counts of observed behaviour (see Flanders, 1970). Studies using the LEI have found that student perceptions of classroom social environments are related to modest and sometimes substantial amounts of the variance in cognitive, affective, and behavioural learning criterion measures (e.g., Randhawa and Fu, 1973; Tisher, 1976; Walberg, 1976; Fraser, 1977). Potential benefits of the LEI measures have been stated by Walberg, Singh and Rasher (1977, p. 48):

Perceptions of the social environment, because of their
predictive validity, convenience, and avoidance of the content
comparability problems of the achievement tests in classroom
research, can serve as useful criteria in educational research
and evaluation. In addition to experimental and correlational
studies, it may be fruitful to obtain such perceptions in one or
more classes over many occasions, perhaps daily or weekly
with randomized interventions in teacher behavior to
elucidate the causal connections with time series analysis.

3. Another widely-used scale for assessing psycho-social environments of classrooms has been devised by Moos (1976,
p. 330). He proposes that 'Vastly different social environments can
be described by common or similar sets of dimensions belonging
to three broad categories: Relationship dimensions, Personal
Development dimensions, and System Maintenance and System
Change dimensions'. Moos suggests that the dimensions 'are
similar across many environments, although vastly different settings may impose unique variations within the general categories'. The dimensions have formed the conceptual framework
for analysing psycho-social environments in settings such as:
families, therapeutic groups, work milieus, university student
living groups, hospital and community programmes, correctional
institutions, and classrooms (see Moos, 1974, 1975). In classroom
research the dimensions are defined by the following scales: (a)
Relationship dimensions by involvement, affiliation, and teacher
support; (b) Personal dimensions by task orientation and competi-
tion; and (c) the System category by order and organization, rule
clarity, teacher control, and innovation. The Classroom Environment Scale consists of 90 true-false items, 10 for each dimension.
Studies have shown that the dimensions discriminate among
classrooms and have moderate relations to a set of children's
outcomes (see Trickett and Moos, 1973; Moos and Trickett, 1974;
Trickett and Quinlan, 1977; Nielsen and Moos, 1978).
4. Although the Walberg and Moos classroom environment
schedules have been shown to have moderate associations with
children's cognitive and affective characteristics, the research has
not included measures of the social-psychological environments
of families. Using data collected on 250 12-year-old children and
their parents from towns in rural parts of Australia, Marjoribanks
(1978a) used canonical analysis to examine relations between

family and school environments and measures of children's school-related affective characteristics. Family environment was defined by six variables which were labelled: parents' expectations for the child, expectations for themselves, concern for the use of English in the home, reinforcement of educational expectations, knowledge of child's educational progress, and the family involvement in educational activities (see: Chapter 2 for a further discussion of the sample and measures, and the Appendix for a copy of the schedule). An equally weighted composite of father occupation, father education, and mother education was used as an indicator of the social status of the families.

A new school environment measure was developed by selecting items from the Walberg and Moos schedules. The selected items had been shown to have moderate concurrent validities in relation to affective characteristics. The new scale is of a Likert-type format consisting of 50 items which attempt to assess children's perceptions of classroom and school learning environments. Scores on the items were analysed using principal component analysis. After eliminating items with small factor loadings (< 0.40) the remaining items were refactored, producing two factor scales with theta reliability estimates of approximately 0.80. The scales were labelled the intellectual orientation of the school, and the punitive nature of the school environment.

The intellectual orientation scale consists of 14 items of the form: 'New ideas are met with immediate enthusiasm in this school', 'Teachers here put a lot of energy and enthusiasm into their teaching', 'Teachers encourage students to think about exciting and unusual careers', and 'In this school teachers go out of their way to help you'. Included in the punitive environment scale are 16 items such as: 'Students in this school are sometimes punished without knowing the reason for it', 'In this school teachers very often make you feel like a child', 'Students are often made to take the blame for things whether they did them or not', 'Those in charge of this school are not very patient with students', and 'Sometimes teachers embarrass students in my classes for not knowing the right answers to questions'. An 'intellectual orientation of the school' and a 'punitive nature of the school environment' score for each child, were obtained from the items that made up the two scales.

The school-related affective characteristics have been discussed previously (p. 50). From two 50-item schedules, seven factor scales were isolated. In the following list the labels used for the seven affective characteristics are presented with some sample items provided to indicate the nature of the scales: (a) enthusiasm for school ('If I missed a mathematics or English lesson I'd be very disappointed', 'We have very interesting lessons in this school', 'Doing well at school is important to me'); (b) academic self-concept ('Most of my teachers think that I am clever', 'When we have tests I usually get good marks', 'I'm very good at my school-work'); (c) friendliness of school ('I have many friends in this school', 'I rarely feel alone in this school', 'I have very few friends whom I like in this school'); (d) dislike for disruptive behaviour ('When the teacher goes out of the room I dislike other children who fool about', 'I dislike other children who get me into mischief', 'It is good to fool about in this class'); (e) educational and occupational expectations ('What is the highest level of education you expect to achieve', 'What type of occupation do you expect to have after leaving school'); (f) alienation-commitment to school ('I shall just get an ordinary job whether I work hard at school or not', 'Success in school hardly matters as it has little to do with success in life', 'People stay at school beyond the age of 16 only to pass examinations'); and (g) child's academic orientation ('My parents encourage me to get good results at school', 'My friends and I think that we will have a good future and we are working towards it', 'I always have confidence in myself when sitting for examinations'). Factor scores on the seven affective scales were computed for each child. In the final sample there were 120 girls and 130 boys.

When the family and classroom measures are combined in regression equations they have moderate relations to the affective scores. Enthusiasm for school and dislike for disruptive behaviour, for example, have multiple correlations with the predictors of 0.54 and 0.43, respectively, for girls and 0.60 and 0.40, for boys. The covariate structure of the relations between the environment and affective measures were examined further using canonical correlation analysis. In the analysis, the six family environment scales, two school environment measures, and family social status formed a set of predictor variables, and the seven affective indicators acted as criterion variables, although no causal inferences are made between the measures. Two significant canonical correlations of 0.691 and 0.509 were obtained for boys and one significant correlation of 0.651, for girls (p's < 0.001).

The relations between the environment measures, boys' affective characteristics, and the two canonical variates are shown in Figure 5.3. In the figure the values are canonical loadings which are the correlations between the original measures and canonical variates of the same battery: predictor measures with predictor

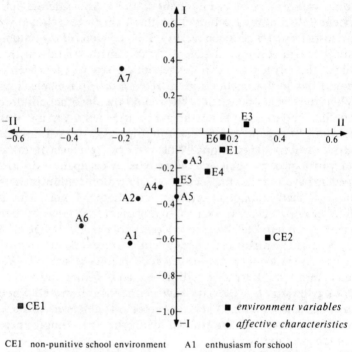

CE1   non-punitive school environment
CE2   intellectually oriented school
E1   parents' expectations for child
E3   parents' concern for language
E4   reinforcement of expectations
E5   knowledge of child's progress
E6   family involvement

A1   enthusiasm for school
A2   academic self-concept
A3   friendliness of school
A4   dislike for disruptive behaviour
A5   expectations
A6   commitment to school
A7   non-academic school orientation

FIGURE 5.3 *Canonical loadings of environment variables and school-related affective characteristics: boys*

canonical variates and criterion measures with criterion canonical variates. Canonical loadings not significant with one of the canonical variates have not been plotted. The loadings show that in relation to the first canonical variate, boys who: perceive the school environment to be non-punitive (CE1) and intellectually oriented (CE2), and to a lesser extent have families in which the parents have knowledge of their son's educational progress (E5), and reinforce their expectations for their sons (E4); have a profile of affective characteristics defined by enthusiasm for school (A1), high commitment to school (A6), and to a lesser extent, positive academic self-concept (A2), high educational and occupational expectations (A5), dislike for disruptive behaviour in school (A4), and a positive academic orientation to school (A7). After removing the variance of the first canonical variate from predictors and criteria, the loadings on the second variate show that boys who perceive the school environment to be punitive (CE1) express alienation from school (A6) even when they perceive the school to be intellectually oriented and have parents who have a concern for language development.

As already indicated, only one canonical variate was significant for the girls' sample. The loadings on the variate suggest that girls who perceive the school environment as being non-punitive, and to a lesser extent have parents with high expectations and who reinforce those expectations, express a positive academic self-concept, a dislike for disruptive behaviour in school, and a high commitment to school.

From these analyses two general propositions are offered: (a) boys who perceive the school environment to be intellectually oriented and non-punitive, and who have the support of an academically-oriented family, express positive school-related characteristics; but (b) children who perceive the school environment to be punitive express negative school-related affective characteristics, even if the family provides academic support and the children perceive the school to be intellectually oriented.

The findings from the study indicate that family and school environment measures can be used conjointly to augment our understanding of children's characteristics. Data from the above study are used in a later section of this chapter, when regression surfaces are constructed in a further analysis of the relations between refined environment measures and children's behaviours.

Teachers' attitudes and children's outcomes

In Chapter 3 (Model 6) it was suggested that in educational research there is a growing awareness of the importance of the relations between children's environments, teachers' attitudes, and children's school performances. Most of the research has been restricted to examinations of the relations between either global environment measures and teachers' attitudes or attitudes and children's performances. The following study is perhaps the only one that has investigated the relations between teachers' attitudes and children's outcomes at different levels of a refined family environment measure.

The Plowden data were used in Chapter 3 (p. 74) to examine relations between teachers' attitudes and children's academic achievement at different levels of family social status. The same data set is adopted in the present analysis of the associations between teacher attitudes, family environment, and academic achievement. A comprehensive family measure was compiled using the following distal and proximal environment measures: father occupation, family income, father education, parents' aspirations for children, parental interest and support for schooling, initiative and responsibility taken by parents towards education, literacy of the home, and parents' interest in helping with schoolwork. As indicated on p. 75, teachers' attitudes to children were obtained by asking teachers to respond to questions such as whether they thought the student: was a hard worker, obedient in class, concentrated on schoolwork, restless in class, and aggressive in school. Williams (1976b) distinguishes between the normative and cognitive attitudes of teachers. Those assessed in the present analysis are normative, reflecting attitudes related to the children's adherence to the norms of classroom behaviour.

In regression models, family environment has significant associations with the achievement scores at different teacher attitudes in each of the three age-cohorts. Except for senior boys' English, and middle girls' English and mathematics achievement, the attitude scores are related to achievement at different family environment levels. Generally the associations between the achievement scores and the predictors are linear; but there are situations in which the relations, after adjusting for design effects, are curvilinear. Some of the differences in the relations are presented in Figure 5.4, which shows the regression-fitted relations between teachers' attitudes and the English achievement of senior girls and boys at different levels of family environment. The curvature of the surface for the boys indicates the possible complexity of relations that may exist between teachers' attitudes of

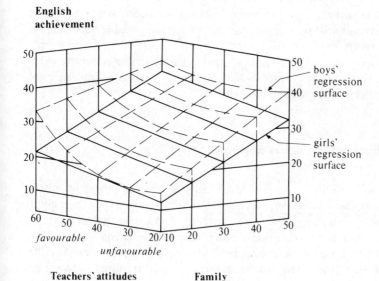

FIGURE 5.4 *Fitted-English achievement scores in relation to teachers' attitudes and family environment: senior Plowden cohorts*

children and achievement scores. At each level of the family environment, as teacher attitudes become more favourable there are increases in the English performance of both girls and boys. At low family environment scores, changes in teachers' attitudes of boys' behaviour, from unfavourable to favourable, are associated with sizeable increments in English performance. Because of the correlational design of the analysis, it is not possible to determine whether the attitudes influence the changes in English performance or whether changes in English scores generate the modifications in attitudes. At high family environment levels, teachers' attitudes are not related to the English scores of boys but continue to be associated with girls' performances. The girls' regression surface reflects most of the surfaces constructed from the data suggesting the propositions that: (a) at each family environment level, changes in teachers' attitudes are associated with modest changes in academic achievement, and (b) at each level of teachers' attitudes, increases in family environment scores are related to sizeable increments in academic performance (see Marjoribanks, 1978d).

A relatively crude index of teachers' attitudes was used in the study but still it is quite a strong mediating variable between the comprehensive family environment measure and children's achievement. The results suggest that school environment research should continue its search for more embracing measures of teachers' attitudes and behaviours.

Ethnographic studies of schools

In educational research, especially in Britain, there is much dissatisfaction among some researchers with the path-analytic type approach to studies of classrooms and schools. As a result, ethnographic techniques increasingly are being adopted to analyse school environments. Wilson (1977) proposes that the rationale underlying the ethnographic methodology is based on two hypotheses about human behaviour. First, the naturalistic-ecological hypothesis, and second, the qualitative-phenomenological hypothesis. In relation to the first hypothesis Wilson (1977, p. 248) indicates that '. . . the ecological psychologist would warn that if one wants ultimately to generalize research findings to schools, then the research is best conducted within school settings where all these forces are intact'. He suggests that 'the inability of classical learning theories to say very much that is meaningful about everyday classroom learning can be explained in part by the absence of these school/organizational forces in the research laboratories where the theories were developed'. In a similar criticism Bronfenbrenner (1977, p. 513) claims that 'much of contemporary developmental psychology is *the* science of the strange behavior of children in strange situations with strange adults for the briefest possible periods of time'.

The qualitative-phenomenological hypothesis states that 'the social scientist cannot understand human behavior without understanding the framework within which the subjects interpret their thoughts, feelings, and actions' (p. 249). That is, an underlying assumption of ethnographic research on classrooms and schools is that children, teachers, parents, and administrators have meaning structures which influence much of their behaviour. Therefore research must attempt to understand these meaning structures, how they develop, and how they affect behaviour.

Znaniecki (1969, p. 21) indicates that data for such research may be obtained from several sources: '(1) the personal experience of the sociologist, both original and vicarious; (2) observation by the sociologist, both direct and indirect; (3) the personal experience of other people; (4) observation by other people, . . . (5) generalizations made by other people with or without scientific purposes in mind'. (See Thomas and Znaniecki's (1927) masterly adoption of these techniques, especially the personal experience of other people, in their analysis of *The Polish Peasant in Europe and America*.)

In school environment research there now exists a number of fine ethnographic studies that have contributed to an enriched understanding of children's and teachers' behaviours (e.g., Cicourel and Kitsuse, 1963; Hargreaves, 1967; Jackson, 1968; Lacey, 1970; Keddie, 1971; Hargreaves *et al.*, 1975; Delamont, 1976). But there are also many classroom studies, using an interpretative approach, that have provided no more than an unstructured journalistic account of classroom activities. Perhaps research adopting the ethnographic approach would benefit from the directive put forward by Karabel and Halsey (1977, p. 61), that what is needed now 'is a concerted effort by adherents of the interpretative school to carry out the program of empirical research it implies and to link its findings with the structural studies that have traditionally dominated the sociology of education . . .'. Such research would profit from interpretative and structural studies of not only classroom and school environments but also of children's family, peer group, and neighbourhood environments.

Regression surface analysis of family and school relations with children's performances

The final study in this chapter is an examination of the relations between children's perceptions of school environments and measures of intelligence, personality, and school-related affective characteristics at different levels of a refined family environment measure (see Marjoribanks, 1979a). Data for the study have been described in detail in Chapter 2 (p. 49) and earlier in this chapter (p. 117). From the six family environment variables described previously, two second-stratum factors were identified from factor analysis and these were labelled: parents' press for achievement (loaded on parents' expectations for the child, expectations for themselves, concern for the use of language within the home, reinforcement of expectations) and parent-child involvement (loaded on knowledge of child's educational progress, and the family involvement in educational activities). Classroom environment is assessed by the two scales: the intellectual orientation of the school, and the punitive nature of the school. For the measures of children's characteristics, personality is defined by the four second-stratum factors of contemplative-impatience, self-reliant-subduedness, adjustment-anxiety, and extraversion-introversion (see p. 50); intelligence by the Otis Intermediate Test – Form AB; and the attitude variables by child's commitment to school and school self-confidence. The sample included 120 girls and 130 boys.

Zero-order correlations showed that there were sex-differences in the relationships. For boys, the family environment has negligible relations to personality and school self-confidence but moderate associations with intelligence and commitment to school. Boys who perceive the school environment as non-punitive have personalities which tend to be more contemplative, subdued, and introvert rather than impatient, self-reliant, and extrovert; and boys who tend to be introvert perceive the school to be more intellectually oriented than those who are extraverts. Also, boys who perceive the school environment as being non-punitive have higher scores on the two school-related affective characteristics than boys who consider the school to have a punitive environment. Generally, the measure of girls' family environment has negligible associations with the criterion variables. But girls who perceive the school environment as being non-punitive are likely to be more contemplative, subdued, adjusted, and have a higher commitment to school and more positive school self-confidence than girls who deem the school environment to be punitive. And girls who perceive the school as being intellectually oriented tend to be more contemplative, subdued, adjusted, intro-vert, and have a higher commitment to school than girls who regard the school to be non-intellectually oriented.

Relationships between measures were investigated further by plotting regression surfaces from models including linear, product, and squared predictor terms. Four surfaces have been plotted in two figures to provide an indication of some of the different relations that are present among the variables and to show some of the gender-differences in the relationships. For the construction of the surfaces the scores on each variable were converted to standard scores with a mean of 50 and a standard deviation of 10.

In Figure 5.5, the surfaces show the regression-fitted relations between children's perception of the intellectual orientation of the school and their commitment to school, at different levels of parents' press for achievement. The shape of the boys' surface

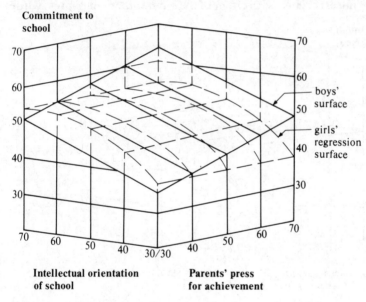

FIGURE 5.5 *Fitted-commitment to school scores in relation to parents' press for achievement and perceptions of the school's intellectual orientation*

reflects regression models in which family and school environment measures both have significant linear relations to the criterion measures. At each press for achievement level, increments in boys' perceptions of the intellectual orientation of the school are associated with increases in boys' commitment to school. Also, at each school environment level, increases in boys' commitment to school are related to increases in parents' press for achievement. The girls' surface in Figure 5.5 represents regression models in which the criterion variables have linear and curvilinear relations to the school environment at different family environment levels, but where the criterion measures are not associated with the family environment factors at different levels of school environment.

In Figure 5.6, the surfaces show the fitted-relations between children's perceptions of the punitive nature of the school environment and intelligence test scores, at different levels of parent-child involvement in the family. The girls' surface is indicative of regression models in which the criterion variables are not associated with either of the environment measures, while

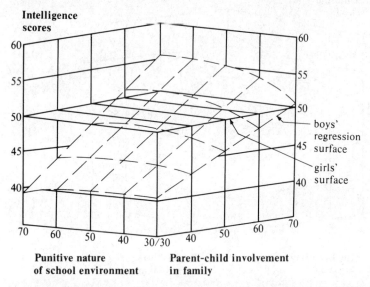

FIGURE 5.6 *Fitted-intelligence scores in relation to parent-child involvement and perceptions of the school's punitive environment*

the boys' surface reflects significant linear, interaction, and curvilinear relationships.

By using complex multiple regression models to generate regression surfaces and by including refined measures of both family and school environments, the present study goes beyond much previous research which has examined the environmental correlates of children's individual characteristics. In Chapter 3 it was concluded that for a more complete understanding of the relations between family environments and children's school-related outcomes it is essential to integrate measures of global social-status characteristics and refined social-psychological environment measures. The studies reviewed in the present chapter suggest that our comprehension of the association between school environments and children's outcomes will be enhanced if studies adopt a methodology incorporating: organizational and structural school measures, social-psychological environment indicators, analyses of curriculum content and the stratification of knowledge, as well as ethnographic investigations of teachers' and children's behaviours. The influences that schools have on children will only be revealed in a meaningful manner when the above-suggested methodology is adopted in conjunction with a similar approach applied to families.

6 Family environments, person variables and children's achievement: an interactionist analysis

Interactionist models of analysis in social psychology propose that the behaviour of individuals is the result of a continuous interaction between persons and the situations they encounter. Typically the model is described by a simple equation of the form: $B = f(P,S)$. Previous chapters have been concerned with showing that variations in children's outcomes are understood more completely when different forms of family environment measures are used in analyses. For ease of presentation, many of the studies reviewed in the earlier chapters have been examined in relation to a situationist model, in which behaviour is explained primarily as a function of the situation ($B = f(S)$). It is the underlying assumption of the book, however, that behaviour is more appropriately explained by an interactionist model. In the present chapter relations are examined between social-psychological family environment measures, person variables, and children's cognitive achievement.

Ideally, interactionist analyses would involve a dynamic, rather than a mechanistic or reactive model of the individual. Investigations adopting a mechanistic model examine only uni-directional 'causality', assuming that behaviour is affected by the person and situation variables. Alternatively, dynamic interaction involves bi-directional analysis which assumes a mutual interdependence of persons-situations and behaviours. In such analyses, situations are considered to be as much a function of the person as the person's behaviour is a function of the situation. But, as Endler and Magnusson (1976, p. 13) indicate, 'we are not yet at a stage in psychology where we have isolated the basic parameters that affect behavior, nor do we know how they interact with each other'. They go on to suggest that 'the methodology and technology to examine the nature of dynamic interaction have not yet been fully developed'. The research examined in the present chapter is restricted to a mechanistic framework of interactionism. But it is hoped that the studies that are reviewed provide support for Endler's (1976, p. 66) contention that 'Concurrent with an investigation of dynamic interaction we must also examine how persons and situations interact (mechanistic interaction) in influencing behaviour'. (See Chapter 1.)

The relations between five person variables and children's cognitive achievement, at different levels of family environment, are examined. The person variables include: intelligence, self-expectations, school-related attitudes, personality, and prior academic achievement. In the analysis involving prior academic performance, relations are investigated between two measures of reading achievement, assessed four years apart, and the intervening family environment. This latter study comes closest to satisfying the requirements of a dynamic model of the individual, as it assumes that early reading performance influences the family environment and that these person and situation variables interact to influence later performance.

Much of the previous research which has analysed the mechanistic interactionist model of behaviour has adopted analysis of variance models that examine the proportion of variance in the behaviour measures associated with person variables, situations, and the interaction of person and situation variables (e.g., see Endler and Hunt, 1969; Moos, 1969, 1970; Argyle and Little, 1972; Endler, 1973). Such statistical models are restricted as they require a grouping of variables into levels which leads to a loss of information, neglect of possible curvilinear relations, and assume that the statistical interaction term is the only appropriate test of the interaction taking place within the research (e.g., see Bowers, 1973; Mischel, 1973). In the present chapter, regression surfaces are constructed as they allow relations between person variables and behaviours to be examined at different levels of the situation measures, and similarly, they permit the associations between situations and behaviours, at different levels of the person variables, to be investigated. Although cognitive achievement is the criterion or dependent variable in each study, it is assumed that persons and situations are likely to be affected by children's performances as well as performances being influenced by the person and situation variables.

Thus regression surface analysis is used in an examination of the relations implied by the titles of the following five studies:

(a) Family environment, intelligence, and academic achievement (an English sample)

(b) Family environment, self-expectations, and intelligence (an English sample)
(c) Family environment, children's school-related attitudes, and academic achievement (an Australian sample)
(d) Family environment, personality, and intelligence (an Australian sample)
(e) Early reading achievement, family environment and later reading achievement; within different social-status groups (an English sample)

Generally the data used in these five studies have been discussed previously and therefore they are not elaborated upon in this present chapter. In each study the regression surfaces are generated from models of the form that have been used throughout the book:

$$Z = aX + bY + cXY + dX^2 + eY^2 + \text{constant},$$

where Z, X and Y represent measures of achievement, person, and situation variables, respectively.

Family environment, intelligence, and academic achievement

Data from the three age-cohorts in the Plowden follow-up study are used to examine the associations between family environment, intelligence, and measures of mathematics and English performance. Although there have been many investigations examining the relative influence of social status and intelligence on children's achievement (see Chapter 3, Model 4), research has not analysed the effects of intelligence on achievement at different levels of refined family environment measures. The family environment score for each child was formed from a combination of: parents' aspirations for the child, parents' interest and support for schooling, initiative and responsibility taken by parent for child's education, literacy of the home, parents' interest in helping with schoolwork, and parents' knowledge of the school environment (see Marjoribanks, 1979b).

Typically, the findings reveal that family environment and intelligence both are related to the achievement measures, and the surfaces in Figure 6.1 reflect the nature of the associations. The surfaces show the regression-fitted relations between family environments and the English performance of senior girls and boys at different levels of intellectual ability. In the Figure, the scores have been converted to standard scores with a mean of 50 and a standard deviation of 10. For girls, the curvature of the surface shows the complexity of relations that may exist between the

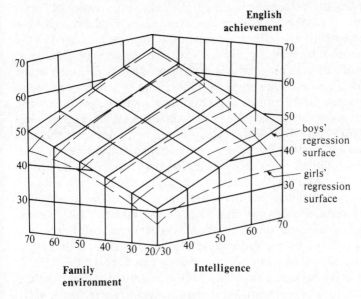

FIGURE 6.1 *Fitted-English scores in relation to intelligence and family environment: senior cohort girls and boys*

measures. At low intelligence levels, increases in girls' environment scores are associated with a negatively increasing change in performance while at high ability levels, improvements in the environment at lower environment levels are associated with size-able increments in English achievement. The boys' regression surface is representative of most of the relations in the study, where there are only significant linear relations between the measures. At each ability level, increases in family environment are associated with similar increments in boys' English scores. The results show, however, that for both girls and boys increments in family environment scores of one standard deviation are associated with only very modest increments in children's achievement, at each level of intelligence. As the family environment score increases from 30 to 40, for example, the increment in boys' English is approximately 4 points at each ability level. In both regression surfaces the curvatures reveal that intelligence is related to performance at each environment score. Generally the results suggest a conclusion which will be examined later in the chapter: that if it can be assumed that the intelligence test scores represent, in part, the result of past environmental influences and prior academic performance, then the 'manipulation' of social-psychological family environment variables of the type measured in the present study may, by themselves, not realize very significant changes in children's school outcomes. That is, if family intervention programmes or parent-school interaction projects are to be successful in influencing children's academic performances, then environment variables other than the social-psychological measures investigated here also need to be explored. It was proposed in Chapter 3 that educational policy should examine a broad range of situation variables including the production of curriculum, the fostering of parental participation in schools, the allocation of educational resources, the training of teachers, as well as more refined social-psychological family variables, for a more meaningful understanding of the variation in children's outcomes. Also, it was recommended in the last chapter that structural analyses of school environments would be embellished if studies included an examination of the content of curriculum or of the stratification of knowledge. And it is possible that the investigations of family environments may be enhanced if the 'content' of family pedagogy is examined. Bourdieu (1973), for example, proposes that there are strong relationships between social status and the cultural capital that families pass on to their children.

In this first investigation of the mechanistic interactionism model, the findings show that situation variables are related to achievement scores at different levels of person measures and, similarly, that changes in person variables are associated with changes in performance scores at different levels of the situation measures.

Family environment, self-expectations and intelligence

Although there have been many investigations of the relations between the affective characteristics of children and their cognitive performance, the findings from the research remain inconsistent and inconclusive (e.g., Malpass, 1953; Brodie, 1964; Finger and Schlesser, 1968; Jackson, 1968; Kahn, 1969; Aiken, 1970; Williams, 1970; Evans and Anderson, 1973; Ainsworth and Batten, 1974; Anderson and Evans, 1974; Husén *et al.*, 1974). Studies show either positive, negative, or sometimes no relations between affective and cognitive variables. The equivocal nature of the findings is related, in part, to the failure of most of the research to examine relations between affective measures and cognitive achievement at different environment levels. That is, most of the investigations have adopted a trait model of analysis in which behaviour is considered to be related primarily to person characteristics $(B = f(P))$, rather than examining an interactionist model. The criticism by Lavin (1965, p. 100) is still appropriate, that the 'disappointing state of affairs' in the research may be due to the circumstance that virtually all studies 'conceive of the individual as if he was operating in a vacuum'. Similarly, Getzels (1969, p. 100) claimed that research relating affective characteristics and achievement 'might be more powerful if the social setting in which educational performance takes place were conceptualized and used as a significant variable with which personality interacts'. That is, Lavin and Getzels are suggesting the adoption of an interactionist framework of analysis. In the following study some of the limitations of prior research are eliminated by investigating relations between self-expectations and children's cognitive performance, within the context of different levels of family environment (see Marjoribanks, 1977d). The importance of self-expectations for explaining variations in children's attainments is described by Braun (1976) in a model he develops to explain how teachers' expectations influence children's outcomes.

Again the data from the Plowden follow-up study are used in the analysis. Self-expectations are assessed by a questionnaire developed by the National Foundation for Educational Research in England, in which children respond to questions such as: 'staying on at school is a waste of time', 'to do well at school is most important', 'other people always seem to be able to do things better than I can', 'all in all I think that I am a failure', and 'no matter how grown up you are adults always treat you like kids'. In each age-cohort, after adjusting raw regression weights for the design effects of the samples, curvilinear and interaction relations between the predictor and outcomes variables were not significant. Family environment and self-expectations had significant linear associations with intelligence, English, and mathematics performance. The findings from the different analyses are reflected in Figure 6.2, which shows the relations between children's self-expectations and intelligence, at different levels of the family environment for both junior girls and junior boys. At each family environment level, increases in the self-expectation

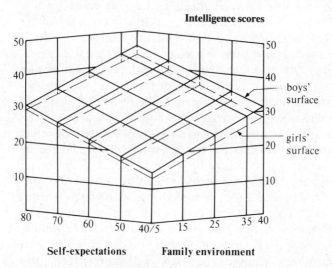

Intelligence scores

boys' surface

girls' surface

Self-expectations   Family environment

FIGURE 6.2 *Fitted-intelligence scores in relation to family environment and self-expectations: junior girls and junior boys*

scores are associated with modest increments in intelligence scores. As the boys' self-expectations increase from say, 50 to 60, the regression-estimated intelligence scores are adjusted by about four points at each situation level. And, at each level of self-expectations, as the environment scores become more favourable there are increments in intelligence. Although the interaction terms in the regression analysis were not statistically significant, the results in Figure 6.2 reveal that both the situation and person variables are associated with the achievement measures, when considered within the context of the other variable. A concentration by interactionist model analysts on detecting significant statistical interaction relations, within analysis of variance designs, may retard the development of the interaction model of behaviour (see also Mischel, 1973).

The analysis of self-expectations suggests the following simple propositions, that: (a) at each level of family environment, increases in self-expectations are related to increments in children's cognitive performance; and (b) at each level of self-expectations, increases in family environment scores are associated with increments in performance scores.

Family environment, children's school-related attitudes, and academic achievement

It was stated in Chapter 1 that Thomas and Znaniecki (1958) constructed a special form of the interactionist model to link social organization and social personality. They proposed that in the field of social reality an effect, whether individual or social, always has a composite cause. The cause contains the subjective social-psychological elements of social reality, namely attitudes, and the objective social elements that impose themselves upon individuals and provoke their reactions and social values. Thomas and Znaniecki claim that there can be no change of social reality which is not the common effect of pre-existing social values and individual attitudes acting upon them, nor any change of individual consciousness which is not the common effect of pre-existing attitudes and social values acting upon them. Thus they propose a bi-directional model of interaction. As Thomas (1966, p. 277) goes on to suggest, 'the cause of a value or an attitude is never an attitude or value alone, but always a combination of an attitude and a value'.

The 'Thomas version' of the interactionist model is adopted in the present study to examine relations between family learning environments, children's attitudes to school, and their academic achievement in school. Children's learning environments are considered to reflect a set of social values which may arouse intellectual reactions. Also, academic achievement scores are defined as social values because of the meanings and reactions that such scores generate for the children themselves, parents, teachers, and peers (see Znaniecki, 1969, p. 69). The research is guided by the question 'to what extent are children's school-related attitudes related to academic achievement at different levels of family learning environments?'

The sample for the analysis includes parents and their 11-year-old children from Anglo-Australian middle and lower social-status families. In the following chapter, the analysis is extended to include families from a set of Australian ethnic groups. For the present investigation there are 140 middle and 250 lower social-status families. Social-status classification is based on an equally weighted composite of father occupation and the education of the mother and the father. Each of the families has an 11-year-old child attending an urban elementary school. Tests devised by the Australian Council for Educational Research were used to assess performance in mathematics, word knowledge, and word comprehension. A semi-structured interview schedule was constructed to assess the family learning environment which was defined by three variables: parents' press for English, aspirations for the 11-year-old child, and satisfaction with schooling. The schedule was used in home interviews with parents and it is an adaptation of the questionnaire discussed in Chapter 2 (see Marjoribanks, 1972a). After using factor scaling techniques (Armor, 1974) to analyse the responses to the questions, the press for English scale consisted of eight items of the form: 'Before the child started school how often did you read to her/him' (a response was obtained from both parents), 'How often would you help the child with her/his English grammar (e.g., tell the child how to construct sentences, when to use certain words)', 'At school, what topic is the child studying in English classes', and 'How particular would you say you are about the way the child speaks English (correct grammar, good vocabulary, . . .)'. The parents' aspirations scale consists of five items such as: 'How much education would you really like the child to receive if at all possible', 'How much education do you really expect the child to receive', 'What kind of job would you really like the child to have when she/he grows up', and 'How long have you had these ideas about the kind of job you would like the child to have'. Two aspects of parental satisfaction with schooling were measured: (a) satisfaction with teaching, consisting of seven items, in which parents were asked to rate the quality of teaching in seven subjects taught to their child; and (b) a 10-point scale labelled 'satisfaction with the school', in which parents were asked to react to statements such as, in the school that my child attends: 'there is not enough homework', 'not enough time is spent on teaching subjects such as reading and arithmetic', 'there is not enough discipline', and 'teachers are very friendly and approachable'. The reliability estimates of the four scales were greater than 0.75.

School-related attitudes of the children were measured using a Likert-type questionnaire that assessed seven attitude sub-scales (also see Chapter 5): (a) enthusiasm for school, (b) enthusiasm for class membership, (c) dislike for disruptive behaviour, (d) relationships with teacher, (e) academic self-image, (f) social adjustment in school, and (g) achievement orientation. (A more complete description of the scales is provided in Chapter 7.) When the scores on the sub-scales were factor analysed, using principal component analysis, two factors were identified. The first factor had a reliability estimate of 0.80, consisted of 29 items, and assessed an affective component of school-related attitudes. It was labelled 'affective commitment to school' and loaded on the scales: enthusiasm for school, enthusiasm for class, dislike for disruptive behaviour, and positive relationships with teacher. A cognitive-behavioural component of school attitudes was measured by the second factor, which consisted of 19 items and had a theta reliability estimate of 0.76. The factor was labelled 'academic adjustment to school' and loaded on the scales: academic self-image, achievement orientation, and social adjustment to school.

Thus the study investigates relations between mathematics, word knowledge, and word comprehension scores and measures of affective commitment to school and academic adjustment to school, at different family environment levels for 11-year-old children, from lower and middle social-status Anglo-Australian families. Because of the relatively small sample size, although larger than in most studies that collect family environment data, the regression surface analysis was not conducted separately for girls and boys. After adjusting for the design effects of the sample, neither the product nor curvilinear terms were significant. Generally, the equations involving affective commitment to school did not account for a significant amount of the variance in the criterion scores. Similarly, the models including the satisfaction variables were not related to achievement. The surfaces constructed in Figure 6.3 reflect the significant associations in the study. The surfaces show the regression-fitted relations between academic adjustment to school and word knowledge scores at different levels of parents' aspirations. In both surfaces, at each level of parents' aspirations, increments in the attitude scores are

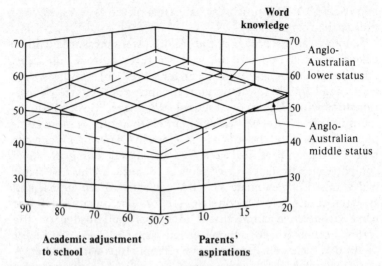

FIGURE 6.3 *Fitted-word knowledge scores in relation to parents'
aspirations and academic adjustment to school*

associated with increases in word knowledge. For middle social-
status children the increases are slightly higher at each level of
parents' aspirations. For example, as the attitude scores increase
from a score of 50 to 90, the regression-fitted word scores for the
middle social-status children increase by approximately 10 points,
and for the lower status children the increase is about six
points, at each level of parents' aspirations. Also at each level of
academic adjustment to school, increases in the aspiration scores
are associated with increments in word knowledge performance.
As the aspiration scores increase from a low of 5 to a high of 20,
the regression-fitted word scores increase by about 10 and 12
points, respectively, for the middle and lower social-status groups
(see also Marjoribanks, 1978e).

Although the changes in performance, related to variations in
attitudes and environment, are only modest the findings provide
tentative support for the Thomas and Znaniecki conceptual framework: that there can be no change of social reality which is not the
common effect of pre-existing social values and individual attitudes acting upon them. For a more complete analysis of the
framework, Thomas and Znaniecki (1958) propose that the dependence is most suitably examined by a comparative analysis of
social groups which are in different positions of transition from

older to newer organizational forms. As mentioned earlier, the conceptual framework is analysed in greater detail in the following chapter using samples including families from different Australian ethnic groups.

Family environment, personality, and intelligence

There have been many investigations of the relations between the personality of children who are of late elementary or early secondary school age, and measures of cognitive performance, but the findings remain inconclusive. Studies of British children, for example, by Jones (1960), Rushton (1966), Savage (1966), Ridding (1967), Eysenck and Cookson (1969), and Savage and Savage (1973) suggest that the extraverted child tends to perform better than the introverted child on measures of cognitive performance. The finding has been supported in Uganda by Honess and Kline (1974) and in a study by Orpen (1976) of Xhosa-speaking blacks and Afrikaans-speaking whites in South Africa. Entwistle and Welsh (1969) found that among bright boys extraversion was related negatively to academic attainment, but for low-ability boys the relation was positive; while Entwistle and Cunningham (1968) revealed that girls who were stable extraverts and boys who were stable introverts formed superior academic groups. It is proposed by Frost (1968) that for girls there is a positive relationship between extraversion and attainment, but for boys the relation is negative; this has the effect of producing an overall U-shaped relationship between children's extraversion and achievement. No significant relations between extraversion and scores on the Raven's Progressive Matrices are reported by Orme (1975), and Jensen (1973a) observed that while extraversion had negligible correlations with intelligence it had low but significant associations with the academic achievement scores of white, Negro, and Mexican-American children. A high correlation between extraversion and reading age was found by Elliott (1972), but a negligible relation between extraversion and intelligence when mental age and reading age were held constant.

For the relation between neuroticism and cognitive performance, Savage (1966), Ridding (1967), and Honess and Kline (1974) found no association, while Callard and Goodfellow (1962), Rushton (1966), Entwistle and Cunningham (1968), and Jensen (1973a) obtained significant negative linear correlations. Eysenck and Cookson (1969) proposed that the relation between neuroticism and performance scores is negative with the regression being slightly curvilinear, while Brown (1970) revealed a definite curvilinear association. But Entwistle and Cunningham (1968) conclude that the relationship between neuroticism and attainment is linear and that the hypothesis of a non-linear relationship must be rejected.

Most of these prior personality studies have used a trait model of behaviour $(B = f(P))$, and adopted restricted statistical techniques. The following study employs regression surfaces in an interactionist analysis of the relations between personality, family environment, and intelligence.

The data for the analysis were collected from 120 girls and 130 boys, in Australian rural towns (see Chapter 5, p. 117). Personality was defined by four second-stratum factors which were generated from Cattell's CPQ (form A), and labelled: contemplative-impatience, self-reliant-subduedness, adjustment-anxiety, and extraversion-introversion. The family environment data (see the Schedule in the Appendix) were collapsed into two global factors: press for achievement and parent-child involvement. The general intellectual ability of the children was assessed using the Otis Intermediate Test – Form AB, which has acceptable reliability estimates and moderate to high concurrent validities in relation to other academic achievement measures. The results of the analysis are summarized in Figure 6.4, which shows relations between intelligence scores and the anxiety-adjustment personality factor, at different levels of press for achievement. Because the samples of girls and boys are small, the findings must be treated with much caution. But the overall results of the analysis suggest the propositions that for boys: (a) at each level of personality, increases in the favourableness of the family environment are related to increments in intelligence, while (b) at each level of family environment, changes in personality factors are not associated with changes in intelligence test scores. And for girls, (a) at each level of personality, changes in the family environment are not associated with changes in intelligence scores, but (b) at each level of family environment, changes in personality are associated with changes in intelligence test scores. That is, these findings tend to provide support for a trait model explanation for girls' perform-

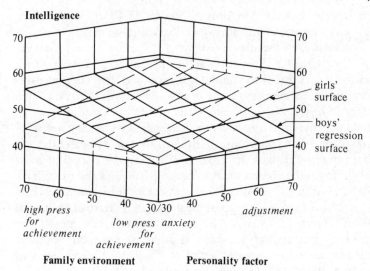

FIGURE 6.4 *Fitted-intelligence scores in relation to the anxiety-adjustment factor and parents' press for achievement*

ances and a situationist account of the boys' scores. But when measures of the children's school environment are included in the investigation (not presented here), an interactionist model is the appropriate explanatory framework for both girls and boys. As indicated earlier, the findings are extremely tentative and further research needs to be undertaken before the equivocal findings of prior research can be fully explained. The inclusion of environment variables into the investigation and the adoption of regression surface analysis do help, however, to explain some of the inconsistencies in previous research, especially the equivocal findings for girls and boys (see Marjoribanks, 1978f).

Early reading achievement, family environment and later reading achievement; within different social-status groups

From an investigation of research on human development, Bloom (1964) constructed a model to account for changes in the cognitive, physical, and emotional characteristics of humans. The model which is expressed in the formula $C_2 = C_1 + f(E_{2-1})$ suggests that the measurement of an individual characteristic at time 2 (C_2) is accounted for by the measurement of the same characteristic at time 1 (C_1) plus some function of the environment between times 1 and 2 (E_{2-1}). From the model it is proposed that: (a) 'the correlation between measurements of the same characteristic at two different times will approach unity when the environment in which the individuals have lived during the intervening period is known and taken into account' (Bloom, 1964, p. 192), and (b) 'the environment will have its greatest effects in the period of most rapid normal development of a characteristic and that its effects will be least in the period of slowest normal development, while its effects will approach zero in the period of no normal change in the characteristic' (p. 200). In the following study the Bloom model of human development is used to examine relations between the reading performance of children and measures of their family environment (see Marjoribanks, 1978g).

The data from the three age-cohorts of the Plowden and Plowden follow-up studies are used to investigate the model. In Chapter 3 it was suggested that social status has a pervasive influence on children's outcomes. Therefore in the analysis the relations between family environment and reading development are examined within different social-status groups as well as for total samples. Also, the size of the samples allows a confident examination of possible gender differences in the relations between the variables.

During the Plowden survey the children in the senior cohort were assessed using the Watts-Vernon reading test, while the middle and junior groups were tested with the N.S. 45 reading test, which was constructed by the National Foundation for Educational Research in England. In the follow-up study the performance of children in the three groups was measured using the Watts-Vernon reading test.

An equally weighted combination of family income, father occupation, and father education is used to estimate the social status of families. In the analysis the sample is divided into middle and lower social-status groups, based on the Registrar General's social class classification in Britain (see Plowden, 1967; volume 2: pp. 99–104). Factor scaling techniques were adopted to examine the family environment indices and a measure of the intervening family environment was obtained by combining measures from both national surveys. The final environment scale includes variables such as: press for achievement, parents' aspirations for the child, knowledge of child's school environment, parent-teacher interaction, parent-child activeness, and press for intellectuality.

The results of the regression surface analysis show that, at each level of initial reading achievement, changes in the family environment scores generally are not associated with significant changes in later reading performance. Variation in later reading scores is related primarily to the linear and squared initial reading scores. As it is not possible to present all the regression surfaces that were generated from the data, four surfaces are plotted in two figures. The surfaces have been chosen to reflect the possible relationships that are present in the regression models. In the figures the reading and environment scores have been converted to standard scores with a mean of 50 and a standard deviation of 10.

The surfaces in Figure 6.5 show the regression-fitted relationships between the initial and later reading scores at different levels of the intervening family environment for the total samples of girls and boys in the senior cohort. Representative of most of the surfaces in the investigation is the shape of the girls' surface,

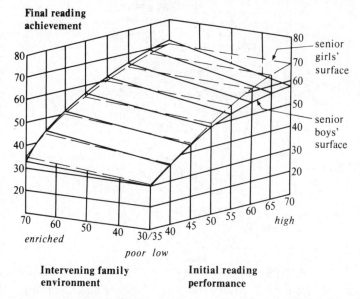

FIGURE 6.5 *Fitted-final reading scores in relation to initial reading performance and family environment: senior girls and senior boys*

as it shows that the relation between initial and later reading scores is not associated significantly with changes in the quality of the intervening family environment. At an initial reading level of 55, for example, the regression-estimated final reading scores for senior girls are 56 and 60 at the extremes of poor and enriched family environments, respectively.

The shape of the surface for the senior boys reflects a small number of regression models in which there is a significant relation between final reading performance and the statistical interaction between initial reading achievement and family environment. At each initial reading achievement level, increases in the quality of the intervening environment are associated with increments in later reading scores, with the increases being greatest at high initial reading and high environment scores. For example, at an initial reading level of 40, the regression-estimated later reading scores associated with poor and enriched environments are 37 and 43 respectively, while at an initial reading performance of 65, the corresponding later scores are 58 and 69.

In Figure 6.6, the surfaces show the regression-fitted relations between family environment and reading scores for middle and

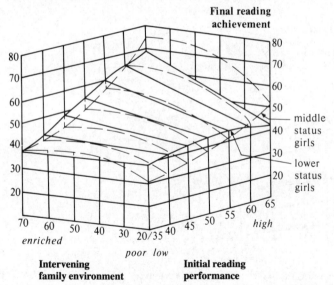

FIGURE 6.6 *Fitted-final reading scores in relation to initial reading performance and family environment: middle age cohort, middle- and lower-status girls*

lower social-status girls from the middle age cohort. The surfaces indicate the potentially complex nature of the relations between environment and cognitive variables. At each initial reading level, increments in the family environment score are associated with increases in later achievement. For middle social-status girls the surface suggests the environment threshold hypothesis: that at each level of initial reading achievement, increases in the quality of the intervening environment are related to sizeable changes in the final reading scores until a certain level of environment is reached. After that threshold level is exceeded further increments in environment scores are not associated with additional increases in reading performance. For both girls and boys, their later reading achievement is depressed relative to their initial scores if the intervening environment is defined as poor.

By using complex multiple regression models to generate regression surfaces and by including prior measures of reading performance in the analysis, the above study goes beyond much of previous research that has investigated the environmental correlates of cognitive development. In general, the present findings suggest the specific propositions that: (a) for children with low initial reading levels, increases in the quality of the intervening family environment are not associated with significant changes in later reading performances; (b) at any initial reading level, children who experience a poor intervening family environment show a decline in their later reading achievement, relative to the performance of other children; and (c) children with high initial reading scores either maintain or increase their relative position in reading achievement, with respect to other children, if they experience an enriched intervening family environment. The findings also indicate that there are variations in the relations between later reading performance and measures of family environment and initial reading achievement, for girls and boys, between the different social-status groups. For example, the initial reading scores expressed in a linear form generally account for more of the variance in the later reading scores for girls than for boys, which suggests that the associations between initial and later performance may be more complex for boys. Also the pattern of significant relations between the predictor variables and the later reading scores differs for girls and boys, within the lower and middle social-status groups. Thus the findings provide support for the claims that both sex and social-status are important variables to be included in analyses of the correlates of cognitive development.

The present results provide only partial support for the acceptance of Bloom's model of human development. Only in the senior cohort did the multiple correlations involving reading performance and environment approach unity. Also there was no regular pattern in the findings to support Bloom's general propositions relating the growth of reading development and the impact of the environment. For example, in the total samples of senior and junior cohort girls and junior boys, the environment was not related to changes in later reading performance at any initial reading level. But for senior boys and middle group girls and boys, increases in family environment scores were associated with increments in later reading performance at high initial reading levels. Also for middle social-status girls in the middle age cohort, changes in the environment were related to sizeable changes in the later reading scores at each initial reading level, while for lower-status girls such an association occurs only at high initial reading scores.

As indicated in Chapter 2, the Bloom model of development generated research that has investigated the environmental correlates of the cognitive and affective characteristics of children. Typically the studies have found moderate to large correlations between assessments of family environments and cognitive scores. These results have often been used to support the proposition that the 'manipulation' of the social-psychological environment of the family is likely to be related to sizeable changes in academic performance. The present analysis reveals the possible intricacies in the relations between the family environment and measures of cognitive development. Tentatively, the results indicate that low reading achievement levels may be less malleable in relation to 'manipulation' of the family environment, as it is measured in the present study, than is sometimes proposed (also see p. 134). The analysis, however, is restricted to an investigation of reading performance and does not include an examination of other situations such as classrooms, neighbourhoods, and peer groups. Only when research includes these other environment measures and additional achievement variables, will the Bloom model relating to cognitive development be fully tested.

The studies reviewed in the present chapter show that, typically, person and situation variables both contribute to an understanding of the variation in children's academic achievement, when considered in the context of each other. That is, the investigations provide support for adopting an interactionist model in educational and social psychological research which is attempting to explain children's behaviours. But the regression model used in the present studies to generate regression surfaces should be considered as only an initial approximation of the complexity of the inter-relationships between person, situation, and behaviour variables. In future research it is hoped that measurement of environments, persons, and behaviours will be improved. All these characteristics are multivariate, and it is likely to be found that different situations and parts of situations will produce different effects on a variety of growth measures and will produce different effects on different individual characteristics depending on the pattern of their initial states. For subsequent research the following equation, which is constructed from the model that Bloom developed and from the results of the studies in the present chapter, might be estimated (also see Walberg and Marjoribanks, 1976):

$$l_{j,t_2} = \sum b_j \, l^{\star}_{j,t_1} + \sum b_k \, E^{\star}_{k,t_{1-2}} + \sum b_{jk}(l^{\star}_{j,t_1}) \, (E^{\star}_{k,t_{1-2}})$$

where l_{j,t_2} is a given individual characteristic, the first term on the right hand side of the model is a weighted composite of a number of antecedent individual characteristics (the asterisk indicates the characteristics are in the optimal mathematical form; for example, linear, quadratic, or logarithmic for prediction); the second term is a similar intervening situation composite, and the last term is a weighted composite of products of antecedent characteristics and situations. Research based on the proposed generalized model would allow for the multiplicity of possible causes in the two domains, of persons and situations, and the possibility that initial characteristics interact with environment measures, influencing later characteristics. The proposed equation does not take into account the possibilities of genetically programmed factors, analogous to sexual maturation effects or adolescent height spurts, that may hasten or impede cognitive growth (Wilson, 1972). Nor does the model explicitly consider the absorption of early environments that produce unobservable propensities which are latent until later developmental stages; but only recently have these effects been claimed, and they are still controversial (McCall, 1970; McCall *et al.*, 1972).

By analysing the longitudinal development of human characteristics and by emphasizing the need for more refined measures of learning environments, Bloom provided the necessary impetus for studies of family environmental influences on cognitive growth. In the present chapter an attempt has been made to build upon Bloom's model and on other interactionist models of behaviour. It is hoped that the proposed interactionist paradigm might be useful in guiding future investigations in environmental social psychology.

7 Ethnicity, family environment, and children's achievement

The controversies generated by the work of researchers such as Eysenck (1971, 1973), Jensen (1969, 1973b, 1973c), Herrnstein (1973), and Shockley (1971a, 1971b) have dramatized the need for refined investigations of the relationships among the constructs of ethnicity, environment, and children's cognitive performance. As Banks (1976, p. 69) suggests, the disputes raised by the controversies are 'unlikely to be resolved until we have a much greater knowledge of the ways in which abilities develop in interaction with the environment'. In the present chapter the general question is examined: to what extent is the learning environment of the family related to ethnic group differences in measures of children's cognitive performance? A comprehensive review of research related to the question is not presented. Instead, readers are referred to Loehlin *et al.* (1975) for an extremely comprehensive, balanced, and critical analysis of the 'race-IQ' issue. From investigations of empirical findings and theoretical arguments, they suggest that at present the following three general conclusions are warranted (p. 239):

1. Observed average differences in the scores of members of different U.S. racial-ethnic groups of intellectual-ability tests probably reflect in part inadequacies and biases in the tests themselves, in part differences in environmental conditions among the groups, and in part genetic differences among the groups. It should be emphasized that these three factors are not necessarily independent, and may interact.

2. A rather wide range of positions concerning the relative weight to be given to these three factors can reasonably be taken on the basis of current evidence, and a sensible person's position might well differ for different abilities, for different groups, and for different tests.

3. Regardless of the position taken on the relative importance of these three factors, it seems clear that the differences among individuals *within* racial-ethnic (and socio-economic) groups greatly exceed in magnitude the average differences between such groups.

Two sets of data are used in the present chapter to examine inter-relationships between ethnicity, family environment, and children's outcomes. The first data set includes Canadian children and their parents from Anglo-Canadian, Canadian Indian, French-Canadian, Jewish, and Southern Italian groups, while the second study involves Australian families from Anglo-Australian, English, Greek, and Southern Italian groups.

Ethnicity and patterns of children's mental ability scores

In an endeavour to overcome some of the shortcomings of prior investigations of ethnic group differences in intellectual ability, Marjoribanks examined relations between a refined family environment measure and ethnic group differences in the levels and profiles of a set of mental ability test scores (see Marjoribanks 1972b, 1972c). Essentially, the research attempts to explore four questions:

(a) What is the relationship between ethnic group membership and mental ability test scores?
(b) What is the relationship between ethnicity and family environment measures?
(c) What is the relationship between family environment and mental ability test performance?
(d) To what extent is the learning environment of the family related to ethnic group differences in mental ability test scores?

The research is guided by the general theoretical position constructed by Ferguson (1954, 1956), suggesting that a mental ability is an attribute of behaviour which through learning attains a crude stability or invariance. The relative stability which characterizes an ability is considered to be the result of over-learning. Within the framework, it is assumed that the limits of ability that are achieved by individuals are related to the 'genetic potential' of the individual and also to the learning environment in which the person develops. Ferguson proposes that we can think of abilities as being a function of the learning that has taken place, and that the learning of a new task is facilitated by those abilities that have already been developed. From the conceptual position it can be hypothesized that if different cultural groups are found to be characterized by different patterns of mental ability test scores, then the groups are also characterized by different environments for learning.

Essentially Lesser (1976, p. 137) puts forward a similar proposition when he asserts that 'people who share a common cultural background will also share, to a certain extent, common patterns of intellectual abilities, thinking styles, and interests'. This latter proposition was generated by Lesser after conducting a series of studies on relations between ethnicity, social status, and patterns of mental ability test scores. Lesser, Fifer and Clark (1965) tested 320 first-grade children from 45 elementary schools in New York City. The children came from four ethnic groups: Chinese, Jewish, Black, and Puerto Rican. Each ethnic group was divided into middle and lower social-status groups, and then each social group was divided into equal numbers of girls and boys. The final sample involved a 4 x 2 x 2 analysis-of-covariance design with 16 sub-groups each composed of 20 children. In the testing sessions each child was tested by an examiner who shared the child's ethnic identity, and Lesser *et al.* (1965) describe the extensive efforts made to achieve as much standardization as possible within the sessions. Four test scores were obtained for each child: verbal ability, number facility, space conceptualization, and reasoning ability.

The results of the study indicated that each ethnic group exhibited its own distinctive pattern of mental ability scores, and that the ability patterns remained invariant across social-status categories. Statistically, this meant that social-status influences on the shapes of the patterns of mental ability test scores within each ethnic group were non-significant, or that the pattern of abilities for middle social-status children within each ethnic group was parallel to the pattern of abilities for lower social-status group children (see Figure 7.3, which shows similar relations).

> For example, the pattern displayed by the middle-class Chinese children and duplicated at a lower level of performance by the lower-class Chinese children differed strikingly from the pattern specific to the Jewish children; and the pattern displayed by the middle-class Jewish children was duplicated at a lower level of performance by the lower-class Jewish children. Parallel statements can be made for the other ethnic groups as well (Lesser, 1976, p. 143).

In a follow-up study involving 208 of the original 320 children, Lesser (1976, p. 149) found that in the sixth grade 'the distinctive ethnic group patterns seem to be operating at least as strongly as they were earlier in the children's lives'.

Marjoribanks's study of Canadian children was, in part, a response to and replication study of the original Lesser analysis, as well as a test of the Ferguson postulate: that if different cultural groups are characterized by different patterns of mental abilities then they are characterized also by different environments for learning. As indicated earlier, members of five ethnic groups residing in Ontario, Canada were included in the study: Anglo-Canadians (Protestants), Canadian Indian (Iroquois), French Canadians (Franco-Ontarians), Jews, and Southern Italians. Approximately 100 11-year-old boys from each ethnic group were selected and tested, using first the California Test of Mental Maturity and then the SRA Primary Mental Abilities Test. The first test-taking session was used to establish examiner-examinee rapport, to ensure that all the boys were able to understand the test instructions, and to establish as far as possible uniform test-taking conditions. In the second test-taking situation, the SRA test was administered and all the testing sessions were conducted by Marjoribanks. Only the scores from the latter test are used in the analysis.

Each boy in the sample was Canadian born and attending a school in which English was the predominant language of instruction. In the Jewish schools a Hebrew studies programme was taken by each boy, and in the schools for the French-Canadians a French studies curriculum was offered. The Canadian Indian students attended schools on an Indian reserve, but many of the parents worked in neighbouring urban centres. The Southern Italian boys attended a Roman Catholic school system which served an urban neighbourhood that was primarily Southern Italian. All of the schools, except those on the reservation, were in urban areas.

Where possible, two parallel pools of 40 families were formed within each ethnic group. The purpose of the substitute pool was to provide a set of alternate families which could be used in the study if families from the first pool did not agree to participate. Within these pools the families were assigned to two categories, classified as middle and lower social-status, with the intention of obtaining 20 middle- and 20 lower-status families within each pool. Social-status classification was based on an equally weighted combination of the occupation of the head of the household and a rating of her (or his) education. For the Southern Italians and Canadian Indians, it was not possible to form completely parallel middle social-status pools, and in the case of the Jewish families it was not possible to duplicate the lower social-status group. The final sample within each ethnic group consists of 37 families, 18 classified as middle- and 19 as lower-social status.

The first set of hypotheses examined are the same as those analysed in the Lesser studies (see Lesser *et al.*, 1965; Stodolsky and Lesser, 1967):

(a) Significant differences exist among groups of children from different social-status and ethnic groups in the *level* of each of the four mental abilities.
(b) Significant differences exist among the social-status and ethnic groups in the *patterns* of children's mental ability test scores.
(c) Significant interactions exist between social status and ethnicity in relations with the level of each mental ability and the nature of the patterns among the abilities.

The profiles of scores shown in Figures 7.1 and 7.2 provide support for the acceptance of the first two hypotheses. On each of the abilities, the middle-status boys have significantly higher scores than the lower-status boys, and generally the level of abilities of the Jewish and Anglo-Canadian groups are significantly higher than the level of abilities of the other three groups. When the ethnic group data are included in multiple regression models as a set of mutually exclusive categories they are related to approximately 45 and 34 per cent of the variance in the verbal and number ability scores, respectively, and 8 and 4 per cent of the variance in the reasoning and spatial scores.

When a multivariate analysis-of-variance technique, which involved the computation of Wilk's lambda criterion, was used to test for differences in the profiles of test scores, the findings indicated that the social-status and ethnic group differences in the profiles of scores were statistically significant (see Rulon and Brooks, 1968; Cooley and Lohnes, 1962). In Figures 7.1 and 7.2 the scores on each ability are converted to standard scores, calculated over the total sample, with a mean of 50 and a standard deviation of 10.

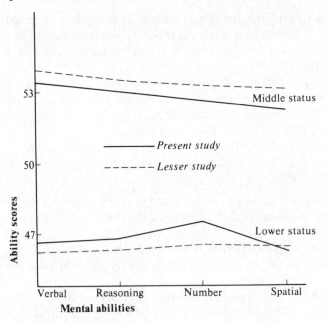

FIGURE 7.1 *Patterns of normalized ability scores for each social-status group*

The results in the figures replicate some of the findings from other research. In Figure 7.1, the patterns of abilities of each social-status group in the original Lesser study have been presented. The two sets of patterns indicate the similarity of the findings from the two studies. Also, the shape of the profile of scores for the Jewish children is similar to the shape obtained in the Lesser studies, in which the Jewish children were characterized by higher verbal and number scores and relatively lower reasoning and spatial scores. Results in the Coleman *et al.* (1966) study of sixth-grade American Indian children are compatible with the present findings relating to the Iroquois boys. Coleman also found that the reasoning scores of the Indian children were higher than their verbal scores, which in turn were higher than number ability scores. In an investigation of children from Western Canada, Vernon (1969) revealed that the spatial ability scores of Cluny Indian children exceeded their number and verbal ability test performance. That is, the findings replicate, in part, the results of a number of studies that have examined the mental

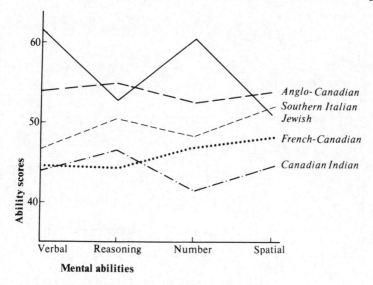

FIGURE 7.2. *Patterns of mental ability scores for each ethnic group*

ability profiles of children from different cultural groups. The replication provides some confidence for the validity of the present study.

The third hypothesis involves a test of the significance of the interaction of social status and ethnicity on the levels and profiles of ability. When levels of ability are examined the interaction is significant only for number ability. Social status has a stronger association with the number ability scores of the French-Canadian boys than with the number scores of the boys from the other four groups. For verbal, reasoning, and spatial scores, the relations to ethnicity are not significantly different across the social-status levels. All of the interaction effects in the Lesser studies were significant, as social status had stronger relations to the ability measures for black children than for the other groups. The relations between the patterns of abilities and the interactions between ethnicity and social status are summarized in Figure 7.3. Only the Canadian Indian middle- and lower-status groups differ significantly from parallelism in the profiles. These initial findings provide answers for the first general question of the study: 'What is the relationship between ethnic group membership and mental ability test scores?'

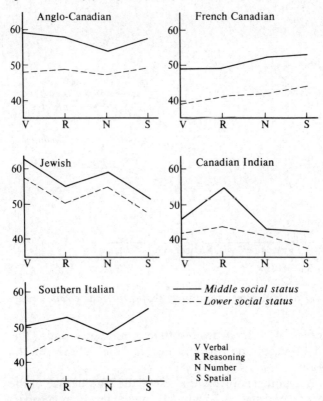

FIGURE 7.3 *Patterns of normalized mental ability scores for ethnic and middle and lower social-status groups*

The second question being explored is: 'What is the relationship between ethnicity and family environment measures?' Family environment is defined by the eight process variables identified in Chapter 2 (see p. 38), which were labelled parents' press for: achievement, activeness, intellectuality, independence, English, a second language, and: mother's dominance and father's dominance. Except for the parental dominance dimensions, ethnicity is related to moderate to large percentages of the differences in the environment scores. In Figure 7.4 the profiles indicate that for the first five environment variables the Jewish and Anglo-Canadian families have scores which are significantly higher than the scores of families from the other three groups. Differences are not significant in press for English, press for

French, and the learning of Hebrew in the Anglo-Canadian, French, and Jewish groups, respectively. Group differences in the profiles of scores are statistically significant, which means that the ethnic groups occupy different regions in the test space for the environment scores.

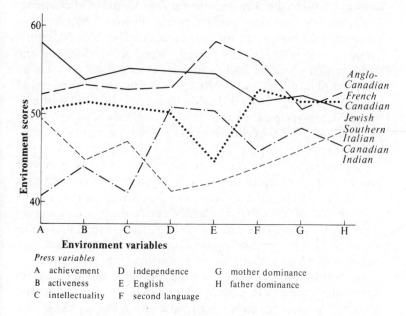

Environment variables

Press variables

A achievement   D independence   G mother dominance
B activeness   E English   H father dominance
C intellectuality   F second language

FIGURE 7.4 *Patterns of normalized environment scores for each ethnic group*

When the relations between the eight process variables and the four mental abilities were examined, a significant canonical correlation of 0.77 was obtained. In a principal component analysis of the eight environment variables, the six press measures loaded strongly on a factor which was labelled the 'learning environment of the family'. When the six measures are combined into a predictor set they have multiple correlations of approximately 0.70, 0.70, 0.25, and 0.40 with verbal, number, spatial, and reasoning abilities, respectively.

Thus the study shows that ethnic groups are characterized by distinctive patterns of: (a) mental abilities and (b) family environment measures; and that the family environment has low to moderate concurrent validities for spatial and reasoning abilities and high concurrent validities for verbal and number performance.

The final question being explored is: 'To what extent is the learning environment of the family related to ethnic group differences in mental ability scores?' A multiple regression model was used to examine the relations among the constructs of ethnicity, family environment, and levels of mental abilities. The amount of variance in the mental ability scores that could be related to ethnic group membership was assessed, after accounting for the variance that could be associated with environment and the co-variation of ethnicity and family environment. In the regression models, ethnic group membership data formed a set of mutually exclusive categories, the scores on the environment variables a set of eight continuous predictor variables, and the mental abilities were the criteria.

The findings indicate: (a) for verbal ability, ethnicity initially is related to 45 per cent of the variance in the test scores, but after accounting for the variance related to the environment and to the co-variation of ethnicity and family environment, the independent contribution of ethnicity is 11 per cent; (b) for number ability, ethnic group membership has an initial association with 34 per cent of the variance in the test scores, while the independent contribution is reduced to 3 per cent; (c) ethnicity does not have a significant independent relation to the spatial scores; and (d) for the reasoning scores, an initial ethnic relation of 8 per cent is reduced to a unique contribution of 6 per cent of the variance. Thus the results show that the variance in the ability scores that may be attributed to ethnicity is reduced after the relations between the environment and the ability scores are taken into account. But, because of the intercorrelation between ethnicity and family environment, the findings may attribute a possible inflated importance to the family environment measure. Therefore the contribution of environment to the variation in the ability scores was calculated after allowing for the contribution of ethnicity and the co-variation of ethnicity and family environment. The relative importance of ethnicity, environment, and the joint contribution of these two variables for the ability scores is shown in Table 7.1. After accounting for the independent or unique influence of the environment, significant ethnic group differences remain in verbal, number, and reasoning ability scores. Only for spatial ability scores are the ethnic group dif-

TABLE 7.1 *Relative contribution of environment and ethnicity in relation to the mental abilities*

| | Variance related to contributions of: | | |
Criterion	Environment	Ethnicity	Co-variation of environment and ethnicity
Verbal	16.0	11.0	34.0
Reasoning	14.0	6.0	n.s.
Number	19.0	3.0	31.0
Spatial	5.6	n.s.	n.s.

n.s. = contribution not significant.

ferences in ability levels not significant. A multivariate analysis-of-variance technique with multiple co-variance adjustments showed that the relation between ethnicity and the profiles of ability scores is reduced significantly after controlling for the relations between family environments and test scores.

As in most western industrialized societies, the Canadian social structure is characterized by a disproportionate representation of ethnic groups in the various levels of the social-status hierarchy. Census data indicate that the ethnic groups classified as British and Jewish are over-represented in the upper levels of the hierarchy and under-represented in the lower levels. French Canadian and Southern Italian groups display a reverse pattern. Canadian Indians are concentrated largely in the lower levels of the status hierarchy. When such differences among ethnic groups persist, it is necessary to determine, as Jensen (1969) suggests: 'To what extent can such inequalities be attributed to unfairness in society's multiple selection processes? . . . And to what extent are the inequalities attributable to really relevant selection criteria?' By examining the verbal, reasoning, number, and spatial ability scores of children from five ethnic groups, the present study in part investigates the relevance of mental ability performances as potential selection criteria. While the analysis is not a direct examination of the genetic hypothesis of ethnic group differences in mental abilities, the results show that the smallest ethnic group, and also social-status, differences are in relation to spatial ability. In an examination of the heritability of mental abilities, including verbal, reasoning, number, and spatial scores, Bock and Vandenberg (1968) conclude that, for boys, spatial ability is not particularly sensitive to between-family environmental differences. Spatial ability showed the largest component of heritable variance, and Bock and Vandenberg suggest that there is justification for including spatial ability in tests which purport to assess innate general ability, especially for boys.

The *ex post facto* nature of the study and its correlational design restrict, of course, the inferences which can be made about causation among the variables. The presence of the large joint environment and ethnicity component in the analysis of the verbal and number abilities, may reflect the finding that children who are members of different ethnic groups have a greater than chance likelihood of being surrounded by distinctive patterns of family learning environments, which in turn are associated with distinctive ethnic patterns of mental abilities. Such an interpretation raises the question of whether ethnic group profiles of family environment variables might in themselves be relevant selection criteria.

The research discussed in this chapter, so far, is susceptible to the criticism that standardized tests are inappropriate or insensitive measures for the assessment of children from different ethnic and social-status groups (see Cicourel *et al.*, 1974; Cole, 1976; Labov, 1972). Gordon (1976b, p. 167) comments that such research 'seems to have neglected the non-cognitive factors involved in learning. . . . I feel that it is important to recognize that the strictly cognitive aspect of intellectual functioning is only one aspect of such functioning and that all behavior, including cognitive behavior, occurs in the context of an integration of affective and cognitive factors.' Commenting specifically on the Lesser-type research, Gordon (1976b, p. 171) suggests that the studies 'fail to consider the compensatory role of motivation. Even though an individual's ability to perform certain cognitive tasks may not be extremely high, his desire to excel may be strong enough to enable him to persevere and master the field requiring the particular skill.'

Although the study of Canadian children involves an examination of family environments and thus moves beyond other Lesser-type analyses, the research includes only a narrow range of mental ability measures and does not include affective variables. In the following study designated as 'the Australian Study', relations are investigated between measures of ethnicity, family environment, school-related attitudes, intelligence, and academic achievement.

Ethnicity, family environment, school-related attitudes and children's cognitive performance

As stated in the previous chapter, Thomas and Znaniecki (1958) developed a general conceptual framework linking social organization and social personality. They claim that there can be no change of social reality which is not the common effect of pre-existing social values and individual attitudes acting upon them, nor any change of individual consciousness which is not the common effect of pre-existing attitudes and social values acting upon them. As Thomas (1966, p. 274) suggests:

> Even if we find that all the members of a social group react in the same way to a certain value, still we cannot assume that this value alone is the cause of this reaction, for the latter is also conditioned by the uniformity of attitudes prevailing in the group; and this uniformity cannot be taken for granted or omitted.

When investigating the interaction between behaviour and measures of an individual's attitudes and social conditions, Thomas proposes that the social conditions should be defined in relation to the meanings that they have for the individual. Karabel and Halsey (1977, p. 58) indicate, however, that emphasis on the meanings that social conditions have for an individual 'often fails to take adequate account of the social constraints on human actors in everyday life'. They propose that in the examination of behaviour there is a 'necessity of integrating structural and inter-actional levels of analysis'. A parent interview schedule was constructed for the Australian study to assess the 'constraints' that parents may establish within family learning environments, and questionnaires were administered to children to measure their attitudes to schooling. The latter measure is considered an attempt, if somewhat superficial, to assess the meanings that education has for the children. It is assumed that the meanings are constructed from a child's interaction with parents, other members of the family, peers, and from experiences within school.

It is suggested by Thomas and Znaniecki (1958) that sets of general relations between social organization and social personality are revealed by investigating social groups that are in varying positions of transfer from older to newer forms of social organization. Families from five Australian social groups are involved in the present analysis, including: middle social-status Anglo-Australian, and lower social-status families from the following groups: Anglo-Australian, English, Greek, and Southern Italian. The Greek and Southern Italian families are representative of Australian social groups that are in positions of substantial transition to newer organizational forms, while the English immigrant families reflect ethnic groups in which the transitions in social organization are likely to be relatively modest.

Although the Thomas and Znaniecki framework has been criticized (e.g. see Bierstedt, 1969; Janowitz, 1966) because of the difficulties that sometimes confront researchers in differentiating between social values and attitudes, the conceptual position is a useful starting point for the following analysis of the relations between family environments, school-related attitudes, and the cognitive performance of children from different Australian ethnic groups.

Data for the analysis were collected from 140 Anglo-Australian middle social-status families, and from lower social-status families from the following groups: Anglo-Australian (250), English immigrants (120), Greek (170), and Southern Italian (120 families). The social-status classification is based on an equally weighted composite of father occupation and the education of the mother and father. Each of the families has an 11-year-old child attending an urban elementary school. In the Southern Italian and Greek families both parents migrated from their respective countries before or just after the birth of their 11-year-old child. The parents indicated that Greek or Italian was the language generally spoken in their respective homes. Families are classified as English if both parents were born in England and had migrated to Australia after they were married, and generally after the birth of the 11-year-old child. Families are defined as Anglo-Australian if both parents were born in Australia and English is the only language spoken in the home.

A set of academic achievement tests was administered to the 11-year-old children within their own classrooms. Testing sessions were conducted by Marjoribanks to obtain as far as possible standardized testing situations and to ensure that all students were able to understand, as far as possible, the test instructions spoken or written in English. The Raven's Progressive Matrices was adopted to assess the intellectual ability of the children, and tests devised by the Australian Council for Educational Research were used to measure achievement in mathematics, word knowledge, and word comprehension. These latter tests are labelled the Classroom Achievement Tests in Mathematics and the Primary Reading Survey Tests.

The school-related attitudes of the children were measured using a Likert-type questionnaire, adapted from a schedule developed originally by the National Foundation for Education Research in England for two studies of streaming in English schools (Barker Lunn, 1969; Ferri, 1971). For the present study, items are used that assess seven attitude sub-scales (see Chapter 5 for a description of a similar attitude measure). The following list includes the labels used for the scales with some sample items provided to show the nature of the scales: (a) enthusiasm for school (I am sorry when school is over for the day, I would leave school tomorrow if I could, school is boring); (b) enthusiasm for class membership, which assesses the favourableness or otherwise of being a member of a particular class in the school (of all the classes in this school my class is the nicest of all, I would rather be in my class than in any other, I hate being in the class I'm in now); (c) dislike for disruptive behaviour (I dislike children who are noisy in class, I like fooling about in this class, when the teacher goes out of the room I fool about); (d) relationship with teacher (I get on well with my teacher, our teacher treats us as if we were babies, my teacher is nice to me); (e) academic self-image, which reflects self-image in terms of schoolwork (I'm useless at schoolwork, when we have work to do I get very good marks, I think that I am pretty good at schoolwork); (f) social adjustment in school, which assesses children's ability to get on well with peers (I have no friends who I like very much in this school, I wish there were nicer children in this class, I have friends who I like very much in this class); and (g) achievement orientation (I work and try very hard in school, doing well at school is most important to me, and I would like to be one of the cleverest students in the school).

Thus the schedule assesses a wide range of school-related attitudes. In the administration of the questionnaire, Marjoribanks read each item to the children to minimize any difficulties associated with understanding the meaning of the questions. From principal component analysis of the responses, two factors were identified. One factor was a cognitive-behavioural component of school attitudes consisting of 19 items and loading on the scales of academic self-image, achievement orientation, and social adjustment to school. This factor was labelled 'academic adjustment to school', and had a theta reliability estimate of 0.76. The other factor consists of 29 items, assesses an affective component of school attitudes, and loads on the scales of enthusiasm for school, enthusiasm for class, dislike for disruptive behaviour, and positive relationship with the teacher. Labelled as 'affective commitment to school', the scale has a reliability estimate of 0.80 (also see p. 139 for a description of the attitude scale).

As indicated in the previous chapter (see p. 138), the family environment was defined by parents' press for English, aspirations for the 11-year-old child, satisfaction with teaching, and satisfaction with school. The interviewing in the homes was conducted by government social survey interviewers who were able to communicate in the primary language of the family.

The data collected on the 800 Australian families are used to examine three sets of relations, involving:

(a) Ethnicity, family environment, school attitudes and academic achievement
(b) Ethnicity, family environment, intelligence and academic achievement
(c) Ethnicity, school attitudes, intelligence and academic achievement

Because of the relatively small sample sizes within each ethnic group, the data are not divided into sex groups for any of the analyses. Although there is no agreement on the extent of gender differences in the relations between environments, attitudes, and cognitive performance (e.g., Deutsch, 1967; Hutt, 1972; Alexander and Eckland, 1974; Maccoby and Jacklin, 1974; Hout and Morgan, 1975; Epstein and McPartland, 1977), the failure to test for gender differences within ethnic groups is a restriction of the analyses (e.g., see earlier chapters in which gender differences have been examined).

The first examination of the relations between the measures involves an analysis of simple correlations. For the results in Table 7.2, ethclass group membership, which has been labelled ethnicity, forms a set of mutually exclusive categories. Relations between ethnicity and the other variables are multiple correlations, while all other associations are zero-order correlations.

TABLE 7.2 *Relations between ethnicity, environment, attitudes, and academic achievement*

	Ethnicity[a]	Press for English	Parents' aspirations	Satisfaction with school	Satisfaction with teaching	Affective commitment	Academic adjustment
Mathematics	0.21†	0.21†	0.08*	0.10*	0.07*	0.07*	0.10*
Word knowledge	0.40†	0.36†	0.07*	0.17†	0.19†	0.09*	0.18†
Word comprehension	0.35†	0.30†	0.06	0.20†	0.17†	0.11*	0.17†
Press for English	0.69†	–	−0.16†	0.25†	0.31†	0.06	b
Parents' aspirations	0.42†	−0.16†	–	b	b	0.02	0.11*
Satisfaction with school	0.25†	0.25†	b	–	0.48†	0.05	0.03
Satisfaction with teaching	0.28†	0.31†	b	0.48†	–	b	0.05
Affective commitment to school	0.12	0.06	0.02	0.05	b	–	0.43†
Academic adjustment to school	0.13	b	0.11*	0.03	0.05	0.43†	–
Intelligence	0.12	0.11*	0.07*	0.08*	0.13†	0.06	0.05

[a] Coefficients associated with ethnicity are multiple correlations in which the ethclass groups form a set of mutually exclusive categories.

b indicates that the correlation < 0.01.

*$p < .05$

†$p < .01$

Except for intelligence and the attitude scores, the findings show that there are group differences in the measures. Particularly interesting is the non-significant relation between ethnicity and the Raven's intelligence measure, which is similar to the lack of an association between ethnicity and spatial ability in the Canadian study. That is, in the two sets of data being analysed in this chapter, ethnicity is not related to those intelligence tests which may be considered to be the most 'culturally-reduced' of the tests being examined. In Table 7.2 the results show also that intelligence and the achievement scores have low to moderate concurrent validities in relation to the environment measures and low associations with the attitude scores. Differences in mean scores between the groups on the cognitive, family environment, and attitude measures are shown in Figure 7.5. Scores on the measures have been converted to standard scores with a mean of 50 and a standard deviation of 10, calculated over the total sample. The profiles show that the Anglo-Australian and English groups have higher scores on the achievement measures, exert stronger parental press for English (which, of course, is not surprising), and tend to be more satisfied with schooling. Southern Italian and Greek parents express stronger aspirations for their children than do parents from the other lower social-status groups.

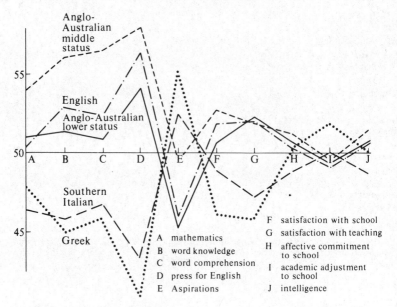

FIGURE 7.5 *Profiles of achievement, environment and attitude scores for each social group*

Ethnicity, family environment, school attitudes and academic achievement

Relationships between family environment, attitudes, and achievement within each social group were investigated further using regression surface analysis. After adjusting significance levels for the design effects of the samples, it was found that product terms (to test for interactions) and quadratic variables (to test for non-linearity) were not significant. The environment and attitude scores are related differentially to the academic achievement scores within different social groups. Some of these differences are displayed in Figures 7.6 and 7.7.

In Figure 7.6, the surfaces show the regression-fitted relations between academic adjustment to school and word knowledge scores at different levels of parents' aspirations (also see Chapter 6, p. 140). The shape of the surfaces for the Anglo-Australian and English children indicate that academic achievement is related to both the attitude and environment measures. For Southern Italian

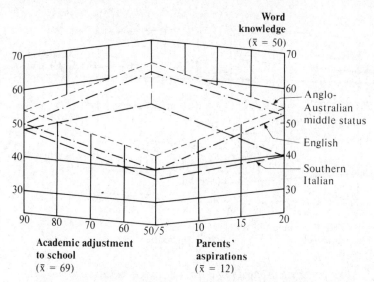

FIGURE 7.6 *Fitted-word knowledge scores in relation to parents' aspirations and academic adjustment to school*

children, word knowledge scores have significant associations with only the attitude scores. At each level of parents' aspirations, increments in the adjustment to school scores are associated with increases in the regression-fitted word knowledge scores, while, at each level of academic adjustment, increases in parents' aspirations are not related to significant changes in the Southern Italian children's word knowledge scores.

Except for the Southern Italian children, the findings show that affective commitment to school scores are not related to children's academic achievement scores at different levels of the family environment measures. In Figure 7.7 the surfaces show the regression-fitted relations between affective commitment to school and word knowledge at different levels of parents' aspirations. The surfaces for the Anglo-Australian and English children reveal that at each level of the affective commitment to school scores, increases in aspiration scores are related to increments in the word knowledge scores. For the Southern Italian children increases in the attitude scores are associated with changes in the word knowledge scores at each level of parents' aspirations.

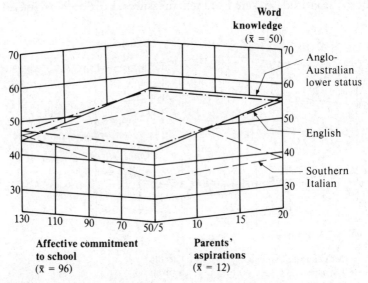

FIGURE 7.7 *Fitted-word knowledge scores in relation to parents' aspirations and affective commitment to school*

The findings from the regression surface analysis provide only partial support for the general theoretical framework, which suggests that children's attitudes are related to academic performance at different levels of the learning environment of the family. There are differential relations between the variables within the social groups. For the Greek children none of the relations between attitudes and achievement, at different environment levels, is significant. It is possible that the extremely low press for English scores within the Greek group present too great an obstacle for the other environment variables and attitude measures to be related to achievement in a 'predictable manner'. Thomas (1966, p. 20) proposes that the more uniform and steady the social influences are on an individual, the more difficult it is for the individual 'to find around him influences which would make him take a course different from other members of the group in acquiring a new attitude. Of course this means also a limitation of the variety of possible attitudes and values that can develop from a given starting point.' Very low press for English scores and extremely high aspiration levels in Greek families may provide a set of social conditions which inhibit interactions between achievement-related social values and children's attitudes. In the Anglo-Australian lower status and Southern Italian samples there are more significant relations between attitudes and achievement at different environment levels than in the other social groups. Social conditions within these two groups may be less extreme than those in the other groups (see Figure 7.5), which suggests the possibility of more varied interactions between social values and attitudes (Znaniecki, 1969).

In general, the environment and attitude scores are not related to mathematics achievement, indicating the need for investigating interactions between further sets of environment variables and attitudes for an understanding of the variation in different academic characteristics. Also, the affective orientation to school measure has few relations to the achievement scores at different environment levels. Levin (1976, p. 285) proposes that 'educational programs that focus on student attitudes may be able to compensate for "disadvantages" in socio-economic background. Indeed this tentative interpretation argues . . . that these background factors now appear to have much their direct effects not on achievement, but on attitude, and through attitude, on achievement.' The present findings suggest that the 'manipulation' of the cognitive-behavioural aspects of school attitudes may influence the academic achievement of low social-status children from certain ethnic groups, at different levels of environment variables. But educational programmes that concentrate primarily on the affective components of school attitudes may have a less immediate impact and possibly a restricted influence on academic performance. Also, the results indicate that parents' satisfaction is not a significant environment variable in any of the relations within the social groups.

It is submitted by Thomas and Znaniecki that in the development of behaviour there is a reciprocal dependence between social organization and individual life organization, and that the dependence is most suitably examined by a comparative analysis of social groups that are in different positions of transition from older to newer social organizational forms. The present study shows that word knowledge and word comprehension scores are related to a cognitive-behavioural component of school-related attitudes at different levels of parents' press for English and parents' aspirations, but that the relations are found only within certain social groups. These initial findings indicate the necessity of conducting studies in educational research that investigate relations between variables within different ethnic groups. Only when such research is undertaken might educators desist from generalizing research findings from one social group to children belonging to other groups.

Ethnicity, family environment, intelligence, and academic achievement

The caveat that research findings in education should not be transmitted, without examination, between different ethnic and social-status groups, applies to many of the propositions that have been formulated in earlier chapters of this book. In the previous chapter, for example, after examining samples of English children it was suggested that at different levels of intelligence, increments in the social-psychological environment of the family are likely to be associated with only modest changes in children's academic achievement. The following analysis of the Australian data (Marjoribanks, 1979c) shows that there are differential ethnic group relations between family environment measures and academic achievement performance, at different levels of intellectual ability. Only some of the differences are able to be presented in the following regression surfaces.

In Figure 7.8, the surfaces show the regression-fitted relations between press for English and word knowledge at different levels of the Raven's intelligence test scores. For the Anglo-Australian children both intelligence and press for English scores have significant linear associations with achievement. At each level of intelligence, increases in the press for English scores, from a low of 5 to a high of 40, are associated with a regression-fitted word knowledge increase of approximately 10 points, at each level of intelligence. Also, as the ability scores increase from a score of 70 to 120, the regression-fitted word knowledge scores increase by approximately 5 points at each environment level. The surface for

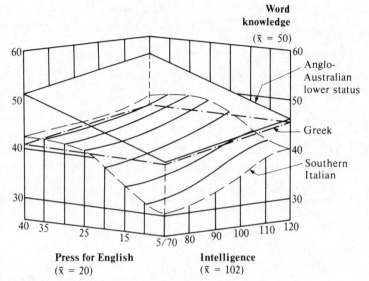

FIGURE 7.8 *Fitted-word knowledge scores in relation to intelligence and press for English*

the Greek children reflects the results of many previous studies that have suggested that academic achievement is not related to the social environment of children with equal intellectual ability. But the curvature of the surface for the Southern Italian children indicates the complex nature of the relations which may exist between intelligence, family environment, and academic achievement. At each level of intelligence, increments in the press for English scores are associated with sizeable increments in word knowledge until a ceiling level of performance is attained. In part, the curvature of the surface reflects an artefact of the data, as there were few Southern Italian parents who exerted a strong press for English.

In Figure 7.9 the surfaces reflect the regression-fitted relations between parents' aspirations and mathematics achievement at different levels of intellectual ability. For middle social-status Anglo-Australian children, parents' aspirations are not related to mathematics performance at different levels of intelligence. But in the lower-status Anglo-Australian group aspirations are associated with mathematics, such that at high aspiration levels there are no differences in mathematics scores between children of equal ability from the two Anglo-Australian social-status groups. For

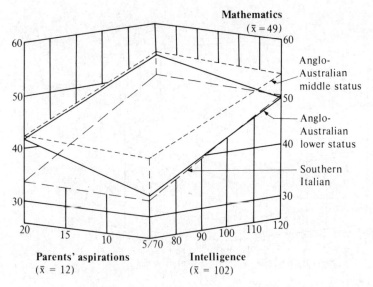

FIGURE 7.9 *Fitted-mathematics scores in relation to intelligence and parents' aspirations*

lower social-status Southern Italian children, increments in parents' aspirations are not related to mathematics achievement at different intellectual levels. The differences in the shapes of the surfaces in Figure 7.9 provide support for the contention of Havighurst (1976) and Frideres (1977) that ethnicity and social status are essential variables to be included in investigations of social and cognitive development.

The surfaces in Figure 7.10 show the relation between satisfaction with schooling and word comprehension scores at different levels of intelligence, for lower social-status Anglo-Australian and Greek children. In the regression model the satisfaction with teaching and satisfaction with school scores were combined into one index of 'satisfaction with schooling'. The shape of the surface for the Anglo-Australian children reflects approximately one-half of the regression models involving the satisfaction variable, in which increments in parents' satisfaction are not related to achievement scores at different levels of ability. The curvature of the surface for the Greek children indicates a complex situation in which increases in satisfaction scores beyond a certain level are related to decreasing achievement scores. The findings within this section of the chapter suggest the general propositions that:

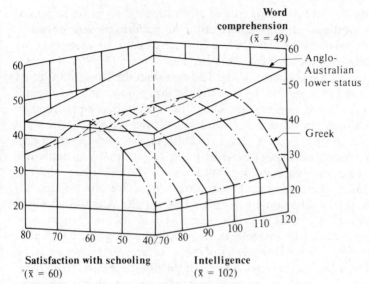

FIGURE 7.10 *Fitted-word comprehension scores in relation to intelligence and satisfaction with schooling*

(a) within Anglo-Australian middle and lower social-status groups there are different socialization processes operating to influence children's academic achievement; (b) for lower social-status families, ethnicity has a pervasive affect on the learning environments that families structure for their children; and (c) there are significant differences in the socialization processes operating within different ethnic groups to affect academic achievement. That is, ethnicity is a significant variable to be taken into account when examining relations between family environments and children's school-related characteristics. As Walberg and Marjoribanks (1976, p. 527) suggest, when investigating the relations between sets of predictors and cognitive performance 'correlational or causal relationships established for one group may not hold for other times, social classes, ethnic groups, or countries'.

Ethnicity, school attitudes, intelligence and academic achievement

In commenting on the Lesser-type studies of the relations between ethnicity and mental ability scores (see p. 162), Gordon (1976b, p. 167) proposes that the research 'seems to have neglected the non-cognitive factors in learning' and that the studies 'fail to study the compensatory role of motivation' (p. 171). He suggests that even though individuals' ability to perform certain cognitive tasks may not be extremely high, their desire to excel may be strong enough to enable them to persevere and master the field requiring the particular skill. The data from the Australian study are used in a brief analysis of the Gordon proposition. In Figure 7.11 the regression surfaces show the relation between academic adjustment to school and word knowledge at different intelligence levels. For the English children, at each level of intelligence, increments in adjustment scores are associated with sizeable increases in the word scores. For Southern Italian children increases in the attitude scores are not related to changes in achievement scores while for the Anglo-Australian children, only at high intelligence levels are increases in attitude scores related to increments in word knowledge performance. The differences in the shapes of these surfaces, and other surfaces not reported here, provide support for the contention that when attempting to understand variation in academic achievement it is necessary to include affective variables as well as measures of intellectual ability and of the environment (see Marjoribanks, 1978h).

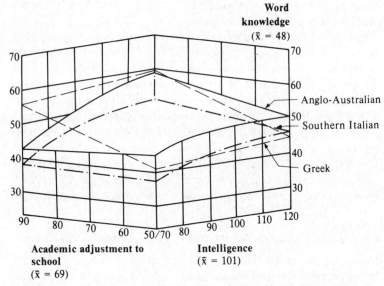

FIGURE 7.11 *Fitted-word knowledge scores in relation to academic adjustment to school and intelligence*

In Chapter 1 it was proposed that the environment surrounding a child may be depicted as a set of nested-situations ranging from global social environments such as social status and ethnicity to proximal social-psychological measures such as parents' aspirations and parents' press for English. Lewin's field theory in social psychology suggests that the proximal family variables may be considered as forming a differentiated network of interconnected systems. The findings of the present chapter suggest that, within the national contexts studied, the environmental regions surrounding children from English-speaking families may be defined as 'near' rather than 'remote' (see Hall and Lindzey, 1970), and that the boundaries of the regions are fluid and weak rather than rigid and strong. That is, each of the social-psychological environment variables that make up the family environment has an opportunity of interacting with the person variables of the child and also the possibility of influencing other environment variables. For non-Anglo children, within English-speaking contexts, the boundaries within the family environmental space of a child may be more rigid and firm, and some of the environment variables may be quite remote from the child. The findings of the analyses suggest that low press for English may, in a sense, encircle a child, restricting the effect of other family environment variables on academic achievement. For example, while non-English-speaking parents may have high aspirations and strong achievement-oriented values, the desired effect of these environment variables on children's outcomes may be tempered if a certain English language environment level is not established within the home. It is likely that press for English acts as a threshold variable in relation to the other 'remote' environment variables, such that until a certain level of press for English is attained other family measures have a reduced influence on the academic achievement of children who are operating in English-speaking classrooms. After the threshold level has been attained, then the other variables within the family environment may begin to exert a more significant influence on children's school-related outcomes. These conclusions, generated from the study of Canadian and Australian children, have educational policy implications such as whether bilingual and bidialectical programmes should be constructed within classrooms and for families. These and other curriculum challenges are considered in the following chapter.

8 Socialization influences on children's outcomes: conclusions

Technical and affective parent socialization influences on children's outcomes

Bidwell (1972, 1973) suggests that the socialization of children can be thought of as having two principal components: first, technical socialization, which attempts to change children's cognitions or involves 'developing intellective and motor skills and learning items of information and systems of thought that organize them' (Bidwell, 1972:1); second, affective socialization, which relates to changes in children's affective states. But Bidwell (1973, p. 415) says that the distinction between technical and affective socialization cannot be sustained empirically with much ease, for the two kinds of activities are interdependent.

Perhaps because of the difficulty in differentiating between the two components, research using refined family socialization measures has generally dealt with either cognitive performance (e.g. Bing, 1963; Dave, 1963; Wolf, 1964; Mosychuk, 1969; Walberg and Marjoribanks, 1976; Williams, 1976a), or with children's affective characteristics (e.g. Strodtbeck, 1958; Rosen, 1959; Weiss, 1974; Brook *et al.*, 1974; Bardsley, 1976). Socialization studies including both outcomes have typically used them as intervening variables in explanations of children's educational and occupational attainments (e.g. Alexander and Eckland, 1975; Featherman and Hauser, 1976; Porter, 1976; Portes and Wilson, 1976; Sewell and Hauser, 1975, 1976; Kerckhoff and Campbell, 1977; Otto and Alwin, 1977). These latter studies have usually adopted the restricted family measure of 'children's perceptions of parents' encouragement for further education'. As Epstein and McPartland (1977, p. 3) propose, 'earlier [socialization] research is limited in coverage of outcomes, and little has been done to chart the developmental nature and origins of the sex differences across grade levels on academic and non-academic outcomes. The studies have been restricted by the lack of proximate measures of family socialization practices.'

Path analytic study: Plowden data

Using the Plowden data (see Chapters 2 and 3) and path analytic techniques, the first section of the present chapter brings together many of the variables used in previous chapters to examine relations between refined parent socialization measures and children's cognitive and affective outcomes. The path model specified in Figure 8.1 indicates that parents' influences are assessed in each cohort at two time periods, which were four years apart. In the first survey, data were collected on family social status, sibsize, and children's reading achievement, while in the follow-up study assessments were made of teacher attitudes and children's peer group orientations, cognitive performance, and affective characteristics. Children's aspirations were measured in the senior-age cohort only, and peer group orientations in the senior and middle age groups.

The model proposes that parents' influences at time 1 are affected by the background factors, and that the two sets of family measures influence children's reading achievement. Parents' socialization influences at a later time are affected by the earlier family measures and by children's reading performance (e.g., Finn, 1972; Nolle, 1973; Shea, 1976). Placement of the 'intervening mechanisms', although more tenuous than the specification of the earlier variables, is guided by previous findings. West and Anderson (1976, p. 615) conclude, for example, that 'information' about children affects teachers' attitudes, which in turn influence children's academic achievement, where 'information' includes 'data about the student's past behavior, socio-economic status, sex, race, medical records, previous grades, previous achievement, and intelligence tests'. Brophy and Good (1970) propose that teachers' attitudes emerge as the result of the achievement or behaviours of students. A behavioural cycle is constructed by Braun (1976) linking teacher input and learner output. In the cycle, teacher attitudes are influenced by children's intelligence test scores, sex, social status, and previous achievement, and then teacher attitudes affect student self-expectations and learner outcomes. Therefore, in the path model, teacher attitudes are placed after peer-group orientations, intelligence, and family measures, as these are assumed to be data used by teachers in forming their attitudes about children.

In the Rehberg and Wisconsin-type models of school processes

Background	Parents' socialization influences (time 1)	Early reading performance	Parents' socialization influences (time 2)	Intervening mechanisms	Children's outcomes
Father's occupation	Parent-teacher relations		Parent-teacher relations		Mathematics achievement
Father's education	Parents' interests		Parents' interests	Peer-group orientations	English achievement
Family income	Parents' aspirations	Reading achievement	Parents' aspirations		Self-expectations
Housing index	Literacy of home		Literacy of home	Teacher attitudes	Educational and occupational aspirations
			Intelligence		
Sibsize	Parents' initiative		Parents' initiative		

FIGURE 8.1 *Specification of parents' socialization influences on children's cognitive and affective outcomes*

and educational attainment (see Shea, 1976), peer-influence variables typically are placed between early academic achievement and scholastic ability measures, and later assessments of achievement and aspirations. Similarly, in the present analysis, peer-group orientations have been situated between intelligence and the outcome variables. It is proposed that children of high ability from academically supportive families have weaker peer-group orientations than lower-ability children who lack parental support.

Five parent socialization variables which were measured for each cohort at both time periods are included in the analysis. The variables are labelled: relations between parents and teachers, parents' interest and support, responsibility and initiative taken by parents over child's education, literacy of the home, and parents' aspirations for the child. An affective socialization influence is defined as parents' support for a child's schooling without emphasizing achievement orientation, while technical socialization stresses cognitive-oriented behaviour. Although the five socialization indices have affective and technical components, parent-teacher relations and parents' interests are classified as affective influences, while parents' initiative and literacy are defined as technical socialization influences. Parents' aspirations could not easily be labelled as primarily affective or technical socialization, which suggests a restriction of the present measures or perhaps a limitation of the conceptual framework. No assumptions are made in the model regarding the causal relations between the achievement and affective outcomes. It is proposed, however, that the achievement outcomes are affected more strongly by the technical socialization and parents' aspiration indices than by the affective socialization scores, while the affective socialization and aspiration measures have stronger effects than the technical socialization influences on the affective outcomes.

Although most of the measures have been described in previous chapters they are presented here again for completeness of the study.

1 Family background variables: Five indicators of family background are assessed: father occupation and family income (each an eight-point scale); father education (five-point scale); a housing index (including whether the family owned its own dwelling, the amenities in the home, and crowding within the home); and the number of children within the family.

2 Parents' socialization influences: In the initial and follow-up Plowden studies a structured interview schedule was used to gather information about the children's family environments. Parents were interviewed in their homes by government social survey interviewers. As already indicated, five socialization variables which were assessed within each cohort during both surveys were chosen for the present study. Each socialization scale consists of six to eight items. The following list includes the labels used for the scales with some sample items provided to indicate the nature of the measures: (a) responsibility and initiative taken by parents over child's education (whether parents had talked to teachers about reading methods used, asked for work for child to do or how to help the child at home, discussed educational matters with principal); (b) parents' interest and support (whether husband helps with the control of the child, whether parents do things with the child at weekends, whether husband takes an interest in how child is progressing at school); (c) literacy of the home (number of books in the home, whether parents read, whether child has library books at home); (d) relations between parents and teachers (whether parents are happy with the arrangements for seeing teachers, feel teachers are interested in what they think about their child's education, feel teachers would prefer to keep parents out of the school); and (e) educational and occupational aspirations (parents want child to stay on at school, to have a professional occupation, to take university entrance examinations).

3 Teacher attitudes: A scale developed by the National Foundation for Educational Research in England was administered to teachers, during the follow-up survey, to assess teachers' attitudes towards the children's school-related behaviour. The scale is of a Likert-type format and requires teachers to rate their students on ten items, such as whether they thought the student was a hard worker, participated in class and school activities, concentrated on schoolwork, was obedient in class, was restless in class and aggressive in school. A teacher attitude score was obtained by summing the scores on the scale items.

4 Peer-group orientations: During the follow-up study parents of senior and middle age cohort children were asked to assess children on 20 items of the form, whether the child: goes around with a group, wants to stay out late at night, spends most spare time at home, dresses up to look older, wants to go on holidays

with friends, and spends many evenings a week out with friends. An orientation measure was obtained by summing the scores on the 20 items.

5 Cognitive performance: In the follow-up survey the children in the three age-groups were tested using the Alice Heim general intelligence test (AH4), the Vernon graded mathematics test, and the Watts-Vernon English comprehension test. During the first survey the senior children were assessed on the Watts-Vernon reading test, and the middle and junior groups were tested using the N.S. 45 reading test, devised by the National Foundation for Educational Research in England.

6 Affective characteristics: Scales constructed by the National Foundation for Educational Research were used in the second survey to measure children's affective characteristics. For the senior cohort, children's educational and occupational aspirations and self-expectations were assessed; in the other two cohorts, self-expectations were measured. The scales are of a Likert-type format, each with 10 items. In the aspirations scale, questions assessed: what academic level the student wanted to attain in English and mathematics, what school examinations the student wanted to take, type of occupation desired, age the student wanted to leave school, how important the student thought it was to stay on at school, whether the student wanted to undertake tertiary education, and how important the student thought it was to do well at school. Included in the self-expectation scale were items such as: all in all I think that I am a failure, on the whole I am satisfied with myself, parents never listen to what young people say because they think they know best, most grown-ups say one thing and do another, no matter how grown-up you are adults always treat you like kids, other people always seem to be able to do things better than I can.

Thus the path study examines the effects of parents' socialization influences on English children's achievement and affective outcomes when measures of social status, previous achievement, intelligence, peer-group orientations, and teacher attitudes are included in the analysis. Because of space limitations, the zero-order correlations and structural coefficients for the path models are not presented. The simple correlations replicate, however, much prior research showing that social status and sibsize have moderate relations to children's cognitive and affective outcomes. Also, the background measures: (a) have more significant associations with teacher attitudes in the junior and middle cohorts than in the senior group; and (b) are generally not related to peer-group orientations in the senior group but have moderate relations, especially for boys, in the middle cohort. Positive teacher attitudes and weaker peer-group orientations are associated with: (a) supportive parent socialization influences and high intelligence and reading scores; and (b) higher outcome scores.

The academic achievement scores generally have moderate to high relations to the technical socialization influences and parents' aspirations and low to moderate associations with the affective socialization measures, while the affective outcomes have low to moderate associations with the socialization indices. Although the zero-order correlations provide tentative support for the proposition that achievement outcomes are related more strongly to technical socialization influences and parents' aspirations than to affective socialization influences, the initial findings do not provide support for the allied proposition that affective characteristics are related more strongly to affective socialization influences.

In the first estimation of the path model all predetermined variables were included as regressors. Independent variables for which path coefficients were not significant were deleted from the equations and then each equation was re-estimated. The coefficients for the resulting models are the ones reported upon in this analysis. Multi-collinearity among the parent socialization variables is considered generally not to be excessive, as few correlations approached 0.30. In each cohort at time 2, however, there are associations of approximately 0.40 between parents' aspirations and literacy, and these correlations complicate interpretations of the models. Rather than trace through the many paths in the models, general patterns of findings are presented and discussed.

Background variables, parent socialization influences (time 1), and reading achievement

Except for parent-teacher relations, the parent socialization indices are influenced moderately by the social background factors, with literacy of the home being the most affected variable. The direct effects of social status and sibsize on reading achievement are generally mediated by the early parent socialization influences. Sibsize continues, however, to have a direct effect on girls' reading performance in the junior and senior cohorts. Literacy is the only socialization measure that has direct effects on reading scores in the junior and middle cohorts. For the senior children the network of direct parent influences on reading becomes more complex. Aspirations and literacy affect reading, with parent-teacher relations also influencing the girls' scores. Thus, in the early elementary school years, reading is affected primarily by the literacy of the home, which is related to family social background. By the end of elementary school, parents' aspirations also begin to develop as an important socializing influence for reading performance.

Background variables, reading achievement, and parent socialization influences (time 1 (t_1), time 2 (t_2))

Relations between parent socialization influences at time 2 and the preceding variables become increasingly complex with increases in the ages of the children. During the second survey the senior children were approximately 15, the middle children 12, and the junior group children 11 years old. Although only one year separates the junior and middle cohorts, the latter group have made the transition to secondary school. In the junior and middle cohorts, parent-teacher relations, responsibility, and parents' interest are influenced mainly by the corresponding socialization variables measured four years earlier. Parents' aspirations (t_2), in these two younger cohorts, are affected directly by reading, prior aspirations, and social background factors, while literacy (t_2), in the junior group and for middle group girls, is influenced by social background, prior literacy, and reading achievement. Literacy in the middle boys' cohort is not influenced directly by reading performance.

In the senior cohort, the technical socialization influences and parents' aspirations are affected directly by networks of earlier socialization measures and background variables. Aspirations (t_2) and literacy (t_2), in boys' families, are related also to reading performance. The findings suggest that parents' socialization influences, especially technical socialization and aspirations, become increasingly susceptible to change as children move from elementary through secondary school.

Intervening mechanisms

1 Background variables, socialization influences, reading and intelligence   Background variables, literacy (t_2), aspirations (t_2), and reading have direct effects on intelligence in the junior cohort. In the middle cohort the specified model is more efficient in accounting for variation in the intelligence scores of girls than of boys. The girls' scores are related directly to social background, reading, parents' responsibility (t_2), and aspirations (t_2). For boys, the effects of the early socialization variables are transmitted through reading scores and the only direct influences on intelligence are sibsize and reading. In the senior cohort, girls' intelligence scores are affected directly by reading and both measures of parents' aspirations. Senior boys' intelligence is affected by the technical socialization measures of literacy (t_2) and responsibility (t_2), and also aspirations. The influence of reading achievement on boys' intelligence is mediated by the later parent socialization influences.

It was suggested earlier that with increases in children's ages parents' aspirations become a more powerful direct socializing influence on children's reading achievement. The present analysis indicates similar relations between the socialization variables and intelligence. That is, the findings suggest the proposition: 'that as children pass from elementary on through secondary school, parents' educational and occupational aspirations for their children become the most dominant parent social-psychological influence on children's cognitive performance.' In Chapter 7 the analysis of families from different Australian ethnic groups indicated, however, the danger of generalizing such findings to other social groups. The latter study suggested that for non-English-speaking families the effects of high aspirations on children's outcomes were mediated by the language environment of the home.

2 Peer-group orientations   Only a small proportion of the variance in peer-group orientations is accounted for in the models. Generally, the results suggest that higher-ability children, having parents who spend time with them in activities at weekends and in the evenings, express lower peer-group orientations than do other children. Parents' aspirations (t_2) have indirect effects, through intelligence, on the peer-group scores. Also in the senior cohort there are direct relations between peer-group orientations and literacy (t_2) in boys' families, and parents' responsibility (t_2) in girls' families. Thus families with strong parent-child interaction, involving affective and technical components, have children who are likely to indicate lower peer-group orientations than children from families without such involvement.

3 Teacher attitudes are predicted more strongly in the junior cohort models than for children attending secondary schools. Such a finding is not unexpected, because of the different teaching structures between elementary and secondary schools. In the junior cohort, positive teacher attitudes are affected directly by favourable reading achievement and intelligence scores and also by supportive parent socialization influences. For the middle-group children, who are in their first year of secondary school, teachers' attitudes towards girls are influenced directly by prior cognitive performance, while for boys the attitudes are affected directly by intelligence, parents' interest, and peer-group orientations.

Strong peer-group orientations have a slightly depressing influence on teachers' attitudes towards the senior children. Attitudes towards senior girls are affected directly also by intelligence and parent socialization indices, and for boys by parents' aspirations and parent-teacher relations. The attitudes assessed in the present analysis are normative, reflecting dispositions related to children's adherence to the norms of classroom behaviour. The results suggest that the normative attitudes of teachers are influenced by both ascribed and achieved characteristics of children, supporting the propositions of Brophy and Good (1970), Braun (1976) and West and Anderson (1976) that teachers use a variety of cognitive and social background data to form their attitudes about children.

Outcome variables

1 Academic achievement   The predetermined variables that have direct effects on academic achievement may be placed into two categories, depending on the strength of the direct effects. These categories are labelled dominant and subsidiary. For girls, the variables with dominant effects on academic achievement in the junior cohort are intelligence, reading, and teacher attitudes; in the middle cohort, intelligence and reading; and in the senior cohort, intelligence, reading, and aspirations (t_2) for mathematics, and intelligence and aspirations (t_2) for English. The dominant variables for boys in the junior cohort are reading and intelligence for English, and reading, intelligence, and teacher attitudes for mathematics; intelligence and parents' aspirations are the dominant achievement-related variables in the middle and senior cohorts. The subsidiary variables for achievement include primarily technical socialization influences; aspirations and reading when they are not acting as a dominant variable, and, within some groups, peer-group orientations. Therefore the dominant variables influencing academic achievement are intelligence, reading, and parents' aspirations, with teacher attitudes operating in the junior cohort. In the middle and senior cohorts, reading is a relatively more important influence on the academic outcomes in the girls' samples, while intelligence and parents' aspirations are more important variables for boys than for girls.

2 Affective characteristics   No clear pattern of relations exists between the predetermined variables and the self-expectation scores, across the cohorts. The dominant variables for girls in the: (a) junior cohort, are parents' aspirations (t_2) and intelligence; (b) middle group, intelligence, reading, and parents' responsibilities (t_1); and (c) for the senior children, teacher attitudes and parents' interest (t_1). The dominant variables for boys in the: (a) junior group are intelligence, aspirations (t_2), and parents' interest (t_2), (b) middle cohort, teacher attitudes and parents' aspirations (t_2); and in (c) the senior group, teacher attitudes, intelligence, and peer-group orientations. The subsidiary variables include a combination of technical and affective socialization influences. In general, parents' aspirations and variables from the intervening mechanisms are the dominant influences on children's self-expectations.

Parents' aspirations, intelligence, and reading are the dominant influences on children's aspirations in the senior cohort. The subsidiary effects are mainly technical socialization influences and background measures. Reading is relatively more important in the girls' sample, while parents' aspirations are more important for boys than for girls. These latter findings of the relative influences of variables between girls and boys are similar to the results for sex-related differences in the relations between the predetermined variables and academic achievement.

The analysis of children in the three age cohorts suggests that as boys pass from elementary on through secondary school, parents' aspirations become an increasingly important determinant of academic achievement and affective characteristics. Parents' aspirations not only have dominant effects on boys' outcomes, but they also influence the intervening mechanisms, in the path models, which in turn have subsidiary influences on the outcome scores. Aspirations at time 2 are related strongly to parents' socialization influences at time 1, especially in the senior cohort. Therefore, to explain the variation in the cognitive and affective characteristics of boys, it is necessary to account for family differences in the early parent socialization influences. But the analysis indicates that the early parent socialization influences are only moderately related to social status and sibsize. Other studies also have shown that parents' aspirations or parental encouragement have only a moderate association with the social status of families (e.g., Duncan *et al.*, 1968; Hauser, 1973; Kerckhoff and Huff, 1974; Alexander and Eckland, 1974, 1975; Sewell and Hauser, 1976). Thus if social-structural forces are defined in relation to status indicators, then the findings for the boys support only in part the proposition by Woelfel and Haller (1971, p. 85), that 'social structural factors determine the expectations of an individual's significant others, which in turn exert causal influences over the person's attitudes. These attitudes then exert directive forces over both academic performance and later educational and occupational attainments.' The results indicate the need to examine social-structural forces other than social-status indicators if differences in parents' socialization influences are to be more fully explained. Social-status measures fail to assess completely the complexity of the social-structural forces that affect the educational influence of families on children. They do not measure, for example, the social tensions which may exist between schools and families from different status groups (e.g., Bernstein, 1977), the variation in cultural capital between families (e.g., Bourdieu, 1973), the social control that different societal groups exert over the development of school curricula (e.g., Davies, 1976); nor do they assess the social power which is available to different groups of families to influence resource allocation in education (e.g., Byrne *et al.*, 1975).

For girls, the present study suggests that prior reading performance has dominant effects on later academic achievement and affective measures, and indirect effects on these outcomes through parent socialization influences and the intervening mechanisms. But the model shows that background factors and parent socialization influences (at time 1) have only modest effects on the reading scores. Again, the findings indicate the need for more sensitive measures of socialization influences and social-structural forces if variation in children's early reading achievement and thus in later cognitive and affective outcomes are to be explained.

From the different sex-related variables that are found to affect the cognitive and affective measures, the study provides partial support for prior research which proposes that the educational selection and allocation processes of girls and boys differ. The findings suggest, somewhat tentatively, that the educational progress of girls and boys may be defined in relation to two general models, which may be labelled ascribed and meritocratic. In the ascribed model, factors such as social status, parent socialization influences, peer-group orientations and teacher attitudes have more important direct effects than previous academic achievement in determining later achievement and school-related affective outcomes. A meritocratic model suggests that school outcomes are related more strongly to previous academic scores than to ascribed socialization influences. The results suggest that boys' educational progress may be aligned more closely to the ascribed model while girls' progress is related more to a meritocratic model.

Bidwell (1972, 1973) proposed that the socialization of children could be defined in terms of the two components of technical and affective socialization. The present study supports Bidwell's claim of the strong interdependence of the two influences. For girls, self-expectations are related directly to affective socialization influences and parents' aspirations, but typically both the achievement and affective outcomes are influenced mainly by the technical socialization and aspiration influences. Possibly the measures of the technical influences are more valid than those for affective socialization. But perhaps it may not be possible to construct indices which can accurately differentiate between the two highly interrelated components of socialization. Although the study shows that parents' aspirations, intelligence, and reading are generally the dominant influences on the outcomes, the intervening mechanisms of teacher attitudes and peer-group orientations also are potentially important variables. That is, the results of this longitudinal analysis support the findings in previous chapters, that any attempts to influence school-related outcomes need to examine children's individual characteristics and measures of family, school, and peer-group learning environments, as well as more global social environment measures. The concluding section of the chapter considers some of the implications for educational practice of the research reported in this book.

Implications of research for educational practice

Development of family–school learning environments

Environments for children's learning will become more favourable when parents and teachers act as partners in the learning process. While such a claim is easy to state, home-school programmes are extremely difficult to construct and implement. Readers are referred to the programmes developed in the British Educational Priority Area Projects for documentation of the practical hazards, but also of the rewards, for those developing learning environments that involve both parents and teachers (e.g., Halsey, 1972; Smith, 1975). Also in a Report prepared for the Secretary of State for Education and Science in Great Britain, entitled *A Language for Life*, Bullock (1975, p. 71) indicates that 'It is no use pretending that the parent can slip easily into the learning situation. There are adjustments to be made and sensitivities on both sides to be respected.' The great delicacy required when establishing parent-teacher learning environ-ments is captured by the following statement in the Report (p. 59):

> They [the parents] do not recognize their own potential in furthering his [the child's] educational development, and not uncommonly they are apprehensive that any attempt to 'teach' him or introduce him to books will conflict with the school's methods and thus confuse him. Moreover, there may be the natural suspicion on the part of the mother that a home visitor is bringing with her a critical attitude to the child's upbringing or the conditions of the home. . . . The father,

whose co-operation is vital, may let his judgment of the situation be coloured by his experiences with 'officialdom' in other contexts. All this makes it an exercise requiring great tact and particular qualities on the part of the visitor. . . . The visitor will have to be tolerant and understanding, imposing no judgment and hinting no censure. She will be setting up learning situations which are designed to advance the child's linguistic and cognitive development, and she will therefore need a good understanding of the processes at work.

Throughout the book the analyses show that there exists a complex network of interrelated family environment variables that are associated with children's cognitive and affective outcomes. These include social-psychological process variables such as parents' educational and occupational aspirations for the child (or parents' pressure), parents' aspirations for themselves, literacy of the family, parent-teacher interactions, parent-child activeness, and parents' reinforcement of their education activities and expectations; as well as family structure characteristics and measures of social status and ethnicity. But the family environment variables which are related to children's school performances are associated also with the psychological or 'person' characteristics of the children. Most existing family-school schemes have adopted a situationism or trait model rather than an interactionism framework of analysis, which has resulted in the programmes achieving only moderate successes. Projects constructed to create more stimulating and exciting family-classroom learning environments for children need to consider the individual child's abilities, present achievement levels, attitudinal and personality characteristics. Also the analyses in the book suggest that the development of family-school environments to change boys' school attitudes and academic performances may not be the appropriate environments for girls. And it must not be assumed that a programme devised for parents and children belonging to one particular social group can easily be adapted for families within other social groups, or indeed, even for families within the same social grouping. There exists great variation in family environments within and between social-status and ethnic groups. In the study of the Australian ethnic groups reported in Chapter 7, for example, Marjoribanks asked the following three questions:

(a) How much education would you really like your child to receive if at all possible?
(b) What kind of job would you really like your child to have after she/he grows up, if at all possible?
(c) How much education do you *really* expect your child to receive?

The percentages associated with the alternate responses to the questions are shown in Table 8.1, and they reflect the variability in

TABLE 8.1 *Parents' responses to expectation questions*

		Anglo-Australian middle status [a]	Percentage of parents responding to alternative — lower social-status groups				
	Possible response		Anglo-Australian	English	Greek	Southern Italian	Serbo-Croatian
Question 1	Postgraduate education	10[b]	5	3	7	6	10
	Graduate from university	30	19	27	66	40	27
	At least some university	13	8	12	7	28	5
	High school plus some professional training college	22	17	14	9	12	18
	Finish high school or, as much as possible	25	49	43	12	14	40
	Leave school as soon as possible	—	2	1	—	1	—
Question 2	Job requiring:						
	postgraduate education	11	6	6	29	21	23
	university degree	15	14	14	32	29	5
	high school graduation and some college training	24	18	16	13	10	18
	the completion of high school	9	15	13	5	10	14
	some high school education	8	17	11	6	12	18
	little education, or parents say 'I don't care'	34	30	40	15	19	23
Question 3	Postgraduate education	4	1	1	3	4	5
	Graduate from university	22	9	11	42	23	14
	At least some university	9	3	10	6	24	5
	High school plus some professional training college	26	20	17	12	17	18
	Finish high school or, as much as possible	37	57	51	36	27	59
	Leave school as soon as possible	2	10	9	1	4	—

a Numbers in each group include: Anglo-Australian middle status (140), and lower social-status Anglo-Australian (250), English (120), Greek (170), Southern Italian (120), and Serbo-Croatian (50).
b All percentages rounded to nearest whole number.

environments that parents create for their children, within and between social groups. A larger proportion of Greek and Southern Italian parents, for example, express higher educational and occupational expectations than do parents from: (a) lower social-status Serbo-Croatian, English, and Anglo-Australian groups, and (b) the middle social-status group. The data for the third question reveal the variation in responses that can emerge when questions are phrased in a slightly different form. When the parents were asked about the education they 'really' expected their child to receive, the proportion of responses indicating university education dropped markedly. But the Greek group continues to have the highest percentage of parents suggesting university education for their children, with the Southern Italian pattern of answers approximating more closely the responses of the middle social-status Anglo-Australians. In Table 8.1, the findings also reveal the great variation in answers between families within the same social group. For the middle social-status group, for example, 26 per cent of the parents responded that they really expected their child to graduate from university or receive post-graduate education, while 39 per cent of the same social group expressed the expectation that their child would either just complete high school or leave school as soon as possible. And, in the lower social-status Anglo-Australian and English groups, 10 and 12 per cent of the parents *really* expected their child to graduate from university, while 67 and 60 per cent, respectively, expressed high school completion or lower educational expectations.

Family–classroom bilingual or bidialectical learning environments

The Australian data also show the possible complexities confronting educators who contemplate the establishment of family-classroom bilingual or bidialectical learning environments. Australia, like many countries, is in the process of accelerating the adjustment of its educational programmes to accommodate the special needs of non-English-speaking minority groups. But education authorities are in the difficult situation of not knowing what types of language schemes should be adopted, nor indeed, what programmes parents want for their children. In the study of Australian families, the following questions were asked as an initial gauge of parents' feelings for bilingual curriculum in schools:

1 When children who are about 10 years old arrive in Australia from non-English-speaking countries, into which of the following school situations do you think the children should be placed?

2 When children start school at the age of 5 or 6 and they are from non-English-speaking Australian ethnic families, in what language do you think the children should be taught? (The question was asked in two sections: first, in relation to children who have just arrived in Australia; and second, for children who have been in Australia for most of their lives.)

3 The same question as above was asked in relation to children who are about 10 or 11 years old and had: (a) just arrived in Australia; or (b) been in the country for most of their lives.

The questions were asked of English-speaking parents as well as those from Greek, Serbo-Croatian and Southern Italian families. In Table 8.2, the findings show significant variation in the responses within and between groups. Responses to Question 1 indicate, for example, that over 60 per cent of Greek parents but only 38 per cent of Southern Italians suggest that children should be placed in either special classes or schools to learn English. Responses for the three Anglo-groups are quite similar to each other, with approximately 60 per cent of the parents suggesting that the children should be placed in ordinary classes with some special English teaching.

Answers to Questions 2 and 3 reveal that for children who have just arrived from non-English-speaking countries, parents from the Anglo-groups support to a greater extent the teaching of the children mainly in their own language, than do the parents of the children themselves. Within the ethnic groups, the findings also show a great deal of variance regarding the language approach that should be adopted in classroom instruction. The results from Tables 8.1 and 8.2 help to reinforce the claim made earlier, that when devising parent-classroom environment projects, the programmes should attempt to assess the psychological and social needs of individual parents and children.

The findings from the Australian study replicate, in part, a study by Hoover (1975), who examined the attitudes of Black American parents to the use of Black English in the classroom. Initially the investigation was generated by the conflict between those

TABLE 8.2 *Parents' responses to language curriculum course questions*

		Percentage of parents responding to alternative					
		Anglo-Australian middle status	lower social-status groups				
	Possible response		Anglo-Australian	English	Greek	Southern Italian	Serbo-Croatian
Question 1 (10-yr-olds)	In special classes set up to teach English to ethnic children	7[a]	5	7	26	14	18
	The local school but placed in special classes where the children spend most of their time learning English	25	32	26	35	24	27
	Local school and placed in ordinary classes but with some special English teaching	64	58	63	37	52	32
	Local school and placed in ordinary classes with no special attention	3	3	3	1	10	23
	Local school but with the children taught mainly in their own language	1	1	1	–	1	–
Question 2 (5- or 6-yr-olds)	Totally in their own language	2 (–)	– (–)	4 (1)	– (–)	3 (3)	5 (–)
	Mainly in their own language with some English	9 (2)	12 (1)	17 (3)	4 (2)	3 (3)	– (–)
	About half English and half in the ethnic-language	37 (13)	32 (12)	21 (13)	33 (24)	38 (28)	36 (18)
	Mainly English and some ethnic-language	27 (31)	27 (28)	23 (26)	45 (35)	35 (31)	– (5)
	All English	25 (54)	29 (60)	34 (57)	18 (38)	22 (36)	59 (7
Question 3 (10- or 11-yr-olds)	Totally in their own language	2 (1)	1 (–)	1 (1)	1 (–)	2 (1)	5 (–
	Mainly in their own language with some English	14 (19)	14 (–)	10 (–)	2 (–)	3 (3)	– (–
	About half English and half in the ethnic-language	29 (19)	29 (5)	27 (–)	23 (17)	35 (28)	36 (
	Mainly English and some ethnic-language	23 (48)	26 (22)	29 (23)	53 (51)	37 (37)	18 (
	All English	32 (12)	31 (73)	33 (76)	21 (32)	23 (32)	41 (8.

[a] All percentages rounded to nearest whole number.
Percentages in parentheses refer to responses related to children who have been in Australia most of their lives while the other figures refer to children who have only just arrived in Australia.

linguists and educators who favour the use of Black English in the classroom and those who are opposed. Hoover suggests that parents 'accept Africanized English in the listening and speaking channels, but not in the reading and writing channels; they accept Africanized English in the home and some community contexts, but generally not in the schools; they accept Africanized English in informal settings, but seldom in formal ones' (p. 101). She concludes that 'it is simplistic to make assumptions about "Black parents' views" or "Middle-class Blacks" without supportive data' (p. 102), and she observes that:

> Many of the reasons why parents objected to Africanized English in some situations can be traced to the racism in our society. . . . Black parents are going to continue to prefer a 'mainstream' language variety in 'mainstream' contexts as long as speech continues to be one of the variables used by employers to deny Blacks jobs, which is a form of racism' (pp. 107–8).

Recommendations of the Hoover investigation suggest that teachers need to be informed more of Black English so that they can better understand the children, and that parents should become involved in adult education programmes in which they become familiar with methodologies of teaching reading and other language arts to speakers of Black English. In a Report to the British Home Secretary, the Community Relations Commission makes similar observations on education of immigrant children in Britain. It is proposed (Tucker, 1974, p. 10):

> That the educational performance of pupils in the school is to no small extent the result of experiences, stimulation and support received at home has gained widespread acceptance. Unfortunately its educational implications are only beginning to be worked out. Practical problems facing school staff of involving parents of immigrants and the difficulty of communicating with non-English-speaking parents is real.

Two types of recommendation are suggested, including the involvement of parents within the school and the need for a more sustained service linking families and schools. The Report goes on to propose that 'a scheme of educational home visits should provide a means of helping the language development of many adults in the minority community, for inadequate [English] parental language can directly and indirectly impair pupil performance' (p. 10).

In programmes of language development for children and

parents, Labov *et al.* (1968b, p. 345) warn, however, of the differences in approaching bilingual and bidialectical education. They suggest that it seems clear that any interference between Non-Standard Negro English (NNE) and Standard English (SE) is more difficult to handle than bilingual education, because the two grammars are so similar. 'Problems of teaching English to speakers of Italian are of a different order from those of teaching the rules to SE and NNE speakers. The Italian speakers have no fixed rules of English structure, but the NNE students have already internalized a set of English rules from earliest childhood.' Similarly, comments by Bullock (1975, p. 287) on West Indian children in England emphasize the complexities that confront educators when structuring programmes for families from different social-status and ethnic groups. It is stated, that for West Indian children:

> The language of childhood and of the home is an English-based Creole, a variety of dialect of English. Jamaican Creole has been extensively studied . . . [and] it is recognized by linguists as being a well-developed language, with a sound system, grammar, and vocabulary of its own, and capable – like other varieties of English – of being used extensively and richly. However, the West Indian situation is very complex, since in most of its schools in the islands a standard form of English, very close to Standard English in England, is the medium of formal education and is the language the children are expected to read and write. There are already, then, linguistic difficulties for pupils and teachers alike in the schools of Jamaica and other Caribbean islands; and there are difficulties, if of a rather different order, for the West Indian children at school in Britain. For most of them the language of infancy and of the home will almost certainly be a form of dialect, though some members of the family will be able to switch to a more standard dialect for certain purposes.

The Report, *A Language for Life,* then makes a claim that may be appropriate for other non-English-speaking families and for children from lower social-status groups, and which is likely to provide one of the most difficult constraints on the development of teacher-parent schemes. It is proposed that (p. 287):

> The child attending school will be likely to have teachers who know no Creole at all and who will expect him to understand

and respond to a dialect that may at first be very strange to him. The teacher's ignorance of Creole, and perhaps his traditional attitudes to non-standard forms of English, will tend to make him dismiss Creole features in the West Indian child's speech as incorrect or 'sloppy' English.

Any scheme which attempts to involve parents, either within the family setting or in the classroom, requires a detailed planning of objectives and the sensitive selection of teachers. It cannot be expected that all teachers will want to participate, especially initially, or have the skills which enable them to operate in such a sharing context. But it is considered desirable that classroom teachers rather than specially trained 'social workers', who are not involved with day-to-day classroom activities, be the people involved in the interactions with parents. (See Gordon (1968) for a review of early American parent-teacher programmes.) Making contact with parents is a difficult task and it is certainly not easy to sustain parent-teacher sharing relationships over a long period. In Marjoribanks' many interviews with parents, however, there typically was a genuine desire by parents to talk about their children's education and to learn more about the teaching of subjects such as English and 'new' mathematics. Transforming these expressed desires and attitudes into actual parental behaviours is, of course, a complex assignment. Parents need to be assured that the time they devote to any programme will have benefits for them and their children, while teachers need to be convinced that the investment involved in creating parent-teacher sharing environments will be related to gains in children's school outcomes.

Family–school learning environment projects

The most successful projects may be those that are: (a) generated by individual schools rather than by larger educational authorities; and (b) involve schools in which the principals exhibit an academic understanding of the processes of children's cognitive and linguistic development, express great care and delicacy in their relations to children, parents, and teachers, and sustain a continuing vitality within the school for the programme. Walberg *et al.* (1976, pp. 2–3) have provided a detailed assessment of the relations between an intensified parenting project and the reading achievement scores of black, inner-city children from a large elementary school in Chicago. The programme was initiated and sustained by the teachers of the school. During the spring of 1975, a joint parent-school staff steering committee formulated seven goals which were directed at both the technical and affective socialization practices of families and schools. The goals were: 'to increase parents' desire to aid children in achieving, to acquaint parents with the means of determining what the child is doing, to increase parents' awareness of the reading process, to establish and/or improve parent-school-community relations, to develop enthusiasm on the part of parents and children toward higher achievement, to work continuously to create a classroom atmosphere that fosters enthusiasm for education, and to evaluate the ability of the programme as to its effectiveness in influencing reading achievement.' Although the goals are quite global and extensive, it was found that, for reading achievement, classes whose parents were intensively involved in the scheme gained approximately 1.1 grade equivalents over the length of the project, while classes whose parents were less intensively involved gained only 0.5 grade equivalents.

In teacher education programmes, both pre-service and in-service, teachers need to be made aware of: (a) the mechanisms of parent-teacher projects that have been successes or failures; (b) the nature of the social-psychological processes that operate in families, classrooms, and peer groups to affect children's school-related performances; (c) the skills and knowledge required to create adult-oriented curricula; (d) the psychological and linguistic processes operating to influence children's cognitive and language development; and (e) the possibilities, but also the difficulties, in attempting to affect family characteristics such as parents' aspirations, the reading habits of the family, parent-child activeness within the family, or parents' achievement-oriented values.

Educational projects that have been structured to assist parents have often been criticized as supporting a cultural deficit theory of education in which the blame for children's school failure is placed upon families and the child, rather than directed at the school. In the early 1970s a theory of cultural differences gained support, suggesting that children from different social groups are not 'deficient' but 'different', and that it is the responsibility of schools to adjust their curricula to match the needs of the children. A new philosophy is now developing, especially in relation to black children in the United States, which has been labelled 'Excellence', and focuses on academic programmes, strict discipline, and high expectations on the part of teachers and school administrators. Proponents of the 'Excellence' approach to school curricula consider that those who are followers of the cultural difference school of thought are 'sentimental egalitarians'. That is, they are those 'who believe in equality on a sentimental basis, ignoring racism and other intervening variables' (Hoover, 1975, p. 9). No matter which theoretical stance an educator chooses to adopt, it is an assumption of this book that as shared family-classroom environments become more stimulating and exciting, then learning experiences of children will become more enjoyable and rewarding. But it is proposed that individualized learning environment programmes need to be matched for children with different individual characteristics, and that no assumptions should be made about children's family environments merely on the basis of social-status or ethnic group classifications.

In future research on the relations between family environments and children's development, measurements of both environments and behaviours can be further improved. Also, if new statistical and methodological techniques are used, such as conducting ethnographic studies to embellish the structural analyses of environments, using longitudinal analyses, testing different mathematical forms of relationships, and constructing more refined environment measures, then it is likely that our understanding of the causal relations between environmental conditions and behavioural development will be enhanced. While the present book has explored a relatively narrow range of children's behaviours it is hoped that subsequent research will expand the range of outcome measures. As Walberg and Marjoribanks (1976, p. 548) have claimed, 'Compared to the variety of agricultural, business, manufacturing, and health indexes, some issued periodically for many decades, data on children's traits, precious though they are, are indeed spotty and unreliable and have not been thoroughly analyzed.' Obviously we need to know much more about how children's characteristics are changing and how educators might assist in that change. Therefore, we need to continue our research on how families, classroom, and peer-group environments interact with each other and with person variables, to influence the meanings that children give to their own learning environments and how they affect children's school-related outcomes.

The findings in this book have identified a set of environmental correlates of children's performances and have shown that any appreciable changes in performance will require sizeable adjustments in the environments that surround children, at different levels of person variables. Generally the adjustments will have to be much more significant than those attempted in most educational research projects to date. It is worth repeating the claim by Halsey (1975, p. 17), that:

> The association of social class [and ethnicity] with educational achievement will not therefore be explained by a theory or eliminated by a policy which falls short of including changes in public support for learning in the family and neighbourhood, the training of teachers, the production of relevant curricula, the fostering of parental participation, the raising of standards of housing and employment prospects, and, above all, the allocation of educational resources.

The analyses of Marjoribanks's and related research indicates that we are still in need of an adequate social theory to account for children's learning. The present book has been an attempt to explore one of the major elements that would contribute to such a proposed theory.

Appendix
Family environment schedule

The following schedule is presented for researchers who may wish to adapt it in studies assessing aspects of the social-psychological environments of families. As indicated in the text, the schedule and variations of it have been used by Marjoribanks in analyses of the environmental correlates of the cognitive and affective characteristics of Australian children. Therefore the wording needs to be adjusted for use within other national settings.

Part A provides general information about the family and an indication of how satisfied parents are with their child's schooling. In Part B, a number of environment variables are assessed:

1 Parents' aspirations for the child (questions 1–13)
2 Parents' aspirations for themselves (14–18)
3 Concern for the use of language (19–42, 46, 47)
4 Parents' reinforcement of aspirations (48–58)
5 Knowledge of child's educational progress (50, 51, 60–3, 73)
6 Family involvement in educational activities (44, 45, 48, 59, 59, 64–71)
7 Press for independence (43, 72, 74, 75)
8 Value orientations (78)

The concern for language measure may be limited to a press for English scale in which only those questions relating to the use of English are adopted. Or the schedule may be expanded to include a separate press for second language scale. For the latter scale, the second language designation is substituted for English, in the relevant language questions.

For some questions, rating scales have been constructed by combining responses from different sets of questions. Researchers may use the composite rating scales or develop separate environment scale scores from the individual items that make up the scales. Other groupings of items may be generated from further analyses of the items.

The present scales have been generated from a consideration of both press-needs theory and a social learning theory of family environments.

Family environment interview schedule

To the parents: The present set of questions are part of a study examining relationships that exist between families and the schools to which families send their children.

We would like to obtain some information from you regarding your feelings about the school your child (name the child) attends and to find out some of your thoughts about education in general. It is hoped that the kind of information that is collected in the study will be used by schools when they are planning their programmes.

The research guarantees anonymity of the family.

Request: It is essential to have a very accurate response to each question. However, if you feel that a question is an invasion of your privacy, feel free not to answer it. We would rather have no response to some questions than inaccurate responses. Your answers to the questions should be related to (name the child).

Thank you very much for your participation in the study.

The first set of questions deal with certain aspects of the family, in order to provide some general information for the study. Then the following questions are about your child (name the child) and the school she/he attends.

For the interviewer:
(a) Each question should be asked of *all* parents, including Anglo-Australian parents, except where it is obvious from a previous answer that a question doesn't apply.
(b) The questions are associated with numbers. Place a *circle* (not a tick) around the number which is closest to the answer supplied.
(c) In the questionnaire, whenever x appears would you substitute the child's name.
(d) An 'other answer' space is provided for most questions. If the responses that are given do not fit easily within the categories that are supplied then write in the response. Also please supply any comments you feel might be useful when the schedule is being scored.

Family environment schedule: part A

1 Date of interview

2 Surname of family

3 First name of child

4 Sex of child   M F

5 Date of birth of child

6 Home address

7 School attended by child

8 Length of interview

9 Who was interviewed (circle appropriate number):
mother 1
father 2
both parents 3
other (specify)

10 In what country was the mother, father, and x born?

	father	mother	child
Australia	1	2	3
Italy	1	2	3
Greece	1	2	3
Yugoslavia	1	2	3
Netherlands	1	2	3
Poland	1	2	3
England	1	2	3
Scotland	1	2	3
Northern Ireland	1	2	3
Wales	1	2	3
Eire	1	2	3
Germany	1	2	3

other country name the country for:
father/mother/child

11 If the parents or child were not born in Australia, in what year did they arrive?
father/mother/child

12 What language is generally spoken in the home?

English	1	German	5
Italian	2	Polish	6
Greek	3	other language (specify)	
Dutch	4		

13 When you are speaking with x what language would you use most of the time?

	father	mother
English	1	1
Italian	2	2
Greek	3	3
Dutch	4	4
German	5	5
Polish	6	6

other language (specify)

14 When x is talking with brothers or sisters or with other children in the home what language does x generally use?

English	I	German	5
Italian	2	Polish	6
Greek	3	Other language (specify)	
Dutch	4		

15 How satisfied would you say you are with the school that x attends?

very satisfied	I	very dissatisfied	4
reasonably satisfied	2	don't know or don't care	5
not really satisfied	3	other answer (specify)	

16 How do you react to the following statements about x's school: would you agree strongly (1), agree (2), don't know (3), disagree (4), disagree strongly (5).

In the school x attends:

		agree strongly	agree	don't know	disagree	disagree strongly
a	There is not enough homework	I	2	3	4	5
b	There is not enough discipline	I	2	3	4	5
c	Children are very friendly	I	2	3	4	5
d	Too much time is spent on subjects such as art, music, drama	I	2	3	4	5
e	Not enough time is spent on reading and mathematics	I	2	3	4	5
f	Teachers are very friendly	I	2	3	4	5
g	Teachers seem to treat all children very fairly	I	2	3	4	5
h	Teachers seem to be very interested in x's education	I	2	3	4	5
i	The methods of teaching seem to be too progressive, too modern	I	2	3	4	5
j	Too much time is spent on special courses for migrant children	I	2	3	4	5
k	Teachers give impression that they want to keep parents out of the school	I	2	3	4	5
l	Children from different ethnic groups mix very well	I	2	3	4	5

m We don't receive enough 1   2   3   4   5
   information about how
   x is performing at
   her/his schoolwork

17 When children who are about 10 years old arrive in Australia from non-
   English-speaking countries, into which of the following school situations do you think they should be placed? (Ask all questions of
   Anglo-Australian parents as well.)
   Read the following alternatives:
   a In special schools set up to teach English to   1
      ethnic children
   b The local school but placed in special classes   2
      where the children spend most of their time
      learning English
   c The local school and placed in ordinary classes 3
      but with some special English teaching
   d The local school and placed in ordinary classes 4
      with no special attention
   e The local school but with the children taught   5
      mainly in their own language
      Other answer (specify):

18 When children start school at the age of 5 or 6 and they are from
   (non-English Australian) ethnic families, in what language do you
   think the children should be taught? (Ask the question in two sections: first, in relation to children who have just arrived in Australia;
   and second, for children who have been in Australia for most of their
   lives.)
   Read the alternatives:

	For children just arrived	*For children resident in Australia for some time*
a Totally in their own language	1	1
b Mainly in their own language with some English	2	2
c About half English and half in the ethnic-language	3	3
d Mainly English and some ethnic-language	4	4
e All English	5	5
Other answer (specify):		

19 When children from (non-Anglo-Australian) ethnic families have
   reached the age of about 10 or 11, in what language do you think they
   should be taught at school? (*Ask the question in two sections: first, in
   relation to children who have just arrived in Australia; and second, for
   children who have been in Australia for most of their lives.*)
   Read the alternatives:

		For children just arrived	For children resident in Australia for some time
a	Totally in their own language	1	1
b	Mainly in their own language with some English	2	2
c	About half English and half in the ethnic-language	3	3
d	Mainly English and some ethnic-language	4	4
e	All English	5	5
	Other answer (specify):		

20 If a school has a large number of children from non-English-speaking countries, how much time in grades 4 and 5 should be devoted to teaching about the history, geography, culture, languages, of those countries?
Read the alternatives:

a	All such subjects should be related to ethnic-countries with little or no attention to Australia	1
b	Mainly related to ethnic-countries with a reasonable amount of Australian history, geography	2
c	About half related to ethnic-countries and half to Australia	3
d	Mainly related to Australia with some time devoted to ethnic-countries	4
e	All the time should be devoted to the study of Australia or other English speaking cultures	5
	Other answer (specify):	

21 At x's school, from what you know, how would you rate the teaching of the following subjects (either very good (1), good (2), don't know (3), poor (4), very poor (5)).

		very good	good	don't know	poor	very poor
a	Mathematics	1	2	3	4	5
b	Reading	1	2	3	4	5
c	English	1	2	3	4	5
d	Sports	1	2	3	4	5
e	Social studies (history, geography)	1	2	3	4	5
f	Art	1	2	3	4	5
g	Music	1	2	3	4	5

22 *a* How many children are in the family?

I   2   3   4   5   6   7   8   9   10

   b Then ask:
   i what are their ages (listing from eldest to youngest, including x)
   ii where do the children live, at home or away
   iii are they male or female
   iv what are their expected occupations if the children are still at school
   v what is the child's present occupation if the child has left school (put university or college, if attending a tertiary institution)

Complete the following table:

Child number	Age of child	Residence Home	Away	Sex M	F	Expected occupation	Present occupation
I		I	2	I	2		
2		I	2	I	2		
3		I	2	I	2		
4		I	2	I	2		
5		I	2	I	2		
6		I	2	I	2		
7		I	2	I	2		
8		I	2	I	2		
9		I	2	I	2		
10		I	2	I	2		
11		I	2	I	2		
12		I	2	I	2		

Family environment schedule: Part B

1, 2 How much education do you *want* x to receive?

Mother	Father	
I	I	postgraduate education (a higher degree)
2	2	graduate from university (a first degree)
3	3	at least some university
4	4	high school plus teacher training college or some other professional training college
5	5	finish high school, or as much school as possible
6	6	leave school as soon as possible other answer:

3, 4 How much education do you really *expect* x to receive?

Mother	Father	
I	I	postgraduate education
2	2	graduate from university

3	3	at least some university
4	4	high school plus professional training college
5	5	finish high school, or as much as possible
6	6	leave school as soon as possible
		other answer:

5, 6 How long have you had these ideas about the amount of education you expect x to receive?

Mother	*Father*	
1	1	since x was born
2	2	before x started school
3	3	just after x started school
4	4	since last year
5	5	just this year

Rating scale for questions 5 and 6 (complete for mother and father)

	Time scale				
	Since x was born	Before x started school	Just after x started school	Since last year	Just this year
Expectations from questions 3 and 4 (average the expectations)					
postgraduate education	6	5	4	3	2
university	5	4	3	2	1
high school and some college	4	3	2	1	1
finish high school	3	2	1	1	1
less than high school completion	1	1	1	1	1

7, 8 What kind of job would you *like* x to have when she/he grows up?

Mother	*Father*	
1	1	job requiring postgraduate education or long period at university (doctor, lawyer, dentist, scientist, professor, . . .)
2	2	job requiring university degree (architect, public servant, engineer, high school teacher, . . .)
3	3	parents have high educational expectations (see questions 3, 4) and they state that 'it is up to the child to decide'.
4	4	job requiring high school graduation and some college training (draughtsman, elementary school teacher, journalist, nurse, . . .)
5	5	job requiring some high school education

| 6 | 6 | job requiring little education or, parents have low educational expectations (see questions 3, 4) and they state that 'it is up to the child to decide' or, 'I don't care'. |

Name of job desired:

Other answer:

9, 10 Do you really think that x *will* become a (name the job just mentioned)?

Mother	Father	
1	1	Yes (emphatically)
2	2	I hope so
3	3	No (I don't think so), or parents indicate that it is up to the child to decide, or parents say they don't care Other answer

Rating scale for question 9 and 10 (complete for mother and father).

Job expectations (*see questions 7 and 8*)	*Yes (emphatically)*	*I hope so*	*No (I don't think so)*
postgraduate education	6	4	2
university degree	5	3	2
high school and college training	4	2	1
high school completion	3	2	1
less than high school	2	1	1
no expectations	1	1	1

11, 12 How long have you had these ideas about the kind of job you would like x to have?

Mother	Father	
1	1	Since x was born
2	2	before x started school
3	3	just after x started school
4	4	since last year
5	5	just this year

Rating scale for questions 11 and 12 (complete for mother and father)

Time period				
Since x was born	Before x started school	Just after x started school	Since last year	Just this year

job expectations (from questions 7 and 8), average the expectations

	Since x was born	Before x started school	Just after x started school	Since last year	Just this year
job requiring postgraduate education	6	5	4	3	2
university degree	5	3	3	2	1
high school graduation and some college	4	3	2	1	1
high school graduation	3	2	1	1	1
less than high school graduation	1	1	1	1	1

13 What grades (or marks) do you expect x to receive in her/his examinations at school?
1 All A's
2 Mainly A's with some B's
3 All B's
4 Mainly B's with some C's
5 Mainly C's or, as long as x passes, or do the best x can
6 Very low expectations, or I don't care
   Other answer:
   (A = 75 to 100; B = 65 to 74: C = 50 to 64.)

14, 15 What level of education would you say most of your close friends and relatives reached?

Mother	Father	
1	1	All or most of them have graduated from university
2	2	Most have graduated from teachers' college or other professional college
3	3	Most have completed high school
4	4	Most dropped out of high school
5	5	Most of them completed elementary school
6	6	Most of them left school before the end of elementary school
		Other answer:

16 *a* What type of job did/does the husband's father have?
1 job requiring highest education level (doctor, dentist, professor . . .)
2 job requiring university degree (architect, high school teacher . . .)
3 job requiring high school plus some professional college training (elementary school teacher, draughtsman . . .)
4 job requiring some high school education
5 job requiring little education (construction worker, farm labourer . . .)
name the job:

b What jobs do the parents have?

Mother	Father	
1	1	job requiring highest education level
2	2	job requiring university degree
3	3	job requiring high school plus some professional college training
4	4	job requiring some high school education
5	5	job requiring little education
6	6	no job
		name the job:

Rating scale for question 16 (husband's occupation level in relation to his father)

	Husband's occupation level				
	little education	some high school	high school plus college	university	highest level
Father's occupation level					
highest level	1	1	1	3	5
university	1	1	2	4	5
high school plus college	1	2	3	5	5
some high school	1	3	4	5	6
little education	2	3	4	5	6

17, 18 *a* Would the parent like to change her/his job, or is she/he happy to stay in present job?

Mother	Father	
1	1	Yes: would like to change
2	2	No: is content to stay in present job
3	3	No job

b If *Yes*, ask: Has the parent made any plans which might allow her/him to change jobs?

1	1	Yes
2	2	No

c If *Yes*, ask: what are the plans?

1	1	already attending courses (school, college . . .)
2	2	taking correspondence courses
3	3	has enrolled in courses to take in the future
4	4	plans to take courses in the future

Other answer:

Rating scale for question 17, 18 (complete for both mother and father):

Occupation level (see question 16b)	not content, is taking courses	not content, is planning to take courses	not content, no plans	content with job
highest level	6	6	5	5
university	6	5	4	4
high school plus some college	6	5	4	3
high school	5	4	3	2
little education, or no job	4	3	2	1

19 *a* What newspapers do you get regularly? List them:
   None

b How many magazines or journals do you have delivered to your home each month?

1 more than six
2 five or six
3 three or four
4 one or two
5 none
   list the magazines:

c How often do you give x an article from a newspaper or a magazine to read?

Mother	*Father*	
1	1	nearly every day
2	2	once or twice a week
3	3	occasionally (less than once a week)
4	4	rarely gives an article
5	5	never gives an article

Rating scale for question 19

	Number of magazines and newspapers received			
	Many, more than 5	3–4	1–2	less than one a week
Rate given to x to read				
nearly every day	6	5	4	3
once or twice a week	5	4	3	2
occasionally	3	2	1	1
rarely	2	1	1	1
never	1	1	1	1

20, 21 *a* How often is English spoken in the home (especially for non-English-speaking families)?

Mother	Father	Child	
1	1	1	all the time
2	2	2	over half the time (most of the time)
3	3	3	half the time
4	4	4	less than half the time
5	5	5	never or hardly ever

b How particular would you say you are about the way x speaks English (good vocabulary, correct grammar . . .)

Mother	Father	
1	1	very strict
2	2	quite strict
3	3	not too particular
4	4	don't really care
5	5	unable to help
		Other answer:

Rating scale for questions 20 and 21 (complete for both parents)

	Concern for quality of English by parents			
	very strict	quite strict	not too particular	don't really care, or unable to help
Amount of English spoken by parent				
All the time	6	5	4	3
Over half the time	5	4	3	2
Half the time	4	3	2	1

less than half the time	3	2	I	I
never or hardly ever	2	I	I	I

22, 23 *For the interviewer:* from your conversation with the parents, rate the quality of the use of English language according to the following criteria

Quality of English	Fluency of expression		pronunciation		vocabulary	
	Mother	Father	Mother	Father	Mother	Father
excellent	6	6	6	6	6	6
very good	5	5	5	5	5	5
good	4	4	4	4	4	4
fair	3	3	3	3	3	3
poor	2	2	2	2	2	2
very poor	I	I	I	I	I	I

24, 25 Complete for both mother and father

Parent's English scores (22, 23)	*Frequency of English*				
	all the time	over half the time	half the time	less than half	never
16–18	6	5	4	3	I
13–15	5	4	3	2	I
10–12	4	3	2	I	I
7–9	3	2	I	I	I
3–6	I	I	I	I	I

26, 27 Does x ever read to you (include, in English if the family is non-English-speaking)

Mother	Father	
I	I	Yes
2	2	No

If yes, ask: how often would x read to you?

Mother	Father	
I	I	every day
2	2	just about every day
3	3	about 3 or 4 times a week
4	4	probably once or twice a week
5	5	less than once a week
6	6	never
		Other answer:

28, 29 How often would you help x with her/his English grammar (e.g. tell x how to construct sentences, when to use certain words)

Mother	Father	
I	I	every day give x some help
2	2	probably nearly every day
3	3	about a couple of times a week
4	4	probably once a week
5	5	less than once a week
6	6	never
		Other answer:

30 *a* What language is usually spoken at mealtime?

Mother	Father	
I	I	English
2	2	French
3	3	Italian
4	4	Greek
		Other:

b With whom does x generally eat her/his evening meal?
  1 both parents present
  2 of the parents, only the mother is present
  3 of the parents, only the father is present
  4 neither of the parents is generally present
  5 generally eats meal alone
  Other answer:

c Who does most of the talking at the meal table?
  1 everybody participates (including both parents)
  2 the two parents do most of the talking
  3 father dominates the conversation
  4 mother dominates the conversation
  5 no-one is allowed to talk
  Other answer:

Rating scale for question 30
  1 English (only at mealtime – both parents present – concern for good language) (see question 20b, 21b). Everyone participates
  2 English (only). One parent present. Concern for good English. Everyone participates
  3 English (only) – parents present. Concern for good English. Parents dominate
  4 Both parents present. No or little concern for good English. Everyone participates
  5 One parent is present. No or little concern for good English
  6 Neither of the parents is present

31, 32 How often do you think you would introduce x to a new (English) word?

	Mother	Father	
	1	1	every day we try and tell x a new word
	2	2	probably, nearly every day
	3	3	a couple of times a week
	4	4	about once every two weeks
	5	5	probably once a month
	6	6	never
			Other answer:

33, 34 For non-English-speaking families:

How particular are you about the way x speaks (state the ethnic language of the family)?

Mother	Father	
1	1	very strict
2	2	quite particular
3	3	not too particular
4	4	don't really care
5	5	unable to help

35, 36 For non-English-speaking families

How important is it to you that (name the ethnic language) should be maintained in the family and that x should speak it fluently?

Mother	Father	
1	1	extremely important
2	2	important
3	3	not really important
4	4	don't care

37, 38 Do you have time to read books? If yes, ask how many books would you generally read in a month?

Mother	Father	
1	1	no books read
2	2	less than one a month
3	3	about one or two a month
4	4	3 to 5 a month (about one a week)
5	5	6 to 10 a month (about 2 a week)
6	6	more than 10

39, 40 *a* When x was small, before she/he started school, did parents ever read to x. If yes, ask how often?

Mother	Father	
1	1	no reading to child
2	2	not very often, less than once a week
3	3	about once a week
4	4	a couple of times a week
5	5	nearly every day (3 to 5 times a week)
6	6	just about every day (6 or 7)

b In what language did the parents generally read to x?

Mother	Father	
1	1	English
2	2	Italian
3	3	Greek
4	4	Dutch
5	5	German
6	6	Polish
		Other language (specify):

41 *a* Does the mother or father ever listen to x read to them?
If yes: ask how often?

Mother	Father	
1	1	just about every day (6 or 7 times)
2	2	nearly every day (3 to 5 times a week)
3	3	a couple of times a week
4	4	about once a week
5	5	less than once a week (not very often)
6	6	never listens

b In what language does x generally read to the parents?

1 English   5 German
2 Italian   6 Polish
3 Greek   Other language (specify):
4 Dutch

42 Does x bring home books to read, either from local library, school library, or friend's place? If yes, ask how many each month?
1 no books brought home, or I don't know
2 1 or 2 (very rarely brings books home)
3 3 to 5 (about 1 a week)
4 6 to 10 (about 2 a week)
5 more than 10

43 *a* Do you think that children who are about 10 years old should be restricted from viewing certain types of TV programmes or should they decide themselves what to watch?
1 should be restricted from certain programmes
2 decide themselves

b What about books and comics; should parents restrict 10-year-olds from reading certain types of material?
1 Yes 2 No

c How often would you check to see what x is reading or watching on TV?
1 never check   4 very regular checks
2 only occasional checks   5 check most viewing and reading
3 quite regular checks

44 If the child has older brothers or sisters ask: How often does x get together with any older brothers or sisters to get help with homework or reading?

very often	1	hardly ever	5
often	2	never, or no	6
sometimes	3	older brothers	
not very often	4	or sisters	

Other answer (specify):

45 If x has younger brothers or sisters ask: How often does x get together with younger brothers or sisters and play at teaching them?

very often	1	not very often	4
often	2	hardly ever	5
sometimes	3	never, or no	6
		younger	
		brothers or	
		sisters	

46 *a* Did any other adults live with you before x started school (i.e. adults who stayed longer than six months)?

1 no other adults 4 4 or 5
2 just one 5 more than 5
3 2 or 3

b How often did these other adults speak English in the home?
1 no adults, or none of them spoke English
2 generally did not speak English
3 half English, half another language
4 mainly English but some other language
5 all English
Other answer (specify):

c How much time did x spend with these other adults?
1 no other adults, or no time 3 quite a lot of time
2 not very much time 4 nearly all the time

47 *a* How many other adults live with you now?
1 no other adults 4 4 or 5
2 just one adult 5 more than five
3 2 or 3

b How often do these other adults speak English in the home?
1 no adults, or do not speak English
2 generally do not speak English
3 half English, half another language
4 mainly English but some other language
5 all English
Other answer (specify):

c How much time does x spend with these other adults?
1 no other adults, or no time

2 not very much time
3 quite a lot of time
4 nearly all the time

48, 49 What recreational activities (if any) do the parents and x engage in together (*at home*)?

Mother Father
1   1   a great variety of activities (some every week)
2   2   quite a few activities (some nearly every week)
3   3   a moderate variety of activities (one or two a month)
4   4   very few or no activities

Rating scale for questions 48 and 49 (for both parents)

English score of parent (see questions 22, 23)
16–18 13–15 10–12 7–9 3–6

Activities with parent					
great variety	6	5	4	3	2
quite a few	5	4	3	2	1
moderate variety	4	3	2	1	1
very few or none	2	2	1	1	1

50, 51 *a* Do you expect x to spend a regular amount of time each day at his studies or homework outside of schooltime?

Mother Father
1   1   Yes
2   2   No

b If yes, ask: How much time do you expect x to spend on her/his work each day?

Mother Father
1   1   More than 2 hours each weekday
2   2   Between 1 and 2 hours each day
3   3   About 1 hour each day
4   4   Less than 30 minutes each day or, as much as the child wants to do
5   5   No time expected

52 If the parents expect x to pursue education after leaving school (see question 3, 4), ask: Have you given any consideration for making financial preparations to send x to college or university?

1 Yes
2 No, not yet
3 No need to make plans: wealthy family

4 Will wait until x finishes high school
Other answer:

If yes, ask: What are the plans?
1 Evidence of financial preparation already in existence (savings, policies, insurance)
2 Enquiries have been made but no action has been taken
3 Considerations has been given, but no enquiries have been made, nor action taken
Other answer:

Rating scale for question 52
1 financial preparation is in existence
2 enquiries have been made, but no action
3 consideration given but no enquiries
4 consideration not yet given
5 will wait until x finishes high school
6 no plans for further education

For use in questions 53 to 58

How often do you praise x or congratulate x for her/his schoolwork?
Mother Father

Mother	Father	
1	1	every day
2	2	nearly every day (a few times a week)
3	3	two or three times a week
4	4	once, or less than once a week
5	5	never praise

Rating scale for question 53 and 54 (complete for both mother and father)

	Job expectations (see questions 7, 8)		
	highest	moderate	low
Amount of praise by parent			
every day or nearly every day	6	5	3
2 or 3 times a week	5	4	2
once or less than once a week	3	2	1
never praise	1	1	1

Rating scale for questions 55 and 56 (complete for mothers and fathers)

Education expectations (see questions 3 and 4)
highest moderate low

Amount of praise by parent	highest	moderate	low
every day or nearly every day	6	5	3
2 or 3 times a week	5	4	2
once or less than once a week	3	2	1
never praise	1	1	1

Rating scale for question 57 and 58 (for both parents)

Expectations of grades or marks (see question 13)
highest moderate low

Amount of praise by parents	highest	moderate	low
every day or nearly every day	6	5	3
2 or 3 times a week	5	4	2
once or less than once a week	3	2	1
never praise	1	1	1

59 *a* In what hobbies or activities is x interested at the moment?
List the hobbies and activities
Not interested in hobbies

b Who seemed to get x interested in these hobbies?
1 both parents initiated the interest
2 mother initiated the interest
3 father initiated the interest
4 the child became interested without any parental involvement
5 someone outside the family initiated the interest

Rating scale for question 59

Number of hobbies

	3 or more	2	1

Initiation of interest

	3 or more	2	1
Both parents	6	5	4
One parent	5	4	3
Not by parents	2	1	1

60, 61 Would you know what topic x is studying (or has just finished studying) in arithmetic or English?

Mother	Father	
1	1	Knows specific topics (e.g. division of fractions)
2	2	Indicates uncertainty about the specific topic (e.g. I think that it is division of fractions)
3	3	Knows general topic (e.g. fractions)
4	4	Indicates uncertainty about the general topic (e.g. I think it is fractions)
5	5	Has no idea of present topics but mentions some earlier topics that were studied
6	6	Has no idea of the topics that have been studied
		Other answer:

62, 63 What grades or marks did x receive in arithmetic and English in her/his *last* test?

Mother	Father	
1	1	Definite knowledge of grades in *both* subjects (e.g. B in arithmetic and C in English)
2	2	Definite knowledge of marks in *one* of the subjects
3	3	Indicates uncertainty about the grades in both of the subjects (e.g. I think a B in arithmetic and probably a C in English)
4	4	Indicates uncertainty about one subject, no knowledge of the other
5	5	Mentions grades from previous tests but unable to indicate the results from the *last* test
6	6	No knowledge of child's grades in either subject
		Other answer:

64 *a* Do you have an encyclopaedia (or almanac, or set of fact books) in the home?

　　1 Yes　　　　2 No

　b If yes, ask: What kind are they? (Fill in the table)

c How long have you had them? (Fill in the table)

	Time had them			
	less than one year	1 to 2 years	3 to 4 years	over 5 years

Type of encyclopaedia or reference book
1
2
3
4
5

d How often do the mother and × get together to look at them?
  1 about once (or more) a week
  2 once or twice a month
  3 never, or not very often
  Other answer:

e How often do the father and x get together to look at them?
  1 about once (or more) a week
  2 once or twice a month
  3 never, or not very often
  Other answer:

Rating scale for question 64
  1 Much discussion of the books (both parents or one parent and other members of the family)
  2 Much discussion of the books with one person in the family
  3 Discussions about once or twice a month with many members of the family
  4 Discussions about once or twice a month with one member of the family
  5 Books present but very rarely are there any discussions
  6 No books present

65, 66 What educational activities have the parents and x engaged in together during the past six months (what visits have you gone on together, what places have you visited together)? List the activities:

Mother	Father	
1	1	engaged in 5 or more educational activities (i.e. activities such as visits to concerts, museums, zoos, historic places)
2	2	engaged in 3–4 activities of high educational value
3	3	engaged in 1 or 2 activities of educational value

4	4	engaged in 4 or more recreational activities (e.g. visits to sporting events)
5	5	engaged in 1 to 3 recreational activities together
6	6	no outside activities
		Other answer:

67 *a* Out of the last four weekends, on how many have you and/or your husband *taken* x on an outing?
   1 on each of the 4 weekends
   2 on 3 of the weekends
   3 2
   4 1
   5 none of them

   b Out of the next four weekends, how many have you and/or your husband planned to take x on an outing?
   1 the 4 of them
   2 probably 3 of them
   3 2
   4 1
   5 none of them

   Rating scale for question 67
   a 1 weekend: 1   2 weekends: 2   3 or more weekends: 3
   b 1 weekend: 1   2 weekends: 2   3 or more weekends: 3

68 Have the parents taken any courses (*outside* the home) over the past two or three years? (e.g. language courses, sculpturing)

Mother	Father	
1	1	Yes
2	2	No

If yes, ask: What are they?

Mother	Father	
1	1	academic subjects: list them
2	2	sculpturing, music, art
3	3	household courses: cookery, sewing
4	4	sports coaching, exercises
		Other courses:

Rating scale for question 68

1	1	parent taken 3 or more educational courses
2	2	2 educational courses
3	3	1 educational course
4	4	2 or more recreational courses
5	5	1 recreational course
6	6	no courses taken by parent

69 *a* Does x take any lessons *outside* of the school? (e.g. music, art, academic subjects, sports coaching)
1 Yes   2 No

  b If yes, ask: What does x take?
1 academic subjects: list them
2 art, classical music, sculpturing
3 popular music (guitar), singing
4 sports coaching, swimming lessons
Others:

  c Whose idea was it that x should take these lessons?
1 both parents initiated the idea
2 mother's idea
3 father's idea
4 child's own idea without parental involvement
5 someone outside the family initiated the idea
Other answer:

Rating scale for question 69

	Number of courses taken			
	educational courses		Recreational courses	
	2 or more	1	2 or more	1
Initiation of interest in courses				
both parents	6	5	4	3
one parent	5	4	3	2
someone outside the family	3	2	1	1

70 *a* What does x generally do between the time she/he comes home from school and the evening meal?
1 does homework, reads, studies
2 takes courses: music, art, sculpturing
3 gets involved in hobby: name the hobby
4 plays games outside of the house
5 watches TV or listens to the radio
Other activities:

  b After your evening meal what does x generally do?
1 homework and then reads (or just reads)
2 homework and then gets involved with hobby (or, just does hobby)
3 reads and watches some TV
4 watches TV or listens to the radio
Other activities:

Rating scale for question 70

afternoon	*evening*
completely recreational 1	completely recreational 1
educational & recreational 2	educational & recreational 2
courses & hobbies 3	courses & hobbies 3

71 *a* About how many hours does x watch TV on Saturday and Sunday?
  1 doesn't watch TV at weekends
  2 less than 1 hour each day
  3 between 1 and 3 hours a day
  4 between 4 and 5 hours a day
  5 more than 5 hours a day

b How about weekdays? How long does x watch it each day?
  1 doesn't watch it
  2 less than 1 hour each day
  3 between 1 and 3 hours a day
  4 between 4 and 5 hours a day
  5 more than 5 hours a day

c What TV programmes does x generally watch?
  1 most are educational (current affairs programmes, science documentaries)
  2 mixture of educational and recreational
  3 all recreational
  4 don't know
    List the regular programmes:

d How often do parents discuss a TV programme with x?
  1 very regularly
  2 occasionally
  3 have only ever discussed one or two programmes
  4 never have had any follow-up discussions
    Other answer:

Rating scale for question 71
  1 mainly educational programmes, much discussion
  2 mainly educational, moderate discussion
  3 mixture of educational and recreational, much discussion
  4 mixture of educational and recreational, moderate discussion
  5 mainly recreational, much discussion
  6 mainly recreational, moderate discussion

72 At what age did you or would you expect x to be allowed to do the following by herself/himself?
  a earn own spending money 6 7 8 9 10 11 12 13 14 15 16
  b be able to undress and go 6 7 8 9 10 11 12 13 14 15 16
    to bed by herself/himself
  c to know her/his way 6 7 8 9 10 11 12 13 14 15 16
    around the neighbourhood
    so she/he can play where

she/he wants to without
getting lost

d to make friends and visit   6 7 8 9 10 11 12 13 14 15 16
their homes

e to stay alone at home at   6 7 8 9 10 11 12 13 14 15 16
night

f to make decisions like   6 7 8 9 10 11 12 13 14 15 16
choosing clothes or
deciding how to spend
money

g to act as a babysitter at   6 7 8 9 10 11 12 13 14 15 16
someone else's home

h to sleep at a friend's home   6 7 8 9 10 11 12 13 14 15 16
overnight

i go to the movies alone   6 7 8 9 10 11 12 13 14 15 16

j go on an overnight trip   6 7 8 9 10 11 12 13 14 15 16
organized by the school

73 Do the parents ever discuss x's progress at school? If Yes, ask
how often?
1 never discuss progress
2 not very often, less than once a week
3 a couple of times a week
4 nearly every day (3 or 4 times a week)
5 every school day

74, 75 If you see that x is having real difficulty with something she/he is
doing (like building a model, fixing a toy, doing homework) what
would you generally do?
Read alternatives

Mother	*Father*	
1	1	generally do it for x
2	2	sit down with x and help
3	3	offer to help
4	4	wait for x to ask for help, and then show x how to do it
5	5	wait for x to ask for help, but insist that x continue to do it by herself/himself

76, 77 What educational level did the parents reach?

Mother	*Father*	
7	7	Higher degree level
6	6	University degree
5	5	High school plus teachers' college or other college
4	4	Finished high school
3	3	Some high school
2	2	Finished primary school
1	1	Less than primary school completed

78 Now for the last question:
How do you react to the following statements (agree strongly (1),
agree (2), don't know (3), disagree (4), disagree strongly (5))

		agree strongly	agree	don't know	disagree	disagree strongly
a	Even when a boy gets married his main loyalty still belongs to his parents	1	2	3	4	5
b	When a girl gets married her main loyalty belongs to her parents	1	2	3	4	5
c	When the time comes for a son to take a job, he should try and stay near his parents, even if it means giving up a good job opportunity	1	2	3	4	5
d	When the time comes for a daughter to take a job, she should try and stay near her parents, even if it means giving up a good job opportunity	1	2	3	4	5
e	Nothing in life is worth the sacrifice of moving away from one's parents	1	2	3	4	5
f	If a family cannot afford to provide education for all their children after high school, then any boys in the family should get preference	1	2	3	4	5

Bibliography

Adams, R. L. and Phillips, B. N. (1972), 'Motivational and achievement differences among children of various ordinal birth positions', *Child Development*, 43, 155–64.

Adler, A. (1959), *The Practice and Theory of Individual Psychology*, Paterson: Littlefield, Adams.

Aiken, L. R. (1970), 'Attitudes toward mathematics', *Review of Educational Research*, 40, 551–96.

Ainsworth, M. E. and Batten, E. J. (1974), *The Effects of Environmental Factors on Secondary Educational Attainment in Manchester: A Plowden Follow-Up*, London: Macmillan.

Alexander, K. L., Cook, M. and McDill, E. L. (1978), 'Curriculum tracking and educational stratification: some further evidence', *American Sociological Review*, 43, 47–66.

Alexander, K. L. and Eckland, B. K. (1974), 'Sex differences in the educational attainment process', *American Sociological Review*, 39, 668–81.

Alexander, K. L. and Eckland, B. K. (1975), 'Contextual effects in the high school attainment process', *American Sociological Review*, 40, 402–16.

Alexander, K. L., Eckland, B. K. and Griffin, L. J. (1975), 'The Wisconsin model of socio-economic achievement: a replication', *American Journal of Sociology*, 81, 324–42.

Alexander, K. L. and McDill, E. L. (1976), 'Selection and allocation within schools: some causes and consequences of curriculum placement', *American Sociological Review*, 41, 963–80.

Altus, W. D. (1966), 'Birth order and its sequelae', *Science*, 151, 44–9.

Alwin, D. F. and Hauser, R. M. (1975), 'The decomposition of path effects', *American Sociological Review*, 40, 37–47.

Alwin, D. F. and Otto, L. B. (1977), 'High school context effects on aspirations', *Sociology of Education*, 50, 259–73.

Anastasi, A. (1956), 'Intelligence and family size', *Psychological Bulletin*, 53, 187–209.

Anderson, G. J. (1970), 'Effects of classroom social climate on individual learning', *American Educational Research Journal*, 7, 135–52.

Anderson, G. J. (1971), 'Effects of course content and teacher sex on the social climate of learning', *American Educational Research Journal*, 8, 649–63.

Anderson, G. J. and Walberg, H. J. (1968), 'Classroom climate and group learning', *International Journal of Educational Science*, 2, 175–80.

Anderson, G. J. and Walberg, H. J. (1974), 'Assessing classroom learning environments', in K. Marjoribanks (ed.), *Environments for Learning*, Slough: NFER.

Anderson, J. G. and Evans, F. B. (1974), 'Causal models in educational research: recursive models', *American Educational Research Journal*, 11, 29–39.

Argyle, M. and Little, B. R. (1972), 'Do personality traits apply to social behaviour?', *Journal for the Theory of Social Behaviour*, 2, 1–35.

Armor, D. J. (1974), 'Theta reliability and factor scaling', in H. L. Costner (ed.), *Sociological Methodology, 1973–1974*, San Francisco: Jossey-Bass.

Bain, R. K. and Anderson, J. G. (1974), 'School context and peer influences on educational plans of adolescents', *Review of Educational Research*, 44, 429–45.

Bajema, C. J. (1963), 'Estimation of the direction and intensity of natural selection in relation to human intelligence by means of the intrinsic rate of natural increase', *Eugenics Quarterly*, 10, 175–87.

Banks, O. (1976), *The Sociology of Education*, New York: Schocken Books.

Banks, O. and Finlayson, D. (1973), *Success and Failure in the Secondary School*, London: Methuen.

Baratz, S. S. and Baratz, J. C. (1970), 'Early childhood intervention: the social science based on institutional racism', *Harvard Educational Review*, 40, 29–50.

Bardsley, W. N. (1976), 'Student alienation and commitment to school: a multivariate analysis of the effects of home and school environments', unpublished doctoral thesis, Australian National University.

Barker Lunn, J. C. (1969), 'The development of scales to measure junior school children's attitudes', *British Journal of Educational Psychology*, 39, 64–71.

Barker Lunn, J. C. (1970), *Streaming in the Primary School*, Slough: NFER.

Bayer, A. E. and Folger, J. K. (1967), 'The current state of birth order research', *International Journal of Psychiatry*, 3, 37–9.

Belmont, L. and Marolla, F. A. (1973), 'Birth order, family size, and intelligence', *Science*, 182, 1096–101.

Bereiter, C. *et al.* (1966), 'An academically oriented pre-school for culturally deprived children', in F. Hechinger (ed.), *Pre-School Education Today*, New York: Doubleday.

Bereiter, C. and Engelmann, S. (1966), *Teaching Disadvantaged Children in the Pre-School*, Englewood Cliffs, NJ: Prentice-Hall.

Bernstein, B. (1961), 'Social class and linguistic development: a theory of social learning', in A. H. Halsey, J. Floud and C. A. Anderson (eds), *Education, Economy, and Society*, New York: Free Press.

Bernstein, B. (1971), *Class, Codes and Control, Volume One*, London: Routledge & Kegan Paul.

Bernstein, B. (ed.) (1973), *Class, Codes and Control, Volume Two*, London: Routledge & Kegan Paul.

Bernstein, B. (1975), *Class, Codes and Control, Volume Three*, London: Routledge & Kegan Paul.

Bernstein, B. (1977), 'Social class, language and socialisation', in J. Karabel and A. H. Halsey (eds), *Power and Ideology in Education*, New York: Oxford University Press.

Bernstein, B. and Davies, B. (1969), 'Some sociological comments on Plowden', in R. Peters (ed.), *Perspectives on Plowden*, London: Routledge & Kegan Paul.

Bidwell, C. E. (1972), 'Schooling and socialization for moral commitment', *Interchange*, 3, 1–27.

Bidwell, C. E. (1973), 'The social psychology of teaching', in R. M. W. Travers (ed.), *Second Handbook of Research on Teaching*, Chicago: Rand McNally.

Bierstedt, R. (1969), *Florian Znaniecki on Humanistic Sociology: Selected Papers*, Chicago: University of Chicago Press.

Bing, E. (1963), 'Effect of childrearing practices on development of differential cognitive abilities', *Child Development*, 34, 631–48.

Bloom, B. S. (1964), *Stability and Change in Human Characteristics*, New York: Wiley.

Bloom, B. S. (1974), Preface in K. Marjoribanks (ed.), *Environments for Learning*, Slough: NFER.

Bock, R. D. and Haggard, E. A. (1968), 'The use of multivariate analysis in behavioral research', in D. K. Whitla (ed.), *Handbook of Measurement and Assessment in the Behavioral Sciences*, Reading, Mass.: Addison-Wesley.

Bock, R. D. and Vandenberg, S. G. (1968), 'Components of heritable variation in mental test scores', in S. G. Vandenberg (ed.), *Progress in Human Behavior Genetics*, Baltimore: Johns Hopkins Press.

Boudon, R. (1977), 'Education and social mobility: a structural model', in J. Karabel and A. H. Halsey (eds), *Power and Ideology in Education*, New York: Oxford University Press.

Bourdieu, P. (1973), 'Cultural reproduction and social reproduction', in R. Brown (ed.), *Knowledge, Education, and Cultural Change*, London: Tavistock.

Bowers, K. S. (1973), 'Situationism in psychology: an analysis and a critique', *Psychological Review*, 80, 307–36.

Bowles, S. and Gintis, H. (1977), 'IQ in the U.S. Class Structure', in J. Karabel and A. H. Halsey (eds), *Power and Ideology in Education*, New York: Oxford University Press.

Bradley, R. H., Caldwell, B. M. and Elardo, R. (1977), 'Home environment, social status and mental test performance', *Journal of Educational Psychology*, 69, 697–701.

Braun, C. (1976), 'Teacher expectation: socio-psychological dynamics', *Review of Educational Research*, 46, 185–213.

Breland, H. M. (1977), 'Family configuration and intellectual development', *Journal of Individual Psychology*, 33, 86–96.

Brodie, T. A. (1964), 'Attitude toward school and academic achievement', *Personnel and Guidance Journal*, 43, 375–78.

Bronfenbrenner, U. (1977), 'Toward an experimental ecology of human development', *American Psychologist*, 32, 513–31.

Brook, J. S., Whiteman, M., Peisach, E. and Deutsch, M. (1974), 'Aspiration levels of and for children: age, sex, race, and socio-economic correlates', *Journal of Genetic Psychology*, 124, 3–16.

Brophy, J. E. and Good, T. L. (1970), 'Teacher expectations: beyond the Pygmalion controversy', *Phi Delta Kappan*, 54, 276–8.

Brophy, J. E. and Good, T. L. (1974), *Teacher-Student Relationships*, New York: Holt, Rinehart & Winston.

Brown, G. (1970), 'An investigation into the relationship between performance and neuroticism', *Durham Research Review*, 25, 483–8.

Bullock, A. (1975), *A Language for Life*, London: HMSO.

Burks, B. S. (1928), 'The relative influence of nature and nurture upon mental development: a comparative study of foster parent–foster child resemblance and true parent–true child resemblance', *Yearbook of the National Society for the Study of Education*, 27, 219–316.

Burton, D. (1968), 'Birth order and intelligence', *Journal of Social Psychology*, 76, 199–206.

Bynner, J. M. (1972), *Parents' Attitudes to Education*, London: HMSO.

Byrne, D., Williamson, B. and Fletcher, B. (1975), *The Poverty of Education*, London: Martin Robertson.

Callard, M. P. and Goodfellow, C. L. (1962), 'Neuroticism and extraversion in schoolboys as measured by the J.M.P.I.', *British Journal of Educational Psychology*, 32, 241–50.

Cattell, R. B. (1963), 'Theory of fluid and crystallized intelligence: a critical experiment', *Journal of Educational Psychology*, 54, 1–22.

Cattell, R. B. and Butcher, H. J. (1968), *The Prediction of Achievement and Creativity*, New York: Bobbs-Merrill.

Cattell, R. B., Eber, H. W. and Tatsuoka, M. M. (1970), *Handbook for the Sixteen Personality Factor Questionnaire (16PF)*, Illinois: Institute for Personality and Ability Testing.

Cicirelli, V. G. (1967), 'Sibling configuration, creativity, IQ and academic achievement', *Child Development*, 38, 481–90.

Cicirelli, V. G. (1975), 'Effects of mother and older siblings on the problem-solving behavior of the younger child', *Child Development*, 11, 749–56.

Cicirelli, V. G. (1977a), 'Children's school grades and sibling structure', *Psychological Reports*, 41, 1055–8.

Cicirelli, V. G. (1977b), 'Effects of mother and older sibling on child's conceptual style', *Journal of Genetic Psychology*, 131, 309–17.

Cicourel, A. V. and Kitsuse, J. I. (1963), *The Educational Decision-Makers*, New York: Bobbs-Merrill.

Cicourel, A. V. *et al.* (1974), *Language Use and School Performance*, New York: Academic Press.

Clausen, J. A. (1966), 'Family structure, socialization and personality', in L. W. Hoffman and M. L. Hoffman (eds), *Review of Child Development Research*, New York: Russell Sage Foundation.

Cole, L. (1954), 'The population consequences of life history phenomena', *Quarterly Review of Biology*, 29, 103–37.

Cole, M. (1976), 'Commentary: cultural differences in the contexts of learning', in S. Messick (ed.), *Individuality in Learning*, San Francisco: Jossey-Bass.

Coleman, J. S. *et. al.* (1966), *Equality of Educational Opportunity*, Washington: Government Printing Office.

Connell, R. W. (1972), 'Class structure and personal socialization', in F. J. Hunt (ed.), *Socialization in Australia*, Sydney: Angus & Robertson.

Connell, R. W. (1974), 'The causes of educational inequality: further observations', *Australian and New Zealand Journal of Sociology*, 10, 186–9.

Cooley, W. W. and Lohnes, P. R. (1962), *Multivariate Procedures for the Behavioral Sciences*, New York: Wiley.

Cooper, H. M. *et al.* (1975), 'The importance of race and social class information in the formation of expectancies about academic performance', *Journal of Educational Psychology*, 67, 312–19.

Dandes, H. M. and Dow, D. (1969), 'Relation of intelligence to family size and density', *Child Development*, 40, 641–4.

Darlington, R. B., Weinberg, S. L. and Walberg, H. J. (1975), 'Canonical variate analysis and related techniques', in D. J. Amik and H. J. Walberg (eds), *Introductory Multivariate Analysis*, Berkeley, California: McCutchan.

Dave, R. H. (1963), 'The identification and measurement of environmental process variables that are related to educational achievement', unpublished doctoral thesis, University of Chicago.

Davies, B. (1976), *Social Control and Education*, London: Methuen.

Davies, I. (1971), 'The management of knowledge: a critique of the use of typologies in educational sociology', in E. Hopper (ed.), *Readings in the Theory of Educational Systems*, London: Hutchinson.

De Bord, L., Griffin, L. J. and Clark, M. (1977), 'Race, sex, and schooling: insights from the Wisconsin Model of the early achievement process', *Sociology of Education*, 50, 85–102.

Delamont, S. (1976), *Interaction in the Classroom*, London: Methuen.

Deutsch, M. (1967), *The Disadvantaged Child*, New York: Basic Books.

Deutsch, M. and Krauss, R. M. (1965), *Theories in Social Psychology*, New York: Basic Books.

Douglas, J. W. B. (1964), *The Home and the School*, London: MacGibbon & Kee.

Duncan, O. D., Haller, A. O. and Portes, A. (1968), 'Peer influences on aspirations: a reinterpretation', *American Journal of Sociology*, 74, 119–37.

Dusek, J. B. (1975), 'Do teachers bias children's learning?', *Review of Educational Research*, 45, 661–84.

Dyer, P. B. A. (1967), 'Home environment and achievement in Trinidad', unpublished doctoral thesis, University of Alberta.

Eggleston, J. (1973), 'Decision-making on the school curriculum: a conflict model', *Sociology*, 7, 377–94.

Elashoff, D. J. and Snow, R. E. (1971), *Pygmalion Reconsidered: A Case Study in Statistical Inference: Reconsideration of the Rosenthal-Jacobson Data on Teacher Expectancy*, Belmont, California: Wadsworth Publishing.

Elliott, C. D. (1972), 'Personality factors and scholastic attainment', *British Journal of Educational Psychology*, 42, 23–32.

Emmett, W. G. (1950), 'The trend of intelligence in certain districts in England', *Population Studies*, 3, 324–37.

Endler, N. S. (1973), 'The person versus the situation – a pseudo issue? A response to Alker', *Journal of Personality*, 41, 287–303.

Endler, N. S. (1976), 'The case for person-situation interactions', in N. S. Endler and D. Magnusson (eds), *Interactional Psychology and Personality*, New York: Wiley.

Endler, N. S. and Hunt, J. McV. (1969), 'Generalizability of contributions from sources of variance in the S-R inventories of anxiousness', *Journal of Personality*, 37, 1–24.

Endler, N. S. and Magnusson, D. (1976), 'Personality and person by situation interactions', in N. S. Endler and D. Magnusson (eds), *Interactional Psychology and Personality*, New York: Wiley.

Entwistle, N. J. and Cunningham, S. (1968), 'Neuroticism and school attainment – a linear relationship', *British Journal of Educational Psychology*, 38, 123–32.

Entwistle, N. J., and Welsh, J. (1969), 'Correlates of school attainment at different ability levels', *British Journal of Educational Psychology*, 39, 57–63.

Epstein, J. L. and McPartland, J. M. (1977), 'Sex differences in family and school influence on student outcomes', paper presented at the annual meeting of the American Sociological Association, Chicago.

Evans, F. B. and Anderson, J. G. (1973), 'The psycho-cultural origins of achievement and achievement motivation: the Mexican-American family', *Sociology of Education*, 46, 396–416.

Eysenck, H. J. (1971), *Race, Intelligence and Education*, London: Temple Smith.

Eysenck, H. J. (1973), *Inequality of Man*, London: Temple Smith.

Eysenck, H. J. and Cookson, D. (1969), 'Personality in primary school children: 1. Ability and achievement', *British Journal of Educational Psychology*, 39, 109–22.

Featherman, D. L. and Carter, T. M. (1976), 'Discontinuities in schooling and the socio-economic life cycle', in W. H. Sewell, R. M. Hauser and D. L. Featherman (eds), *Schooling and Achievement in American Society*, New York: Academic Press.

Featherman, D. L. and Hauser, R. M. (1976), 'Sexual inequalities and socio-economic achievement in the U.S., 1962–1973', *American Sociological Review*, 41, 462–83.

Ferguson, G. A. (1954), 'On learning and human ability', *Canadian Journal of Psychology*, 8, 95–112.

Ferguson, G. A. (1956), 'On transfer of the abilities', *Canadian Journal of Psychology*, 10, 121–31.

Ferguson, L. R. and Maccoby, E. E. (1966), 'Interpersonal correlates of differential abilities', *Child Development*, 37, 549–71.

Ferri, E. (1971), *Streaming: Two Years Later*, London: NFER.

Finger, J. A. and Schlesser, G. E. (1968), 'Academic performance of public and private school students', *Journal of Educational Psychology*, 54, 118–22.

Finifter, B. M. (1972), 'The generation of confidence: evaluating research findings by random sub-sample replication', in H. L. Costner (ed.), *Sociological Methodology, 1972*, San Francisco: Jossey-Bass.

Finn, J. D. (1972), 'Expectations and the educational environment', *Review of Educational Research*, 42, 387–410.

Flanders, N. A. (1970), *Analyzing Teacher Behavior*, New York: Addison-Wesley.

Forer, L. K. (1977), 'Bibliography of birth order literature in the 70's', *Journal of Individual Psychology*, 33, 122–41.

Fraser, B. (1977), 'Pupil perceptions of the climate of Australian science classrooms', paper delivered at the annual meeting of the Australian Research in Education Association, Canberra.

Fraser, E. (1959), *Home Environment and the School*, University of London Press.

Frideres, J. (1977), 'Introduction to special issue, Ethnic Families: Structure and Interaction', *Journal of Comparative Family Studies*, 8, 145–7.

Frost, B. P. (1968), 'Anxiety and educational achievement', *British Journal of Educational Psychology*, 38, 293–301.

Getzels, J. W. (1969), 'A social psychology of education', in G. Lindzey and E. Aronson (eds), *The Handbook of Social Psychology, Volume Five*, Reading, Mass.: Addison-Wesley.

Gordon, E. W. (1976b), 'Group differences versus individual development in educational design', in S. Messick (ed.), *Individuality in Learning*, San Francisco: Jossey-Bass.

Gordon, I. J. (1968), *Parent Involvement in Compensatory Education*, University of Illinois Press.

Gordon, M. T. (1976a), 'A different view of the IQ-achievement gap', *Sociology of Education*, 49, 4–11.

Gorsuch, R. L. and Cattell, R. B. (1967), 'Second stratum personality factors defined in the questionnaire realm by the 16 PF', *Multivariate Behavioral Research*, 2, 211–23.

Hall, C. S. and Lindzey, G. (1970), *Theories in Personality*, New York: Wiley.

Haller, A. O. and Portes, A. (1973), 'Status attainment processes', *Sociology of Education*, 46, 51–91.

Halsey, A. H. (1972), *Educational Priority: EPA Problems and Policies*, London: HMSO.

Halsey, A. H. (1975), 'Sociology and the equality debate', *Oxford Review of Education*, 1, 9–23.

Hargreaves, D. H. (1967), *Social Relations in a Secondary School*, London: Routledge & Kegan Paul.

Hargreaves, D. H., Hester, S. K. and Mellor, F. J. (1975), *Deviance in Classrooms*, London: Routledge & Kegan Paul.

Harré, R. and Secord, P. F. (1972), *The Explanation of Social Behaviour*, Oxford: Blackwell.

Hauser, R. M. (1973), 'Disaggregating a social-psychological model of educational attainment', in A. S. Goldberger and O. D. Duncan (eds), *Structural Equation Models in the Social Sciences*, New York: Seminar Press.

Hauser, R. M. (1978), 'On "a reconceptualization of school effects" ', *Sociology of Education*, 51, 68–72.

Hauser, R. M., Sewell, W. H. and Alwin, D. F. (1976), 'High school effects on achievement', in W. H. Sewell *et al.* (eds.), *Schooling and Achievement in American Society*, New York: Academic Press.

Havighurst, R. J. (1976), 'The relative importance of social class and ethnicity in human development', *Human Development*, 19, 56–64.

Hemphill, J. K. (1956), *Group Dimensions: A Manual for their Measurement*, Columbus, Ohio: Ohio State University.

Herrnstein, R. J. (1973), *I.Q. in the Meritocracy*, Boston: Atlantic Press.

Hess, R. D. and Shipman, V. C. (1965), 'Early experience and the socialization of cognitive modes in children', *Child Development*, 36, 869–88.

Heyns, B. (1974), 'Social selection and stratification in schools', *American Journal of Sociology*, 79, 1434–51.

Higgens, J. V., Reed, E. W. and Reed, S. C. (1962), 'Intelligence and family size: a paradox resolved', *Eugenics Quarterly*, 9, 84–90.

Hoffman, L. (1972), 'Early childhood experiences and women's achievement motives', *Journal of Social Issues*, 28, 129–55.

Honess, T. and Kline, P. (1974), 'Extraversion, neuroticism and academic attainment in Uganda', *British Journal of Educational Psychology*, 44, 74–5.

Honzik, M. P. (1967), 'Developmental studies of parent-child resemblance in intelligence', *Child Development*, 28, 215–28.

Hoover, M. E. R. (1975), *Appropriate Use of Black English by Black Children as Rated by Parents*, Stanford: Center for Research and Development and Teaching.

Hout, M. and Morgan, R. W. (1975), 'Race and sex variations in the causes of the expected attainments of high school seniors', *American Journal of Sociology*, 81, 364–94.

Howarth, E. (1976), 'Were Cattell's "personality sphere" factors correctly identified in the first instance?', *British Journal of Educational Psychology*, 67, 213–30.

Hudson, L. (1966), *Contrary Imaginations*, London: Methuen.

Hudson, L. (1968), *Frames of Mind*, London: Methuen.

Hunt, J. McV. (1961), *Intelligence and Experience*, New York: Ronald Press.

Husén, T., Fägerlind, I. and Liljefors, R. (1974), 'Sex differences in science achievement and attitudes: a Swedish analysis by grade level', *Comparative Education Review*, 18, 292–304.

Hutt, C. (1972), 'Sex differences in human development', *Human Development*, 15, 153–70.

Jackson, P. W. (1968), *Life in Classrooms*, New York: Holt, Rinehart & Winston.

Janowitz, M. (ed.) (1966), *W. I. Thomas on Social Organization and Social Personality: Selected Papers*, University of Chicago Press.

Jencks, C. (1972), *Inequality: A Reassessment of the Effect of Family and Schooling in America*, New York: Basic Books.

Jensen, A. R. (1969), 'How much can we boost IQ and scholastic achievement?', *Harvard Educational Review*, 39, 1–123.

Jensen, A. R. (1973a), 'Personality and scholastic achievement in three

ethnic groups', *British Journal of Educational Psychology*, 43, 115–25.
Jensen, A. R. (1973b), *Educability and Group Differences*, London:
Methuen.
Jensen, A. R. (1973c), *Educational Differences*, London: Methuen.
Jones, H. G. (1960), 'Relationship between personality and scholastic
attainment', *Bulletin of British Psychological Association*, 40, 42.
Kahl, J. A. (1961), ' "Common Man" boys', in A. H. Halsey, J. Floud and
C. A. Anderson (eds), *Education, Economy, and Society*, New York:
Free Press.
Kahn, S. B. (1969), 'Affective correlates of academic achievement',
Journal of Educational Psychology, 60, 216–21.
Kandel, A. B. and Lesser, G. S. (1969), 'Parental and peer influences on
educational plans of adolescents', *American Sociological Review*, 34,
213–23.
Karabel, J. and Halsey, A. H. (eds) (1977), *Power and Ideology in
Education*, New York: Oxford University Press.
Keddie, N. (1971), 'Classroom knowledge', in M. F. D. Young (ed.),
Knowledge and Control, London: Collier-Macmillan.
Keeves, J. P. (1972), *Educational Environment and Student Achievement*,
Stockholm: Almquist & Wiksell.
Keeves, J. P. (1974), 'Educational environment and student achievement',
in K. Marjoribanks (ed.), *Environments for Learning*, Slough:
NFER.
Kehle, T. J. (1974), 'Teachers' expectations: ratings on student
performances as biased by student characteristics', *Journal of
Experimental Education*, 43, 54–60.
Kellaghan, T. (1977), 'Relationship between home environment and
scholastic behavior in a disadvantaged population', *Journal of
Educational Psychology*, 69, 754–60.
Kellaghan, T. and Macnamarra, J. (1972), 'Family correlates of verbal
reasoning ability', *Developmental Psychology*, 7, 49–53.
Kennett, K. F. and Cropley, A. J. (1970), 'Intelligence, family size and
socio-economic status', *Journal of Biosocial Science*, 2, 227–36.
Kerckhoff, A. C. and Campbell, R. T. (1977), 'Black-white differences in
the educational attainment process', *Sociology of Education*, 50, 15–27.
Kerckhoff, A. C. and Huff, J. L. (1974), 'Parental influence on educational
goals', *Sociometry*, 37, 307–27.
Kish, L. (1965), *Survey Sampling*, New York: Wiley.
Labov, W. (1972), *Language in the Inner City*, Philadelphia: University of
Pennsylvania Press.
Labov, W. *et al.* (1968a), *A Study of the Non-Standard English of Negro
and Puerto Rican Speakers in New York City. Volume 1*, New York:
Columbia University.
Labov, W. *et al.* (1968b), *A Study of the Non-Standard English of Negro
and Puerto Rican Speakers in New York City. Volume 2*, New York:
Columbia University.
Lacey, C. (1970), *Hightown Grammar: The School as a Social System*,
Manchester University Press.
Lambert, R., Bullock, R., and Millham, S. (1973), 'The informal social

system', in R. Brown (ed.), *Knowledge, Education and Cultural Change*, London: Tavistock.

Lavin, D. E. (1965), *The Prediction of Academic Performance: A Theoretical Analysis and Review of Research*, New York: Russell Sage Foundation.

Lee, P. C. and Gropper, N. B. (1974), 'Sex-role culture and educational practice', *Harvard Educational Review*, 44, 369–410.

Lesser, G. S. (1976), 'Cultural differences in learning and thinking styles', in S. Messick (ed.), *Individuality in Learning*, San Francisco: Jossey-Bass.

Lesser, G. S., Fifer, G. and Clark, D. H. (1965), 'Mental abilities of children from different social-class and cultural groups', *Monographs of the Society of Research in Child Development*, 30 (4, Serial No. 102).

Levin, H. M. (1976), 'A new model of school effectiveness' in W. H. Sewell, R. M. Hauser and D. L. Featherman (eds), *Schooling and Achievement in American Society*, New York: Academic Press.

Lewin, K. (1935), *A Dynamic Theory of Personality*, New York: McGraw-Hill.

Lichtenwalner, J. S. and Maxwell, J. W. (1969), 'The relationship of birth order and socio-economic status to the creativity of pre-school children', *Child Development*, 40, 1241–7.

Loehlin, J. C., Lindzey, G., Spuhler, J. (1975), *Race Differences in Intelligence*, San Francisco: Freeman.

McCall, R. B. (1970), 'Intelligence quotient pattern over age: comparisons among siblings and parent-child pairs', *Science*, 170, 644–8.

McCall, R. B., Wachs, T. D. and Wilson, R. S. (1972), 'Similarity in developmental profile among related pairs of human infants', *Science*, 178, 1004–7.

Maccoby, E. E. and Jacklin, C. N. (1974), *The Psychology of Sex Differences*, Stanford University Press.

McDill, E. L. and Coleman, J. S. (1965), 'Family and peer influences in college plans of high school students', *Sociology of Education*, 38, 112–26.

McDill, E. L., Rigsby, L. C. and Meyers, E. D. (1969), 'Educational climates of high schools; their effects and sources', *American Journal of Sociology*, 74, 567–86.

McDill, E. L. and Rigsby, L. C. (1973), *Structure and Process in Secondary Schools*, Baltimore: Johns Hopkins University Press.

Malpass, L. F. (1953), 'Some relationships between students' perceptions of school and their achievement', *Journal of Educational Psychology*, 44, 475–82.

Marjoribanks, K. (1972a), 'Environment, social class, and mental abilities', *Journal of Educational Psychology*, 63, 103–9.

Marjoribanks, K. (1972b), 'Ethnic and environmental influences on mental abilities', *American Journal of Sociology*, 78, 323–37.

Marjoribanks, K. (1972c), 'Ethnicity and learning patterns: a replication and an explanation', *Sociology*, 6, 417–31.

Marjoribanks, K. (1974), 'Another view of the relation of environment to mental abilities', *Journal of Educational Psychology*, 66, 460–3.

Marjoribanks, K. (1976a), 'Sibsize, family environment, cognitive performance, and affective characteristics', *Journal of Psychology*, 94, 195–204.

Marjoribanks, K. (1976b), 'Birth order, family environment, and mental abilities', *Psychological Reports*, 39, 759–65.

Marjoribanks, K. (1977a), 'Environmental correlates of Australian children's performances', unpublished manuscript.

Marjoribanks, K. (1977b), 'Educational deprivation thesis: a further analysis', *Australian and New Zealand Journal of Sociology*, 13, 12–17.

Marjoribanks, K. (1977c), 'Socioeconomic status and its relation to cognitive performance as mediated through parental attitudes', in Oliverio, A. (ed.), *Genetics, Education and Intelligence*. Amsterdam: ASP Biological and Medical Press.

Marjoribanks, K. (1977d) 'Affective and environmental correlates of cognitive performance', *Journal of Educational Research*, 70, 3–8.

Marjoribanks, K. (1978a), 'Family and school environmental correlates of school-related affective characteristics: an Australian study', *Journal of Social Psychology*, 106, 181–9.

Marjoribanks, K. (1978b), 'Birth order, age spacing between siblings, and cognitive performance', *Psychological Reports*, 42, 115–23.

Marjoribanks, K. (1978c), 'The stratification of socialisation processes: a further analysis', *Educational Studies (England)*, 4, 105–10.

Marjoribanks, K. (1978d), 'Teacher perceptions of student behavior, social environment and cognitive performance,' *Journal of Genetic Psychology*, 133, 217–28.

Marjoribanks, K. (1978e), 'Ethnicity, family environment, school attitudes and academic achievement', *Australian Journal of Education*, 22, 249–61.

Marjoribanks, K. (1978f), 'Personality and environmental correlates of cognitive performance and school-related affective characteristics: a regression surface analysis', *Alberta Journal of Educational Research*, 24, 230–43.

Marjoribanks, K. (1978g), 'Bloom's model of human development: a regression surface analysis', *International Journal of Behavioral Development*, 1, 193–206.

Marjoribanks, K. (1978h), 'Ethnicity, school attitudes, intelligence and academic achievement', *International Journal of Psychology*, 13, 167–78.

Marjoribanks, K. (1979a), 'Family and school environmental correlates of intelligence, personality, and school-related affective characteristics', *Genetic Psychology Monographs*, 99, 165–83.

Marjoribanks, K. (1979b), 'Intelligence, social environment, and academic achievement: a regression surface analysis', *Journal of Experimental Education* (in press).

Marjoribanks, K. (1979c), 'Ethnicity, family environment and cognitive performance: a regression surface analysis', *Journal of Comparative Family Studies* (in press).

Marjoribanks, K. and Walberg, H. J. (1975a), 'Ordinal position, family environment, and mental abilities', *Journal of Social Psychology*, 95, 77–84.

Marjoribanks, K. and Walberg, H. J. (1975b), 'Family environment: sibling constellation and social class correlates', *Journal of Biosocial Science*, 7, 15–25.

Marjoribanks, K. and Walberg, H. J. (1975c), 'Birth order, family size, social class and intelligence', *Social Biology*, 22, 261–8.

Marjoribanks, K., Walberg, H. J. and Bargen, M. (1975), 'Mental abilities: sibling constellation and social class correlates', *British Journal of Social and Clinical Psychology*, 14, 109–16.

Mischel, W. (1973), 'Toward a cognitive social learning reconceptualization of personality', *Psychological Review*, 80, 252–83.

Moore, T. (1967), 'Language and intelligence: a longitudinal study of the first eight years. Part I. Patterns of development in boys and girls', *Human Development*, 10, 88–106.

Moore, T. (1968), 'Language and intelligence: a longitudinal study of the first eight years. Part II. Environmental correlates of mental growth', *Human Development*, 11, 1–24.

Moos, R. H. (1969), 'Sources of variance in responses to questionnaires and in behavior', *Journal of Abnormal Psychology*, 74, 405–12.

Moos, R. H. (1970), 'Differential effects of psychiatric ward settings on patient change', *Journal of Nervous and Mental Disease*, 5, 316–21.

Moos, R. H. (1974), *Evaluating Treatment Environments*, New York: Wiley.

Moos, R. H. (1975), *Evaluating Correctional and Community Settings*, New York: Wiley.

Moos, R. H. (1976), *The Human Context: Environmental Determinants of Behavior*, New York: Wiley.

Moos, R. H. (1979), *Evaluating Educational Environments*, San Francisco: Jossey-Bass.

Moos, R. H. and Trickett, E. J. (1974), *Classroom Environment Scale Manual*, Palo Alto, California: Consulting Psychologists Press.

Mosteller, F. and Moynihan, D. P. (eds) (1972), *On Equality of Educational Opportunity*, New York: Random House.

Mosteller, F. and Tukey, J. W. (1968), 'Data analysis, including statistics', in G. Lindzey and E. Aronson (eds), *Handbook of Social Psychology, Volume Two*, Reading, Mass.: Addison-Wesley.

Mosychuk, H. (1969), 'Differential home environments and mental ability patterns', unpublished doctoral thesis, University of Alberta.

Murray, C. (1971), 'The effects of ordinal position on measured intelligence and peer acceptance in adolescence', *British Journal of Social and Clinical Psychology*, 10, 221–7.

Murray, H. (1938), *Explorations in Personality*, Oxford University Press.

Nash, R. (1973), *Classrooms Observed*, London: Routledge & Kegan Paul.

Nesselrode, J. R. and Baltes, P. B. (1975), 'High order factor convergence and divergence of two distinct personality systems: Cattell's HSPQ and Jackson's PRF', *Multivariate Behavioral Research*, 10, 378–407.

Nielsen, H. D. and Moos, R. H. (1978), 'Exploration and adjustment in

high school classrooms: a study of person-environment fit', unpublished manuscript, Stanford University: Social Ecology Laboratory.

Nisbet, J. D. (1953), 'Family environment and intelligence', *Eugenics Review*, 45, 31–42.

Nolle, D. B. (1973), 'Alternative path analytic models of student-teacher influence: the implications of different strokes for different folks', *Sociology of Education*, 46, 417–26.

Nuttall, E. V., Nuttall, R. L., Polit, D. and Hunter, J. B. (1976), 'The effects of family size, birth order, sibling separation and crowding on the academic achievement of boys and girls', *American Educational Research Journal*, 3, 217–23.

Oldman, D., Bytheway, B. and Horobin, G. (1971), 'Family structure and educational attainment', *Journal of Biosocial Science*, Supplement 3, 81–91.

Orme, K. (1975), 'Personality, ability and achievement in primary school children', *Educational Research*, 17, 199–201.

Orpen, C. (1976), 'Personality and academic attainment: a cross-cultural study', *British Journal of Educational Psychology*, 46, 220–2.

Otto, L. B. and Alwin, D. F. (1977), 'Athletics, aspirations, and attainments', *Sociology of Education*, 50, 102–13.

Peaker, G. F. (1967), 'The regression analysis of the national survey', in B. Plowden, *Children and their Primary Schools, Volume Two*, London: HMSO.

Peaker, G. F. (1971), *The Plowden Children Four Years Later*, London: NFER.

Picou, J. S. and Carter, T. M. (1976), 'Significant-other influence and aspirations', *Sociology of Education*, 49, 12–22.

Plowden, B. (1967), *Children and their Primary Schools*, London: HMSO.

Poole, A. and Kuhn, A. (1973), 'Family size and ordinal position: correlates of academic success', *Journal of Biosocial Science*, 5, 51–9.

Porter, J. N. (1976), 'Socialization and mobility in educational and early occupational attainment', *Sociology of Education*, 49, 23–33.

Portes, A. and Wilson, K. L. (1976), 'Black-white differences in educational attainment', *American Sociological Review*, 41, 414–31.

Randhawa, B. S. and Fu, L. L. (1973), 'Assessment and effect of some classroom environment variables', *Review of Educational Research*, 43, 303–23.

Record, R. G., McKeown, T. and Edwards, J. H. (1969), 'The relation of measured intelligence to birth order and maternal age', *Annals of Human Genetics, London*, 33, 61–9.

Ridding, L. W. (1967), 'An investigation of the personality measures associated with over- and under-achievement in English and arithmetic', *British Journal of Educational Psychology*, 37, 397–8.

Rist, R. C. (1977), 'On understanding the processes of schooling: the contributions of labeling theory', in T. Karabel and A. H. Halsey (eds), *Power and Ideology in Education*, New York: Oxford University Press.

Rosen, B. C. (1956), 'The achievement syndrome: a psychocultural dimension of stratification', *American Sociological Review*, 21, 203–11.

Rosen, B. C. (1959), 'Race, ethnicity, and achievement syndrome',
    American Sociological Review, 24, 47–60.
Rosen, B. C. (1961), 'Family structure and achievement motivation',
    American Sociological Review, 26, 574–84.
Rosen, H. (1974), 'Language and class', in D. Holly (ed.), Education or
    Domination, London: Arrow Books.
Rosenbaum, J. S. (1975), 'The stratification of socialization processes',
    American Sociological Review, 40, 48–54.
Ross, K. N. (1976), Searching for Uncertainty, Melbourne: Australian
    Council for Educational Research.
Rubovits, P. C. and Maehr, M. L. (1973), 'Pygmalion black and white',
    Journal of Personality and Social Behavior, 25, 210–18.
Rulon, P. J. and Brooks, W. D. (1968), 'On statistical tests of group
    differences', in D. K. Whitla (ed.), Handbook of Measurement and
    Assessment in Behavioral Sciences, London: Addison-Wesley.
Rushton, J. (1966), 'The relationship between personality characteristics
    and scholastic success in 11-year-old children', British Journal of
    Educational Psychology, 36, 178–84.
Sampson, E. E. (1965), 'The study of ordinal position: antecedents and
    outcomes', Progress in Experimental Personality Research, 2, 175–228.
Savage, R. D. (1966), 'Personality factors and academic attainment in
    junior school children', British Journal of Educational Psychology, 36,
    91–2.
Savage, R. D. and Savage, J. F. (1973), 'A longitudinal investigation of
    personality characteristics and scholastic attainment in junior school
    children', Durham Research Review, 30, 742–7.
Schooler, C. (1972), 'Birth order effects: not here, not now!',
    Psychological Bulletin, 78, 161–75.
Scottish Council for Research in Education and Population Investigation
    Committee (1949), The Trend of Scottish Intelligence, University of
    London Press.
Sewell, W. H. and Hauser, R. M. (1972), 'Causes and consequences of
    higher education: models of the status attainment process', American
    Journal of Agricultural Economics, 54, 851–61.
Sewell, W. H. and Hauser, R. M. (1975), Education, Occupation, and
    Earnings, New York: Academic Press.
Sewell, W. H. and Hauser, R. M. (1976), 'Causes and consequences of
    higher education: models of the status attainment process', in W. H.
    Sewell, R. M. Hauser and D. L. Featherman (eds), Schooling and
    Achievement in American Society, New York: Academic Press.
Shea, B. M. (1976), 'Schooling and its antecedents: substantive and
    methodological issues in the status attainment process', Review of
    Educational Research, 46, 463–526.
Shockley, W. (1971a), 'Negro IQ deficit: failure of a "malicious
    coincidence" model warrants new research proposals', Review of
    Educational Research, 41, 227–48.
Shockley, W. (1971b), 'Models, mathematics, and the moral obligation to
    diagnose the origin of Negro IQ deficits', Review of Educational
    Research, 41, 369–77.

Skovholt, T., Moore, E. and Wellman, F. (1973), 'Birth order and academic behavior in first grade', *Psychological Reports*, 32, 395–8.

Smith, G. (1975), *E.P.A.: The West Riding Project, Volume Four*, London: HMSO.

Sørenson, A. B. (1977), 'The structure of inequality and the process of attainment', *American Sociological Review*, 42, 965–78.

Sørenson, A. B. and Hallinan, M. T. (1977), 'A reconceptualization of school effects', *Sociology of Education*, 50, 273–89.

Spady, W. G. (1976), 'The impact of school resources on students', in W. H. Sewell, R. M. Hauser and D. L. Featherman (eds), *Schooling and Achievement in American Society*, New York: Academic Press.

Spencer, W. A. (1976), 'Interpersonal influences on educational aspirations: a cross-cultural analysis', *Sociology of Education*, 49, 41–6.

Stodolsky, S. S. and Lesser, G. S. (1967), 'Learning patterns in the disadvantaged', *Harvard Educational Review*, 37, 564–93.

Strodtbeck, F. L. (1958), 'Family interaction, values and achievement', in D. C. McClelland (ed.), *Talent and Society*, Princeton, NJ: Van Nostrand.

Sumner, R. (1972), *Achievement in Secondary School: Attitudes, Personality and School Success*, London: NFER.

Sumner, R. and Warburton, F. W. (1972), *Achievement in Secondary School*, Slough: NFER.

Thomas, W. I. (1966), *Social Organization and Social Personality, Selected Papers*, University of Chicago Press.

Thomas, W. I. and Znaniecki, F. (1927), *The Polish Peasant in Europe and America, Second Edition*, New York: Alfred A. Knopf.

Thomas, W. I. and Znaniecki, F. (1958), *The Polish Peasant in Europe and America*, New York: Dover Publications.

Tisher, R. P. (1976), 'Variations in the environment of self-paced classrooms: their nature, determinants and effects', *Australian Journal of Education*, 20, 1–10.

Toman, W. (1969), *Family Constellation: Its Effect on Personality and Social Behavior*, New York: Springer.

Trickett, E. J. and Moos, R. H. (1973), 'Social environment of junior high and high school classrooms', *Journal of Educational Psychology*, 64, 93–102.

Trickett, E. J. and Quinlan, D. M. (1977), 'Three domains of classroom environment: an alternative analysis of the classroom environment scale', unpublished manuscript, Yale University.

Tucker, P. (1974), *Educational Needs of Children from Minority Groups*, London: Community Relations Commission.

Tuddenham, R. D. (1948), 'Soldier intelligence in World Wars I and II', *American Psychologist*, 3, 54–6.

Tupes, E. and Shaycoft, M. (1964), *Normative Distribution of AEQ Aptitude Indexes for High School Age Boys*, Lackland, Texas: Air Force Base Technical Documentary Reports.

Vernon, P. E. (1969), *Intelligence and Cultural Environment*, London: Methuen.

Walberg, H. J. (1971), 'Models for optimizing and individualizing school learning', *Interchange*, 3, 15–27.

Walberg, H. J. (ed.) (1974), *Evaluating Educational Performance*, Berkeley, California: McCutchan.

Walberg, H. J. (1976), 'The psychology of learning environments', in L. S. Shulman (ed.), *Review of Research in Education, Volume Four*, Itasca, Illinois: Peacock.

Walberg, H. J. and Anderson, G. J. (1968), 'Classroom climate and individual learning', *Journal of Educational Psychology*, 59, 414–19.

Walberg, H. J. and Marjoribanks, K. (1976), 'Family environment and cognitive development: twelve analytic models', *Review of Educational Research*, 46, 527–51.

Walberg, H. J. *et al.* (1976), 'School based family socialization', unpublished manuscript, University of Illinois at Chicago Circle.

Walberg, H. J., Singh, R. and Rasher, S. P. (1977), 'Predictive validity of student perception: a cross-cultural replication', *American Educational Research Journal*, 14, 45–9.

Waller, J. H. (1971), 'Differential reproduction: its relation to IQ test score, education, and occupation', *Social Biology*, 18, 122–36.

Warburton, F. W. (1972), 'The relationship between personality factors and scholastic attainment', in R. M. Dreger (ed.), *Multivariate Personality Research*, Baton Rouge, LA: Claitor's Publishing Division.

Warren, J. R. (1966), 'Birth order and social behavior', *Psychological Bulletin*, 65, 38–59.

Weiss, J. (1969), 'The identification and measurement of home environmental factors related to achievement motivation and self esteem', unpublished doctoral thesis, University of Chicago.

Weiss, J. (1974), 'The identification and measurement of home environmental factors related to achievement motivation and self esteem', in K. Marjoribanks (ed.), *Environments for Learning*, London: NFER.

West, C. K. and Anderson, T. H. (1976), 'The question of preponderant causation in teacher expectancy research', *Review of Educational Research*, 46, 613–30.

Wilkins, W. E. (1976), 'The concept of a self-fulfilling prophecy', *Sociology of Education*, 49, 175–83.

Williams, R. L. (1970), 'Personality, ability, and achievement correlates of scholastic attitudes', *Journal of Educational Research*, 63, 401–3.

Williams, T. (1976a), 'Abilities and environments', in W. H. Sewell, R. M. Hauser and D. L. Featherman (eds), *Schooling and Achievement in American Society*, New York: Academic Press.

Williams, T. (1976b), 'Teacher prophecies and the inheritance of inequality', *Sociology of Education*, 49, 223–36.

Wilson, K. L., and Portes, A. (1975), 'The educational attainment process: results from a national sample', *American Journal of Sociology*, 81, 343–63.

Wilson, R. S. (1972), 'Twins: early mental development', *Science*, 175, 914–17.

Wilson, S. (1977), 'The use of ethnographic techniques in educational research', *Review of Educational Research*, 47, 245–65.

Wiseman, S. (1967), 'The Manchester survey', in B. Plowden, *Children and their Primary Schools, Volume Two*, London: HMSO.

Woelfel, J. and Haller, A. O. (1971), 'Significant others, the self-reflexive act and the attitude formation process', *American Sociological Review*, 36, 74–86.

Wolf, R. M. (1964), 'The identification and measurement of environmental process variables related to intelligence', unpublished doctoral thesis, University of Chicago.

Yates, A. (1966), *Grouping in Education*, New York: Wiley.

Young, M. F. D. (1971), 'An approach to the study of curricula as socially organized knowledge', in M. F. D. Young (ed.), *Knowledge and Control: New Directions for the Sociology of Knowledge*, London: Collier-Macmillan.

Zajonc, R. B. (1976), 'Birth configuration and intelligence', *Science*, 192, 227–92.

Zajonc, R. B. and Markus, G. B. (1975), 'Birth order and intellectual development', *Psychological Review*, 82, 74–88.

Znaniecki, F. (1969), *On Humanistic Sociology, Selected Papers*, University of Chicago Press.

Author index

Subject index